# CHINA'S GREAT LEAP
The Beijing Games and
Olympian Human Rights
Challenges

# CHINA'S GREAT LEAP

## The Beijing Games and Olympian Human Rights Challenges

## MINKY WORDEN

*With contributions from:*

Joseph Amon ■ Bao Tong ■ Frank Ching ■ Jerome Cohen ■ Geoffrey Crothall ■ Mei Fong ■ Arvind Ganesan ■ R. Scott Greathead ■ Han Dongfang ■ Sharon K. Hom ■ John Kamm ■ Phelim Kine ■ Nicholas Kristof ■ Jimmy Lai ■ Martin Lee ■ Liu Xiaobo ■ Christine Loh ■ Emily Parker ■ Richard Pound ■ Sophie Richardson ■ Kenneth Roth ■ Mickey Spiegel ■ Kadir van Lohuizen ■ Wang Dan ■ Dave Zirin

SEVEN STORIES PRESS

New York ■ London ■ Melbourne ■ Toronto

Seven Stories Press
140 Watts Street
New York, NY 10013
www.sevenstories.com

In Canada: Publishers Group Canada, 559 College Street, Suite 402, Toronto, ON M6G 1A9

In the UK: Turnaround Publisher Services Ltd., Unit 3, Olympia Trading Estate, Coburg Road, Wood Green, London N22 6TZ

In Australia: Palgrave Macmillan, 15–19 Claremont Street, South Yarra, VIC 3141

Library of Congress Cataloging-in-Publication Data

Worden, Minky.
  China's great leap : the Beijing games and Olympian human rights challenges / Minky Worden ; with contributions from Joseph Amon ... [et al.]. -- Seven Stories Press 1st ed.
    p. cm.
  Includes bibliographical references and index.
  ISBN 978-1-58322-843-2 (pbk.)
    1. Olympic Games (29th : 2008 : Beijing, China) 2. Olympics--Political aspects--China. 3. Human rights--China. 4. Civil rights--China. I. Title.
  GV722008 .W67 2008
  796.48--dc22
                        2008008867

College professors may order examination copies of Seven Stories Press titles for a free six-month trial period. To order, visit http://www.sevenstories.com/textbook or send a fax on school letterhead to (212) 226-1411.

Book design by Jon Gilbert

Printed in the USA.

9  8  7  6  5  4  3  2  1

FOR MY FATHER AND MOTHER, who met at a badminton tournament, and who let me go to China over their very sensible objections.

"I very openly criticize the tendency to use culture for the purpose of propaganda, to dismiss the true function of art and the intellect. It is not opposition to the state, but rather in fighting for individualism and freedom of expression, freedom of human rights and justice. If you read newspapers today you see the problems created by this structure and by the effort to maintain power. It is against everything that human society should be fighting for."

—AI WEIWEI, designer of the Beijing National Stadium, known as the "Bird's Nest," interviewed by *The Guardian* on his decision not to attend the opening ceremony of the Beijing Games. Ai Weiwei has said that his perspective as an artist is shaped by the trauma millions of Chinese suffered during the Cultural Revolution, when Ai's father, the poet Ai Qin, was forced into exile, and to clean public toilets during the Chinese Communist Party's purge of writers and intellectuals.

# CONTENTS

## PART III: Polluted Air, Unclean Business Practices

### PHOTO ESSAY: Migrant Workers Race the Clock
KADIR VAN LOHUIZEN

## PART IV: The Political Backdrop of the Beijing Games

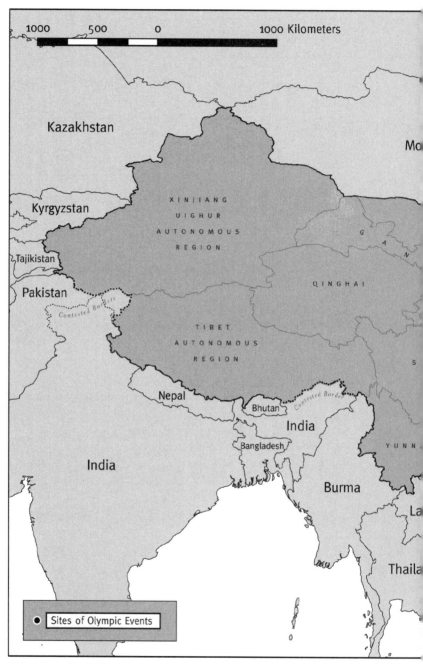

Map of China

# ACRONYMS AND ABBREVIATIONS

| | |
|---|---|
| API | Air Pollution Index |
| BOCOG | Beijing Organizing Committee for the Olympic Games |
| CCP | Chinese Communist Party |
| CCTV | China Central Television |
| CNPC | China National Petroleum Corporation |
| CPJ | Committee to Protect Journalists |
| CPL | Criminal Procedure Law |
| DPRK | Democratic People's Republic of Korea |
| HIV/AIDS | Human Immunodeficiency Virus / Acquired Immuno-deficiency Syndrome |
| HRIC | Human Rights in China |
| ICCPR | International Covenant on Civil and Political Rights |
| IOC | International Olympic Committee |
| NATO | North Atlantic Treaty Organization |
| NGO | Nongovernmental organization |
| NOC | National Olympic Committee |
| NPC | National People's Congress |
| PRC | People's Republic of China |
| RELC | Reeducation-through-labor Center |
| RTL | Reeducation through Labor |
| SARS | Severe Acute Respiratory Syndrome |
| SEPA | State Environmental Protection Administration |
| SPC | Supreme People's Court |
| TOP | The Olympic Partner program, the highest level of corporate sponsorship ("TOP sponsor") |
| UDHR | Universal Declaration of Human Rights |
| WHO | World Health Organization |

# A Lever for Change in China

BY NICHOLAS KRISTOF

NICHOLAS KRISTOF, *a* New York Times *columnist and former Beijing bureau chief, won a Pulitzer Prize in 1990 with his wife Sheryl WuDunn for their reporting on the 1989 Tiananmen Square democracy movement. He was awarded a second Pulitzer Prize in 2006 for his commentaries on Darfur. He is the author with Sheryl WuDunn of* China Wakes: The Struggle for the Soul of a Rising Power *(1998) and* Thunder from the East: Portrait of a Rising Asia *(2001).*

Chinese is a language of elegant four-character expressions redolent of history and culture. Yet it is also enriched by earthy rural vulgarities, like one that peasants use to express skepticism about Potemkin Villages and government propaganda efforts to make everything look beautiful for foreigners. The Chinese expression goes like this: *lu fen dan'r, biaomian'r guang* (on the outside, even donkey droppings gleam).

A peasant vulgarity is perhaps an inappropriate welcome mat for a book full of wise commentary by leading experts on China. But all of China will appear buffed and shiny for the 2008 Olympics. Most of that will be real, and the lavish new high-rises are a tribute to an economy that has lifted more people out of poverty more quickly than any in history. Interspersed with the many genuine triumphs will be donkey droppings. The challenge for the outsiders facing all that dazzle will be to figure out what is what.

The 1964 Tokyo Olympics were the coming out party for Japan on the international stage, and the Seoul Olympics in 1988 filled the same role for South Korea. China is not a new power—it has dominated the world economy for most of the last 3,000 years—but it suffered a calamitous period in the nineteenth and twentieth centuries and sees the Olympics as its moment to regain international respect.

Unfortunately, countries sometimes preen and seek international respect in strange ways. The Mexican government tried to suppress unrest ten days before the opening of the 1968 Olympics by shooting students, in what came to be known as the Tlatelolco massacre. South Korean forces initially clubbed and imprisoned protesters before the 1988 Seoul Games. (One student told me in an interview in 1987 that the South Korean president was a dictator; the president proved the student's point by imprisoning him.)

When China first sought the Summer Olympics, for the year 2000, the International Olympic Committee made an inspection of Beijing in March 1993 to evaluate the bid. My wife and I were living in China then, and we saw how the Communist Party left nothing to chance. Factories were closed down so that the air would be cleaner. Electricity was shut off in neighborhoods that the delegation wouldn't visit, to ensure that there could be a double-dose of electricity around the stadiums. Every taxi was ordered to buy and display a "Beijing 2000" bumper sticker. The homeless were shipped out of town, and "neighborhood committees" were ordered to beautify their districts.

So before the International Olympic Committee visit to Beijing, there was a knock on the door at the home of Wang Chaoru, a forty-one-year-old mentally retarded man. The Wangs lived in a working-class area in southern Beijing, far from the sports venues that the Olympic delegation was going to visit, and it is hard to see how Wang Chaoru could have harmed things. But the neighborhood committee had orders to make everything perfect, and perhaps the head of the committee feared that he might wander out to a main street and gawk in an awkward manner as the Olympic visitors' limousines hurtled by. So the head of the neighborhood committee and two policemen arrested Wang Chaoru—without an arrest warrant or any other document, and without any suggestion that he had ever broken any law.

"I don't want to go," Wang cried out, as his mother later recounted. "Mama! Papa!" He tried to hide, but the policemen dragged him away. (The full story is in *China Wakes*, the book I wrote with my wife, Sheryl WuDunn.) Then, just hours before the Olympic visitors actually touched down in Beijing, the police beat Wang Chaoru to death. His parents were allowed to view the body, which was covered with blood and bruises, and then the police officials invited them to a hearty lunch to make things up—the parents couldn't touch the food, of course. Finally the officials handed the parents 5,000 yuan—the equivalent of about 600 dollars—and told them to keep quiet.

In the aftermath of revelations about Guantánamo and Abu Ghraib, it is clear that Chinese security officers are not the only ones who can operate with an intoxicating mix of brutality and impunity. We Americans have much to answer for as well. More broadly, the old East European variety of Communism was boring because it was simultaneously impoverishing and repressive. In contrast, China's Communist Party is intellectually fascinating because it is simultaneously repressive and empowering. It presides over remarkable increases in wealth and over tumbling infant mortality rates—but also over a public security apparatus that is ruthless in punishing dissidents.

Certainly the Communist Party never ordered Wang Chaoru's death; it was probably an accident, the result of bored police with time on their hands and clubs in their hands. But it is equally true that if China had the rule of law, or a free press, or independent courts and systems of accountability, Wang Chaoru would probably be alive today. Police brutality is a risk in any country, but in a country like China, with something on the agenda like the Olympics, it's easier for zeal to slip into overzealousness.

In more recent years, we have seen again how the Communist Party's desire to showcase Beijing for the Olympics can steamroll the rights of its own people. There used to be a "Petitioners' Village" in southern Beijing, where out-of-towners would gather to appeal for help from central authorities against injustices by local officials. I always thought of it as an odd tribute to the faith that many peasants had in the Communist Party; they believed that if only the center knew what was going on, the injustice would be remedied.

Instead, officials saw the Petitioners' Village as an eyesore. So they tore it down, put a wall around it, detained petitioners and sent them back to their villages to be battered by the same local officials who had caused the problems in the first place. When the village was half-demolished, I slipped inside late one evening—on the theory that at 9 p.m., almost no Chinese government office is still functioning. But Public Security works 24/7. After conducting a few interviews by candlelight, I slipped out again—just as a bunch of police cars roared up and the police fanned out, asking everybody, "Where is the foreigner?" If only the Communist Party tried as hard to root out injustice as it tries to root out foreign journalists.

Yet if the petitioners are already paying a price for the Olympics, there are also opportunities ahead. After all, the South Korean Olympics not only led to arrests in Seoul but were a major source of leverage in bringing democracy to the country. Likewise, human rights groups are trying to embarrass China into improving its human-rights image in the run-up to the Olympic Games—and it has worked to some extent.

The best example is Darfur, the war-torn region in western

Sudan where China wields an important influence through its economic and political support for Khartoum. The actress Mia Farrow and Eric Reeves, a professor of English literature at Smith College, have led an effort to use the Olympics to shame China into more responsible behavior in Sudan. This effort was not, as it was often reported, an attempt at an Olympic boycott but rather an attempt to "brand" the Games the Genocide Olympics unless China improved its behavior. And it has helped. The Chinese government initially reacted with fury, but it also appointed a special envoy in May 2007, and put far more pressure on Khartoum. If UN peacekeepers do get to Darfur, it will be largely thanks to the "Genocide Olympics" campaign, and no doubt there are already some in Darfur who are alive today only because of the pressure linked to the Olympic Games.

The world has a new lever available to try to win better behavior from China. The question is: will the world use it?

# PART I

# RECENT CHINESE HISTORY AND THE OLYMPIC CONTEXT

# CHAPTER 1

# Overview: China's Race for Reform

BY MINKY WORDEN

*When US President George W. Bush announced in the fall of 2007 that he had accepted an invitation by Chinese President Hu Jintao to attend the 2008 Beijing Olympic Games, the American leader said, "The eyes of the entire world will fall on Beijing." The hope of the twenty-five contributors to this anthology is that the light cast by the Olympic flame will illuminate the darker corners of China today, and that unprecedented contact with the international community could lead to positive and permanent change for the Chinese people.* MINKY WORDEN *is Media Director at Human Rights Watch. She has worked in Hong Kong as an adviser to Democratic Party chairman Martin Lee and in Washington, DC as a speechwriter at the US Department of Justice. She is the coeditor of* Torture, *published in 2005 by the New Press.*

When Beijing first sought the Olympic Games in the early 1990s, China was still recovering from the upheavals of the 1970s Cultural Revolution and adapting to the 1980s market revolution. In the wake of the 1989 Tiananmen Square crackdown, the Chinese government needed to find a way to reengage with the world community, sweep away the televised images of tanks in Tiananmen Square, and boost domestic credibility.

In 1990, paramount leader Deng Xiaoping came up with a plan: he announced that "China will apply to host the Olympics." The marketing slogan officials devised to woo International

Olympic Committee officials in China's 1993 bid was, "A More Open China Awaits the 2000 Games," splashed in English on billboards and walls in Beijing. As Chinese journalist Li Datong put it, "A successful application would go a long way to boosting national pride, and would heal a lot of the damage done to the regime . . . However, when the application was made in 1993, the sounds of the gunshots in Beijing were still ringing in people's ears. China was also not as powerful then as it is now. It was entirely predictable that the bid failed."[1]

To secure the 2008 Summer Games, the Chinese government came back to the Olympic bidding table better prepared. Beijing committed to major reforms, such as allowing international reporters unfettered access across the country. Top officials made human rights improvements a cornerstone of their case to be an Olympic host. In July 2001, in his final presentation to win the Games at the Moscow vote, Beijing Mayor and Bidding Committee president Liu Qi proclaimed, "I want to say that the Beijing 2008 Olympic Games will have the following special features: They will help promote our economic and social progress and will also benefit the further development of our human rights cause."[2] Veteran International Olympic Committee leader Richard Pound, who was present at both bids by China, confirms in his chapter that, "Part of its presentation to the IOC members was an acknowledgment of the concerns expressed in many parts of the world regarding its record on human rights, coupled with a preemptive suggestion that the IOC could help increase progress on such matters by awarding the Games to China." Public pledges aside, Beijing is also contractually bound by the many commitments involved in the selection process of Olympic host cities, detailed by Human Rights in China's executive director Sharon K. Hom in her chapter, "The Promise of a 'People's Olympics.'"

Yet today China continues to abuse basic human rights and to jail more journalists than any country in the world, often for reporting on abuses committed by local and central authorities. Some of these abuses are directly linked to the Olympics, such as the death of a forty-one-year-old mentally retarded man caught up in a sweep to beautify the city for an International Olympic Committee inspection tour, as described by *New York Times* columnist Nicholas Kristof in his introduction, or the more recent demolition of the village of petitioners seeking to have their grievances heard by the leaders in Beijing.

It is essential to understand China today, with 20 percent of the world's population, a rapidly growing economy, and a government emerging as a global political force. This book sets out to explain the realities of China in transition, with expert guidance from Chinese writers, China observers and human rights experts who have closely studied the country's revolutions and evolutions.

With these perspectives and analyses, this book is designed to be a resource for those attending or simply watching the 2008 Beijing Games who want to understand the human rights concerns shaping the world's most populous nation. We also hope members of the Chinese government will read *China's Great Leap* as constructive criticism to chart the future, offered by experts who care deeply about China and its people.

## LESSONS FROM SEOUL

When South Korea was attempting to win the right to host the 1988 Olympics, it was, like China today, undemocratic. South Korea's transition from military dictatorship to democracy and its first democratic presidential election in 1987 were the direct result of the prospect of riots at the time of the Olympic bid, making the Seoul Games an indispensable spur to political reform. As Richard Pound writes in his chapter, "Olympian Changes: Seoul and Beijing," the "new spotlight shining on South Korea in the period leading up to the Seoul Games had an important effect on the speed with which the South Korean leadership was willing to move in the direction of political reform."

China in 2008 is not a perfect parallel to South Korea in 1988, and surely there are no guarantees for a similar Olympics-driven political evolution. The 2008 Olympic Games will highlight China's emerging role on the world stage as much as its economic progress and its sports prowess. But like leaders in South Korea a generation ago, the Chinese authorities believe they can control the Olympic process, and they are confident that they can deflect any internal or external pressures for reform that the Olympics create.

Sports writer Dave Zirin's cautionary historical perspective, "The Ghosts of Olympics Past," recalls the 1936 "Nazi Games" in Berlin. The Berlin Games originated the Olympic Torch Relay and in some respects foreshadowed the nationalistic spectacle the Games are today. The Olympics have also occasionally resulted in violent repression, as in the Tlatelolco Square massacre just before the start of the 1968 Mexico City Games. Chinese authorities have warned of the triple treat of terrorism, separatism and extremism and have assigned 80,000 security guards to the Games. But of course the best way to defuse the prospects for demonstrations would be to remove the underlying root of potential unrest—the frustration that can swell when basic rights are denied.

This book was conceived to examine China at a key moment of transition and with the theme that the entire nation will be affected in ways the Chinese government anticipates—the debut of massive new infrastructure in Beijing—but also in ways the Chinese government does not anticipate. History suggests the likely exposure of cracks in China's great wall of control. Another important theme that emerges from this collection is that even if the Games do not produce permanent reforms, they may well produce permanent pressures for reform. For example, international journalists will traverse China, reporting under the somewhat loosened "temporary regulations" put in place for the Games. But once the regulations expire in October 2008, will journalists accept a reversion to the old controls? Other key areas in need of durable reform include the rule of law, Internet freedom, labor rights, health and environmental crises, protections for civil society and political accountability. With scores of world leaders attending the Beijing Olympics, the opportunities for external pressure to reform could also be unprecedented.

## CHINA'S GREAT LEAP BACKWARD

The title of this book, *China's Great Leap*, refers to one of the darkest periods in China's long history. A campaign launched by Chinese Communist leader Mao Zedong in 1958, the Great Leap Forward sought to industrialize agrarian China by collectivizing farms and attempting to turn villages and peasant households into centers of steel production. Across the country, backyard stoves were set up, unsuccessfully, to smelt steel. Farmers left fields untended. One of the world's worst famines followed, with deaths from this period estimated to be 20 million or more. When Deng Xiaoping and other party leaders managed to take control and reverse the Great Leap Forward's catastrophic course, Chairman Mao responded by launching the Cultural Revolution.

During the Cultural Revolution, from 1966 to his death in 1976, Mao unleashed the Chinese people against each other in a decade of political, social and economic chaos. Intellectuals, artists, writers and those who simply had contacts with the outside world were denounced and sent to the countryside to perform manual labor and "learn from the peasants"—or worse. Millions died, were jailed or were "purged" as Mao's power struggle took over the country. Today, many Chinese families carry with them shocking stories of disrupted education, unhinged careers and shattered lives.[3] After Mao's death on September 9, 1976, Deng Xiaoping, who had been put under house arrest by Mao in his last days,[4] became the country's new "paramount leader" in 1978. He managed to correct some of Mao's worst excesses through economic opening and other reforms. As described by author Frank Ching in his chapter "From Mao to Now," China has changed markedly in the three decades since Mao's death. Under Deng's leadership, ordinary Chinese people regained an element of control over their lives and China opened somewhat to the outside world. Intellectuals and others began to hope that there could be space to seek further reforms.

## THE TIANANMEN SHADOW

In May and June of 1989, students led academics, intellectuals, labor leaders and others into Tiananmen Square in central Beijing to protest corruption and to demonstrate for democracy. Because the demonstration coincided with a visit by Mikhail Gorbachev and the first Chinese-Soviet summit in thirty years, the world's media happened to be on hand to cover the protests. Contributors Wang Dan, Han Dongfang, Liu Xiaobo and Bao Tong all served prison terms following the Tiananmen Square crackdown for challenging the party in this period.

In the spring of 1989, Wang Dan was a principal student leader of the Tiananmen Square protests against party corruption and for democratic reform. Han Dongfang organized workers to join the protests and press for independent trade unions—exposing that Communist China was and is no workers' paradise. Liu Xiaobo, a scholar of Chinese literature at Beijing Normal University, led a hunger strike in the square. Unlike the protesters, Bao Tong was a rising star in the party constellation as director of the Chinese Communist Party Office of Political Reform and as Political Secretary to Premier Zhao Ziyang. That is, until Bao and

Zhao backed the demonstrators. Zhao was stripped of his powers and placed under house arrest, while Bao was charged with "revealing state secrets and counter-revolutionary propagandizing," convicted and sentenced to seven years in prison. In his chapter, "Modern Games, Old Chinese Communist Party," Bao writes from Beijing where he and his family still live under virtual house arrest, and where in spite of—or maybe in part because of—this predicament he remains an influential internal critic.

Today the shadow of Tiananmen Square still hangs over China's leaders. Although those leaders who sent the tanks against demonstrators in 1989 have died or left center stage, the Chinese government has not reversed its position on the Tiananmen democracy movement. As former student leader Wang Dan writes in "Five Olympic Rings, Thousands of Handcuffs," the country's prisons are still filled with those who, like him, sought reform through peaceful criticism of the government. Yet the years since the Tiananmen crackdown offer a glimmer of hope. While openly criticizing the government remains off limits, there is far more economic and personal freedom for millions of ordinary citizens. People have more choice, including the ability to leave rural areas of China to seek better pay in China's Special Economic Zones and more prosperous provinces.

Indeed, an estimated 150 million migrant workers are on the move inside the country—a margin of error that itself speaks volumes about the government's inability even to track, much less manage, such changes. Some 4 million migrant workers have contributed to Beijing's massive Olympic makeover. In her chapter, "Building the New Beijing," Pulitzer Prize–winning *Wall Street Journal* reporter Mei Fong brings to life the experience and sacrifices many migrant workers building the new Beijing made to support their families and create a better life for their children. This stark reality is also captured in the photo essay by award-winning photographer Kadir van Lohuizen, "Migrant Workers Race the Clock."

The cost of just six of these Olympic venues—among them the National Stadium, known as the "Bird's Nest," and the National Aquatics Center, known as the "Water Cube"—is expected to total some US $2.5 billion. But as Han Dongfang and writer Geoffrey Crothall explain in their chapter, "China's Olympic Dream, No Workers' Paradise," without basic labor reforms and protections, workers in Beijing and across China are being exploited, from child labor on assembly lines to deadly working conditions on construction sites. In addition to the human cost of building the new Beijing, environmental advocate Christine Loh's chapter, "Clearing the Air," underlines the huge environmental cost of China's fast-paced economic growth in recent years, as evidenced by the polluted air of Beijing. This problem has been compounded by the construction of dozens of new Olympic venues and hotels for the Games. In their zeal to clear the air in August, Chinese weather officials have even used anti-aircraft guns to shoot chemicals into the clouds over Beijing to induce rain.[5]

An estimated 30,000 journalists will fan out across China in the summer of 2008 to cover the Games and more broadly cover the way Chinese people and society are evolving. In a chapter titled, "A Gold Medal in Media Censorship," Human Rights Watch researcher Phelim Kine sets out why the lack of a free media poses a far greater danger to the country's safety than press reports that may shine an unflattering light on the complex realities of modern China. "The truths of corruption, public health scandals, environmental crises, and abusive local authorities may be inconvenient," he writes. But the impulse to "smother the reporting of these truths has contributed measurably to other global debacles, including recalls of tainted food and toys." Product safety and public health in China are growing global concerns. Public health and AIDS expert Joseph Amon's chapter, "High

Hurdles to Health in China," explores the tragic human cost of suppressing the truth in health crises, as in the deadly SARS (Severe Acute Respiratory Syndrome) outbreak in 2002–2003 and the country's ongoing HIV/AIDS crisis.

## RULE OF LAW VERSUS RULE BY LAW

One key reform with great potential to transform China is the rule of law. China today has many laws, but so long as the Chinese Communist Party is above the law, the country will only have "rule *by* law." Without due process and with the frequent use of administrative detention for up to four years (known as or *laojiao*, or "reeducation through labor"), China is able to use the legal system to repress most critical voices. But as Jerome Cohen, who has spent decades studying and working in China's legal system, explains in his chapter, "A Slow March to Legal Reform," there are reasons for cautious optimism, including recent efforts by the Supreme People's Court to bring down the number of state executions.

Another area requiring reform is freedom of religion. Although "freedom of religious belief" is ostensibly guaranteed by Article 36 of China's Constitution, religious freedom expert Mickey Spiegel's chapter, "Worship Beyond the Gods of Victory," details numerous constraints faced in China by evangelical Protestants, underground Catholics, Uighur Muslims, Falun Gong practitioners and Tibetan Buddhists. The Chinese government's harsh crackdown on Tibetan demonstrations in March 2008, as this book was going to press, was met with global condemnation and calls for a boycott of the Beijing Games.

The small, vibrant society of Hong Kong is in some ways an oasis in China. Not only does it still enjoy the rule of law (a legacy from colonial Britain), it also boasts more newspapers than any city in the world. It has long been a place where refugees from China fled for basic rights not available on the mainland. But as

Hong Kong democracy leader Martin Lee writes in his chapter, "Democracy with Chinese Characteristics," the territory's human rights are being undermined by Beijing, which doesn't understand the delicate framework of freedoms that have made Hong Kong one of the world's most prosperous economies. Without democracy, Hong Kong's minority of popularly elected leaders will not be able to defend the territory from laws that would impinge freedoms. And because China has long followed Hong Kong's example in the economic realm, if the world cannot encourage Beijing to preserve the example of the human rights and rule of law in this small but influential corner of China, then it will be much harder to put in place key legal and other reforms on the mainland.

## CHINA'S IMAGE

With international confidence in some Chinese products undermined, and with Beijing's economic and political support for repressive regimes like Sudan, Burma and North Korea exposed, former American Chamber of Commerce head John Kamm's chapter, "A Marathon Challenge to Improve China's Image," explains why Chinese leaders face their worst image crisis since Tiananmen Square. With an estimated half-million attendees and a television audience of many millions, China is seeking the world's spotlight to showcase the country's strength, stability and unity. The last time there was as much attention on China as the Games will bring was in the spring of 1989, when the side of China on display was a desperate and deadly one. For the Games' opening, Tiananmen Square will feature in Olympics celebrations as a staging ground not for protests against corruption and calls for democracy, but to showcase the nation's unity with parades and speeches.

As former top Communist Party official Bao Tong asks, "What makes the Beijing 2008 Summer Olympics different from previous Olympic Games held in other countries? The answer is that no other government has been quite as eager to use the Games to enhance its international prestige. The Chinese government fervently hopes thereby to boost its domestic support and to regain people's trust."

The corporate sponsors of the Games of course hope the 2008 Summer Olympics will boost corporate profiles and bottom lines in and out of China. Arvind Ganesan, an expert in corporations and human rights, proposes in his chapter, "The Race for Profits," that leading sponsors like General Electric and McDonald's should recognize their own self-interest in pressing for Beijing to follow through on its pledges for press and other freedoms. Lawyer R. Scott Greathead points out in "China and the Spielberg Effect" that corporate sponsors and external Olympic advisers— such as director Steven Spielberg prior to his resignation in February 2008 over China's inaction in Darfur—are uniquely well placed to deliver messages of concern about human rights policies, both international and domestic.

## "LOVING THE MOTHERLAND"

In her chapter on Chinese nationalism, "Dragons Win," writer Emily Parker explains that another constant in Chinese government rhetoric is *aiguozhuyi,* or loving the country. China today has largely moved beyond the violent Maoist tactics used in the Great Leap Forward or Cultural Revolution. Its leaders are more sophisticated and care about the government's public image, so intimidation and warnings to "love the country" are preferred methods to keep critics in line. Princeton Professor Perry Link has described the Chinese government's strategy as "not so much a man-eating tiger or fire-snorting dragon as a giant anaconda coiled in an overhead chandelier. Normally the great snake doesn't move. It doesn't have to. It feels no need to be clear about its prohibitions. Its constant silent message is 'You yourself decide.' After which, more often than not, everyone in its shadow makes his or her large and small adjustments—all quite 'naturally.'"[6]

Since China does not have a political system with democratic electoral outlets for expressing nationalistic sentiments, the less attractive side of Chinese nationalism has occasionally surfaced, as after NATO's accidental 1999 bombing of the Chinese Embassy in Belgrade when US Ambassador Jim Sasser was trapped in his Embassy for four days while an angry mob pelted the building with stones. Chinese nationalist fervor also erupted in violent anti-Japanese demonstrations in 2005.

This book contains voices of Chinese citizens who deeply love their country. It is at some level remarkable that Wang Dan, released from prison in 1993 as a bargaining chip in Beijing's first campaign to win the 2000 Games (he was rearrested soon thereafter), nonetheless supports China's hosting of the Games. Like Bao Tong, the Chinese writer and former academic Liu Xiaobo also resides in Beijing. In "Authoritarianism in the Light of the Olympic Flame," Liu analyzes the Communist Party's historic reliance on nationalism as a way to buttress its popularity in the absence of true democratic legitimacy. While Liu concedes that "nationalist pride may swell in the short term" during the Beijing Olympics, he also cautions that the long-term interests of the Chinese people will not be served absent meaningful human rights reforms.

Indeed, working for political and human rights reform remains an area of great peril in China today. Leading human rights advocate Hu Jia, who had used the Internet to inform the outside world about HIV/AIDS, peasant protests and legal cases, became a human rights case himself when he was hauled away from his wife and baby daughter on December 27, 2007. After being denied contact with his lawyers on the grounds that his case involved "state secrets," Hu was sentenced on April 3, 2008 to three and a half years of imprisonment. One month before his arrest, Hu had deplored the "human rights disaster" in China while testifying via webphone at a hearing of the European Parliament's Subcommittee on Human Rights. He had also signed an open letter with the human rights lawyer Teng Biao, affirming their "belief that there can be no true Olympic Games without human rights and dignity."[7]

## A "MORE OPEN" CHINA?

The Olympics are often associated with the economic and physical transformation of a host city, but could the Beijing Games contribute to a revolution of an even wider scope, leading to greater openness and transparency, an expansion of basic freedoms and the rule of law in China? Despite setbacks in the short term, there is reason for hope in the long term. As Olympic expert Richard Pound points out, "No host country of the Olympic Games has ever been the same after the Games as it had been before, especially countries that had been closed or particularly authoritarian."

In examining China's march to human rights reform, this book seeks to take the long view—beyond the 2008 Olympics—and to enable readers to understand why it is vital that China develops not only as a rising global power, but also one that is responsible and transparent in its polices at home and abroad. As several writers in this volume suggest, the Chinese government needs to showcase its achievements on a grand scale because its source of legitimacy is not the ballot box, but a succession of self-selecting party leaders. One certain by-product of a successful Olympics is to prop up the government's domestic legitimacy. But could the Olympics also nudge China into a more responsible role on the foreign policy stage? In "Challenges for a 'Responsible Power,'" China foreign policy expert Sophie Richardson posits that Chinese leaders are taking small but measurable steps to address the crisis in Darfur, engage the Burmese junta, and contribute larger numbers of troops to international peacekeeping efforts such as the UN force in Lebanon.

With a faster flow of information and accelerating external pressures to reform, the big open question is how much positive impact the international community can have in China. Jimmy Lai is a media magnate who has built a publishing empire on the belief that Chinese people want choice. In "Physical Strength, Moral Poverty," Lai writes that changes in the morals and political ambitions of the Chinese people have occurred in ways still largely imperceptible to outside observers, but with the right external pressures could accelerate greatly.

It is a time of great change for the Chinese people, whose economic and social lives are fortunately improved from a generation ago. The status quo seems to exist only in the political areas. However, those who wish to see progress inside China should remember that the Chinese government is not monolithic, and external pressures to reform can only help domestic reformers inside China's system who are already working internally for the same goals.

Could domestic and international pressure in the context of the Olympics achieve significant human rights change? In his chapter, "A Dual Approach to Rights Reform," Human Rights Watch executive director Kenneth Roth concludes, "Difficulty does not warrant despair." As BOCOG President Liu Qi said, "China will live up to its words and will turn its words into deeds."[8] That is, the world should take the Chinese government at its word—that improving human rights is a top priority in the context of the Olympic Games—and work to achieve that vital goal. With intelligent, consistent and principled external pressure over time, there could be truly Olympian changes on the horizon for the people of China. Then the 2008 Beijing Games might not be merely a race for medals or a race for profits—instead, they could sound the starting gun of China's ultimate race for reform.

# CHAPTER 2

# From Mao to Now: Three Tumultuous Decades

BY FRANK CHING

*Three decades separate the death in 1976 of Mao Zedong from the launch of the Summer Olympic Games in Beijing in 2008. During this period China has experienced both continuity—resisting the fate of the former Soviet Union by remaining a one-party, Communist state—and extraordinary change. The country has evolved from pronounced isolation to a marked desire for recognition as a major actor on the world stage, with a thirst for the spotlight which will shine on it during the Beijing Olympics.* FRANK CHING *has covered China for nearly forty years, including as the first correspondent for the* Wall Street Journal *in postwar China. He provides an eyewitness account of these turbulent times leading to the present.*

Chairman Mao Zedong was a towering figure who dominated the People's Republic of China from its establishment in 1949 until his death in 1976. He continued to wield his influence after death as his chosen successor, Hua Guofeng, attempted to wrap himself in the Great Helmsman's mantle by preaching: "We will resolutely uphold whatever policy decisions Chairman Mao made, and unswervingly follow whatever instructions Chairman Mao gave." Under Hua, China was going to be governed by a dead man. But, fortunately for China, the post-Mao succession struggle was resolved in 1978 when Deng Xiaoping, twice purged by Mao, emerged triumphant after having accused Hua of practicing the "Two Whatevers."

The about-turn in Chinese politics was dramatic. In spring 1978, China's parliament, the National People's Congress, had reaffirmed Hua's position as the nation's leader and hailed the "tremendous victory" of Mao's "Great Proletarian Cultural Revolution"—a disastrous campaign that had brought the country to the brink of bankruptcy. The parliament echoed Mao's call for grasping "the key link of class struggle" and adopted a new Constitution that declared, "The state upholds the leading position of Marxism-Leninism-Mao Zedong Thought in all spheres of ideology and culture."

By the end of 1978, however, the Chinese Communist Party had reversed course. At the pivotal third plenary session of the central committee of the eleventh Party Congress—a session dominated by Deng—held in December, the party forswore class struggle and announced that it would in the future focus on economic development.

Though I was based in Hong Kong in those days, writing for the *Asian Wall Street Journal*, I took advantage of the semi-annual trade fair in Canton (now Guangzhou) to cadge visas from the Foreign Ministry and, from Guangzhou, I would make my way up to Shanghai and Beijing where, in late 1978, I was able to witness dramatic events firsthand.

Deng was able to achieve his triumph of partly ridding the country of Mao's dogmatism through a prolonged campaign calling on the party to be pragmatic rather than doctrinaire. He did this by quoting a Maoist dictum: "Seek truth from facts." In May 1978, an article that shocked the nation, "Practice Is the Sole Criterion of Truth," appeared in all the country's major newspapers.

It was earth-shaking because it preached a simple notion: truth can be verified only through practice, and is not found in the writings of Marx, Engels, Lenin or Chairman Mao. When, on October 1, 1978—China's National Day—Hua also chimed in with, "We must emancipate our minds and seek truth from facts," it was clear that Deng had gained the upper hand.

## "SEEKING TRUTH FROM FACTS" AND THE
## DEMOCRACY WALL ERA

In this new environment, handwritten posters began to appear spontaneously in the Xidan District of Beijing, on a long brick wall that was quickly dubbed "Democracy Wall." Many called for the full rehabilitation of Deng Xiaoping and other senior revolutionaries purged in the Cultural Revolution; others called for a reassessment of Mao; still others called for democracy or aired personal grievances, demanding justice. The area became a beehive of activity, day and night.

On November 28, 1978, I went to Democracy Wall. A huge crowd had gathered, awaiting the arrival of the American columnist Robert Novak, who had interviewed Deng Xiaoping earlier that day and had promised to tell the people what China's new leader had to say. Thousands bundled up against the cold, sat on the frozen ground near Democracy Wall. Novak himself did not show up, but John Fraser of the *Globe and Mail* came to say that among other things, Deng had disclosed that Marshal Peng Dehuai, a former defense minister dismissed by Mao in the 1950s for criticizing his Great Leap Forward policies, would be posthumously rehabilitated.

These words were greeted warmly by the crowd, many of whose members would only have been toddlers during the Great Leap years, when Mao fanatically sought to industrialize China through the creation of 600,000 backyard furnaces to be used in steel production, and set unrealistic targets for grain output. These efforts ultimately led to mass starvation. But as far as the throng at Democracy Wall was concerned, the main message imparted by Deng at his meeting with Novak was his assessment of their darling—the posters spread across this wall in Xidan. Deng, it turned out, had told Novak: "Democracy Wall in Xidan is a good thing!"

The crowd's excitement was palpable. "Vice Premier Deng is supporting us!" one exuberant young man shouted with joy, throwing his hat high in the air. Because voices did not carry very far in the open air, only those seated in the front could hear what was said. To spread the word, those seated in the front turned around and repeated the words in unison, with the message being repeated by people a few rows back, the process continuing until the message had reached even people in the very back. The exhilarated multitude then rose and surged into Changan Boulevard in the direction of Tiananmen Square, about twenty minutes away, singing the Chinese national anthem. I found myself propelled along, without my feet touching the ground, as I was carried away on a sea of humanity.

The following week, another wall poster appeared, authored by an electrician at the Beijing Zoo named Wei Jingsheng, entitled "The fifth modernization: Democracy." Deng had echoed the call by Zhou Enlai for the "four modernizations": of agriculture, industry, science and technology, and defense. Now a worker, theoretically the master of the country, was calling for a fifth modernization, something that the Communist Party to this day is reluctant to accept. He was to spend nearly two decades in prison for his beliefs.

## NORMALIZING RELATIONS

A few days later, I was able to interview Ambassador Leonard Woodcock, head of the United States Liaison Office in Beijing, which functioned in lieu of an embassy since China and the United States did not yet have diplomatic relations with each other. Washington at the time still treated the Kuomintang government in Taiwan as the legitimate government of China. The ambassador was convinced that the time had arrived for Washington to normalize ties with Beijing. "I have the feeling that this is about the time that that can be done," he said. "The feeling on both sides is good, and how long it will last I don't know."

On December 15, 1978, exactly a week after my article containing those words was published in the *Asian Wall Street Journal*, President Jimmy Carter announced that, beginning January 1, 1979, the United States would sever its ties with Taiwan and establish diplomatic relations with China. In the joint communiqué announcing this, the United States and China asserted that "neither should seek hegemony in the Asia-Pacific region or in any other region of the world and each is opposed to efforts by any other country or group of countries to establish such hegemony." The second part of that statement was clearly directed at the Soviet Union. China and the United States had entered into a de facto alliance. Days later, the Chinese Communist Party held the third plenary session of the eleventh central committee, which decided on a dramatic change in direction for the party and the nation. An editorial in the *People's Daily* explained: "Modernization will be the central task for the whole party from now on, so long as there is not a large-scale enemy invasion. All other work, including the party's political work, will focus on and serve this central task."

The die was cast. Beginning then, China would single-mindedly focus on economic development, seeking to attract foreign investment, earn foreign exchange through exports and raise the standard of living of its people. World revolution was no longer its goal. The fact that normalization of relations with the United States occurred at almost exactly the same time as the change in the party's direction was no coincidence. Deng knew that if China was to modernize, it would need the West, and particularly America, because of its capital, technology and markets.

Beijing swiftly made use of its enhanced global status by seeking to lure Taiwan to "return to the embrace of the motherland." On January 1, 1979, the day the United States cut off ties with

Taiwan, China broadcast a "Message to Taiwan Compatriots" appealing for early reunification between the two sides, separated since 1949 when the defeated forces of Chiang Kai-shek were swept off mainland China onto Taiwan. In return, Beijing pledged to immediately halt the shelling of the offshore island of Quemoy (Jinmen), which had been going on since the 1950s. But Taiwan's initial response was unyielding. Chiang Kai-shek had died in 1975 but his son, Chiang Ching-kuo, was now president. He responded to Beijing's overtures with an adamant policy of "three no's": No contact, no negotiation and no compromise with the Communists.

At the time, no American journalists were allowed to be based in Beijing. However, we were allowed to fly to the Chinese capital to cover the establishment of bilateral relations and, on January 5, 1979, Deng Xiaoping himself met with us. Each of us was allowed to ask one question. When it was my turn, I asked Deng if China was interested in purchasing weapons from the United States. He answered that China was interested in importing all kinds of advanced equipment from the United States, but he was not sure if the United States would be willing to sell weapons to China.

The next day, the entire transcript of the questions and answers appeared on the front page of the *People's Daily*, together with a photograph. I was standing directly behind Deng, peering at his head to see if the black hair he sported was natural or dyed.

## REFORM AND OPENING

The normalization of Sino-American relations changed my life. It meant that for the first time, American news organizations would be allowed to open bureaus in Beijing. China decided that the first four American newspapers to be allowed into the country would be the *Wall Street Journal*, the *New York Times*, the *Washington Post* and the *Los Angeles Times*. The *Journal* asked me to be its first Beijing bureau chief. I was happy to accept.

My first task upon arrival in Beijing was to get myself accredited and, for that purpose, I went to the Chinese Foreign Ministry to meet the head of the Press Department, a man named Yao Wei. "You don't need permission to interview anyone in China," he told me. Unfortunately, he forgot to tell anyone else, because every time I tried to interview someone, the person would say, "I don't have permission to talk to you." Once, I wanted to interview the manager of the International Club, who was renting out space to foreign companies to use as offices, but he refused to believe that he did not need permission to talk to me. I telephoned the Foreign Ministry and asked the lady on the other end to simply tell him that he could talk to me without permission. The manager asked the lady for her name and title, and then agreed to talk. He had received permission. At the time, I had two rooms in the Peking Hotel, one of which functioned as my home and the other as an office. There were no offices or apartments for rent. There were no scheduled press conferences, no spokespersons, and, worst of all, no telephone numbers—all of which were ostensibly state secrets.

Deng Xiaoping's government announced two national priorities, beginning in the 1980s: economic development and national reunification. Where economic development was concerned, Deng set the ambitious goal of doubling the level of China's gross domestic product as of 1980 in ten years and then redoubling it again by 2000. As it turned out, this goal was achieved by 1995, five years ahead of schedule. This major national reorientation necessitated changes in Chinese foreign policy as well. In order to ensure a tranquil environment in which to focus on economic development, Beijing set about making friends with all of its neighbors, redefining disputed borders and ending its support for insurgent movements in Southeast Asia. It developed what it called an independent foreign policy of peace, in which all nations are considered friends.

Deng's other goal was that of national unification. Although at the time Hong Kong was a British colony and Macau was under Portuguese sovereignty, Beijing's eye was on Taiwan. China knew that it could take back Hong Kong and Macau at any time. In fact, it had rejected an offer from the socialist government of Portugal to return Macau in the 1970s because it knew that such a move would cause pandemonium in Hong Kong as it would inevitably be seen as a prelude to the takeover of the British colony. In Taiwan, the ruling Kuomintang still claimed to be the legal government of all China. Unlike Hong Kong or Macau, Taiwan was under ethnic Chinese rule, but Beijing considered it intolerable to have Taiwan remain politically separate from the mainland.

## GROUNDWORK FOR HONG KONG'S HANDOVER

Gradually, Deng and his associates came up with the idea of "one country, two systems" whereby Taiwan would be able to continue its capitalist way of life after reunification while the mainland would adhere to socialism. This idea was first disclosed in 1981 in a major speech by Ye Jianying, chairman of the National People's Congress, where, for the first time, the term "special administrative region" appeared.

To prepare the groundwork for unification with Taiwan, the following year China adopted a new constitution with an article that declared: "The state may establish special administrative regions when necessary. The systems to be instituted in special administrative regions shall be prescribed by law enacted by the National People's Congress in the light of the specific conditions." However, fate intervened. The British were worried about the future of their colony because while Hong Kong Island and the Kowloon peninsula had been ceded to the United Kingdom, the New Territories had been obtained in 1898 under a ninety-nine-year lease. That lease would expire on June 30, 1997.

The People's Republic of China had taken the position that all three treaties under which Britain had obtained various parts of Hong Kong were "null and void" because they were "unequal treaties" that had been obtained through gunboat diplomacy from a weakened Qing Dynasty. Chinese maps showed Hong Kong as "British occupied." China took the position that at some point in the future when "the time was ripe," it would take back Hong Kong. In the meantime, for its own purposes, Beijing was happy to allow Hong Kong to continue under the British.

Britain, however, could not take the position that the treaties were irrelevant. The expiration of the New Territories lease could deprive Britain of the legal right to administer 92 percent of the territory. During much of the 1960s and 1970s when China was in the grip of the Cultural Revolution, the British realized that the country was in such chaos that there was no one with whom to negotiate. However, London felt that the pragmatic Deng Xiaoping was someone with whom it could strike a deal. And so, in March 1979, shortly before I moved to Beijing, Sir Murray MacLehose, the Governor of Hong Kong, paid a rare visit to China and held talks with Deng Xiaoping. According to a Chinese source present at the meeting, Deng told MacLehose in no uncertain terms that Hong Kong was Chinese territory and would have to return to Chinese control at some point, possibly even before 1997 or during that year. That is to say, the lease was irrelevant.

As a Beijing-based correspondent for whom Hong Kong was home, I was extremely interested in China's position on the future of the colony. MacLehose's visit was followed by a long period with no new developments, either on the British or the Chinese side. However, the British could not afford to let the issue die. They felt that they needed another piece of paper to give them the legal authority to continue to run Hong Kong. Hence the British kept pushing China to take a position. But while Beijing was prepared to allow British administration to continue as a "legacy of history," it was not prepared to sign a new treaty with Britain extending colonialism in China into the twenty-first century.

And so, one evening in mid-1982 when I had dinner with a well-placed source who was an adviser to Deng, I was told that Beijing had decided to "put on the agenda" the return of Hong Kong to Chinese control. My source would not be any more specific but it was clear that the British would not be allowed to administer Hong Kong beyond 1997. With a heavy heart, I reported this exclusive story in the *Wall Street Journal*. It appeared on July 23, 1982, and began: "China has decided against extending Britain's lease over most of Hong Kong and will 'recover' its sovereignty over the colony, according to usually well-informed sources."

While China's previous policy had been to focus on the return of Taiwan while leaving Hong Kong in British hands, it now decided that it would take back Hong Kong in 1997 and turn it into a "special administrative region" as a model for Taiwan. China's decision gave Hong Kong the jitters and created an incredible new phenomenon: the cake run. In May 1984, lines of worried customers clutching coupons received as gifts at bridal receptions stood in line outside the forty-seven cake shops, known as Maria's, demanding cakes. They cleaned out the stores. It was a symptom of the underlying worries of the populace, most of whom were refugees from the Communists or the children of such refugees.

Despite Hong Kong's obvious nervousness, in December 1984, Britain and China signed the Sino-British Joint Declaration on the Question of Hong Kong, under which the colony would revert to Chinese sovereignty on July 1, 1997. China would adopt a policy of "one country, two systems," and Hong Kong as a special administrative region would be given a "high degree of autonomy" with "Hong Kong people administering Hong Kong" for fifty years. In April 1987, Portugal signed an agreement to return Macau to China in 1999. Deng's agenda for national reunification was making progress.

## TIANANMEN DEMONSTRATIONS

Meanwhile, Deng's economic reforms, in particular the introduction of a market economy, had led to rapid development but also increased polarization and the level of serious corruption. On April 15, 1989, the death of former party leader Hu Yaobang from a heart attack provided a catalyst for rallying disaffected citizens throughout China. Hu had been forced out as party leader in 1987 because of his refusal to crack down on student protestors. His death provided an opportunity for students to demonstrate against the party and government in the guise of mourning the death of a liberal leader.

For six weeks, student protesters filled Tiananmen Square, demanding a meeting with the country's leaders. On May 20, martial law was proclaimed in Beijing. Then, on the night of June 3, armed troops were ordered to clear the square. In the resulting violence, hundreds if not thousands of people were killed.

In Hong Kong, people were glued to their TV sets night after night, fearing the worst in the days preceding the crackdown. Menacing tanks lumbering into Beijing were shown on television screens around the world, as were scenes of dead and wounded civilians being taken to hospital on crude wooden carts pushed by hand. There was panic in Hong Kong, whose citizens identified with the Beijing students and feared that they would soon share the same fate.

Overseas, there was universal condemnation of China, led by the United States. Overnight, China became an international pariah. The de facto Sino-American alliance unraveled. Mikhail Gorbachev's Soviet Union clearly posed no threat, and Washington no longer felt any need to provide special treatment to Beijing, especially where human rights were concerned. From 1989 on, China's human rights record became the target of condemnation by the West. The United States and its European allies imposed economic sanctions on China. World Bank loans were discontinued. Western leaders refused to visit China or be seen with its leaders. Even Japan imposed sanctions, cutting off yen loans.

Faced with this situation, China did everything it could to end its international isolation. Where Hong Kong was concerned, the Chinese demanded that British Prime Minister John Major personally travel to Beijing to sign an agreement on the financing of a new Hong Kong airport. The British leader looked somber and unsmiling whenever he appeared with his Chinese counterpart, Premier Li Peng, one of the hardliners responsible for the Tiananmen massacre. Within Hong Kong, Britain was pilloried for agreeing to turn over millions of British subjects to a Communist dictatorship, one that had been proved willing to shed its own citizens' blood. Over the next few years, Hong Kong experienced a "brain drain," as a half million people, some 10 percent of the population, would leave the colony to seek refuge abroad, largely in Canada, Australia and the United States.

Surprisingly, perhaps, the Tiananmen massacre did not slow down the improvement of relations between Taiwan and mainland China. Taiwanese manufacturers transferred more than fifty production lines to the mainland for manufacturing shoes, umbrellas and furniture between August and October 1989. Taiwanese investors rushed in to fill the vacuum left by their Western counterparts. In 1992, Taipei and Beijing reached agreement on the "one China" principle and, the following year, held high-level "nongovernmental" talks in Singapore. But the resulting euphoria was short-lived because in 1995, President Lee Teng-hui was granted a visa by the United States, precipitating a crisis as China conducted military exercises in the Taiwan Strait.

## OLYMPIC BID FAILURE

China's priority was still to break through the invisible blockade imposed by the West. In September 1990, Beijing hosted the Asian Games (also known as Asiad), which helped to alleviate the country's isolation. China began to think of another, bigger athletic event that would do even more to end the international isolation: the hosting of the Olympic Games in 2000. A successful bid would show that China had regained the acceptance of the international community. The holding of the Games would vindicate China's crackdown, showing that the country had emerged more stable and prosperous than before.

Accordingly, President Yang Shangkun told Juan Antonio Samaranch, president of the International Olympic Committee, when the two men met during the Asian Games, that China would apply for hosting the 2000 Olympics. At the closing ceremony of the Beijing Asiad on October 7, 1990, a banner struck across the Dongcheng District of Beijing declared, "We have successfully hosted the Asiad, and we can successfully host the Olympic Games." Beijing Mayor Chen Xitong formally applied for the 2000 Summer Games to be held in his city. The whole country responded, as students called on the youth of the nation to support the bid. The government and the people were finally united in a common effort. The Chinese people, it seemed, felt that hosting the Olympic Games would show that China would be seen as a part of the world again.

In April 1991, a Beijing 2000 Olympic Games bid committee was set up with Mayor Chen as president and Sports Minister Wu Shaozu as the executive president. On December 4, Vice Mayor Zhang Baifa, the executive vice president of the Beijing Bid Committee, handed Beijing's application to Samaranch at the IOC headquarters in Lausanne, Switzerland. Premier Li Peng, in a

1991 letter to the International Olympic Committee, said that China would try "to make the 2000 Olympic Games a grand celebration in sports, marking the advent of a new millennium with a better prospect of peace and friendship." For China, of course, the Games would provide an important opportunity to win back international respect after Tiananmen Square, and a chance to unite the Chinese people behind a nationalistic cause.

For the next two years, the city went all-out to prepare to host the Olympics. However, almost immediately, strong opposition emerged. In the United States, the House of Representatives, in a nonbinding resolution, voted overwhelmingly to oppose holding the Olympics in China because of the Chinese government's poor record on human rights. Even in Hong Kong, where I was then living, significant voices were raised against the idea, saying that China had not "earned" the right to such an honor. Comparisons were drawn to the 1936 Olympics, which Hitler was given the right to host in Berlin, allowing him a springboard to preach Nazi racist theories.

Others, however, pointed out that, in recent experience at least, hosting the Olympics had often had positive consequences, as with Tokyo in 1964 and Seoul in 1988. The Seoul Olympics, in particular, were credited with having provided momentum for South Korea's transition to democracy. Despite opposition to letting the authoritarian South Korean government host the Games at that time, there was widespread agreement after the event that the Olympics had helped South Korea on the road toward democracy. The year before the Games were held, strongman Chun Du-hwan declared an amnesty, releasing 2,335 political dissidents—including his most implacable foe, Kim Dae-jung, who would later become the nation's president—and stepped down to pave the way for presidential elections.

By early 1993, in the race to host the Millennium Olympics, Beijing was clearly ahead of most of its competitors—Berlin, Brasilia, Istanbul and Manchester—with only Sydney as a possible threat.

However, the magnitude of the opposition to China was reflected when, just days before the vote, the European Parliament passed a resolution denouncing the human rights situation in Tibet and opposing Beijing's bid. The chairman of Beijing's bid committee, Chen Xitong, responded, "The closed China of the past has now opened its doors. We fervently want to know more about the world and to have more friends in the world know about us. Hosting the 2000 Games will open our door still wider."

But it was not to be. On September 23, 1993, the International Olympic Committee voting in Monte Carlo chose Sydney over Beijing by a vote of 45 to 43. Sydney's close victory was greeted triumphantly in the United States. "This is a good day for those who are struggling for freedom in China and a proud day for the Olympic movement," Senator Bill Bradley said. He and fifty-nine other senators had sent a letter to the International Olympic Committee urging it to reject Beijing's bid. There was relief that the Olympics would not be besmirched by being held in China.

However, the picture changed drastically when it transpired that hundreds of thousands of dollars went into scholarships and gifts for International Olympic Committee members and their relatives and Salt Lake City Olympic Committee leaders were forced to resign amid this bribery scandal.[1] This was followed by the revelation that the Australians had given US $70,000 to two IOC members the night before the vote—for which the margin of Australia's victory was exactly two.[2]

Actually, it was not at all clear that human rights would be further hurt rather than served if Beijing were allowed to host the Olympics. The official slogan used by China during the campaign was: "A more open China awaits the 2000 Olympics." China itself knew that hosting the Olympics, which would inevitably attract many thousands if not millions of visitors, would result in a more open China. The chairman of China's bid committee, Zhang Baifa, said: "The Olympic Games would help us promote reforms."

## HANDOVER JITTERS

Meanwhile, the handover clock installed in Tiananmen Square was counting down the days before Hong Kong would "return to the embrace of the motherland." The Western media saw mostly gloom and doom in the colony's future, as reflected in *Fortune* magazine's article "The Death of Hong Kong," and in the titles of such books as *The End of Hong Kong, The Fall of Hong Kong* and *The Last Days of Hong Kong.*

In an attempt to redress the balance, I wrote an article in the May/June 1997 issue of *Foreign Affairs* magazine titled "Misreading Hong Kong," which appeared just before the handover. I knew that China was not poised to crack down on Hong Kong, but had been spurred to take it over from a legal-minded British government. Moreover, because Hong Kong was such a success under the British, China, concerned with saving face, could not allow it to fail under Chinese rule.

And so, on June 29, 1997, the night before handover night, I was poised precariously on a stool in pelting rain outside the Royal Hong Kong Jockey Club telling viewers of *Good Morning America* what I felt lay in store for the new special administrative region. The next night, I acted as commentator on the English-language World channel of Asia Television from early evening until about 4 o'clock in the morning. By the time I walked home—there were no taxis anywhere—the British were gone. Hong Kong had become part of China.

## OLYMPIC BID, TAKE TWO

The failure of Beijing's bid for the 2000 Olympics was an unexpected setback for China. But the momentum was revived within a few years when the cry went out: Beijing will host the 2008

Summer Olympics. Those opposed to China's earlier bid again cranked up their lobbying machinery. A new resolution introduced in the US Congress said, "The Olympic Games in the year 2008 should not be held in the People's Republic of China because the deplorable human rights record of the People's Republic of China violates international human rights standards." One sponsor of the resolution, Representative Tom Lantos, declared, "It is completely inconsistent with the Olympic ideal to hold the Games in Beijing."

China responded by accusing the legislators who sponsored the resolution of violating the spirit of the Olympic movement by injecting politics into the Games. Chinese officials lobbying for votes in Moscow promised that foreign journalists would be free to write about anything during the Games, even stories unrelated to the Olympics. Voices opposed to China's bid were further muted when even certain prominent Chinese dissidents supported their government's efforts, believing that holding the Olympics in China would be good for Chinese society as a whole. "I strongly hope China can host the Olympics," said Wei Jingsheng, who was released from prison as part of China's attempt to improve its image and win the Olympics bid. "This is a matter for 1.2 billion people." Wang Dan, a student leader who served a prison term for his role in the pro-democracy movement in Tiananmen Square—and who contributes a chapter to this volume—also supported Beijing's bid.

In the end, while meeting in Moscow on July 13, 2001, the International Olympic Committee voted to give China the right to stage the 2008 Olympics. Beijing scored a landslide victory, receiving fifty-six votes, more than twice the twenty-two received by Toronto, the runner-up. It turned out that the opposition to Beijing was manifestly weaker than it had been eight years before. Even Taiwan, swayed by the strong support expressed by its business community, backed Beijing's bid. The neutral stance adopted by the Bush administration was seen as giving the green light to China. Even the human rights community was less vociferous in opposition. Human Rights Watch said, "There can be a positive impact on a tightly controlled society from hosting an international event." The expectation was that in the intervening seven years, China would be on its best behavior, fearful of having this prize wrenched from its hands.

China scored another victory in 2001, when in December of that year, after fifteen years of negotiations, China finally gained entry into the World Trade Organization. It would be treated as an equal by other members of the international trading community and would be expected to abide by its rules, which China would help to shape.

Meanwhile, the Chinese leadership, echoing Deng's original target, announced it would double the country's 2000 gross domestic product in ten years, and then seek to double it again by 2020—calling for a growth rate of 7 percent a year. Since 2000, China has not reported an annual growth rate lower than 8 percent, so it is again set to reach its target ahead of schedule. However, a steep price is being paid in terms of air and water pollution as well as unsafe food and drugs—the subject of international headlines in July 2007 when China executed a former director of the State Food and Drug Administration who had been convicted of corruption and of allowing the sale of tainted drugs.

In December 2006, Beijing moved to keep a promise it had made to the International Olympic Committee. It unveiled liberalized rules for foreign reporters from January 1, 2007, to October 17, 2008, a month after the end of the Paralympics, after which the old, more restrictive rules would presumably be reinstated. Article 6 of the new regulations said: "To interview organizations or individuals in China, foreign journalists need only to obtain their prior consent." That is to say, the government's approval is not required. It appeared that what Chinese Foreign Ministry official Yao Wei had told me some twenty-eight years earlier—"You don't need permission to interview anyone in China"—is finally coming to pass, even if only temporarily and just in the case of foreign journalists.

After a hiatus of 150 or more years following the decline of the Qing dynasty, China is preparing once again to play on the world stage a role proportional to the importance of its size, history, and geography. While the bid to host the Olympics in Beijing, first made in 1993, was meant to break through the country's diplomatic isolation and to unite its people, the 2008 Olympics have now assumed a much more important symbolic role. The Games are now seen by people both in and outside the country as the "coming out" of China, serving as a rebirth, as it were, after generations of foreign dominance and domestic oppression.

# CHAPTER 3

# The Promise of a "People's Olympics"

BY SHARON K. HOM[1]

*In February 2001, the* Washington Post *quoted a plea by Beijing's Deputy Mayor Liu Jingmin, a top Olympic official: "By applying for the Olympics, we want to promote not just the city's development, but the development of society, including democracy and human rights." Did such public and private assurances swing IOC votes in Beijing's favor?* SHARON KANG HOM *is the Executive Director of Human Rights in China and professor of law emerita at City University of New York School of Law. She is the coeditor of* Challenging China *(2007), and the editor of* Chinese Women Traversing Diaspora: Memoirs, Essays, and Poetry *(1999). In November 2007, the* Wall Street Journal *named her one of "Fifty Women to Watch" in 2008.*

In November 1998, as Salt Lake City was bidding for the right to host the 2002 Winter Olympics, a local TV station leaked a 1996 document according to which the bid committee had set up a "scholarship fund" for the relatives of International Olympic Committee (IOC) members. Although the document turned out to be a forgery, the information was subsequently confirmed by investigations conducted by the United States government, the US Olympic Committee and the IOC. The scope of the corruption and bribery that finally came to light totaled more than US $1.2 million in benefits to IOC members and their families, including cash payments, scholarships, jobs, paid vacations, medical expenses, and shopping sprees. The 300-page SLOC ethics panel report reported another US $1 million in travel and shopping reimbursements with untraceable payments.[2]

In the aftermath of the Salt Lake City scandal, there were resignations, expulsions, warnings, and sanctions against IOC members except at the very top. IOC President Juan Antonio Samaranch declined to resign, and the IOC gave him a vote of confidence, enabling him to finish his term, which ended in 2001. But Salt Lake City was just the tip of the iceberg. Further investigations of Olympic bids revealed a widespread culture and practice of corruption and bribery of IOC members, as revealed in the cases of Atlanta (gifts, travel, scholarships, job assistance), Nagano (destruction of expense records, US $13,000 sword given to Samaranch) and Sydney (sports funding totaling about US $1 million for eleven African countries, lavish hotels and restaurants for seventy-two IOC members).

Clearly, reforms were called for if the IOC was to recover from its seriously tarnished image. An independent Ethics Commission was established in 2000, with the mandate to provide opinions and recommendations to the IOC Executive Board on cases submitted by the IOC president and to give advice at the request of IOC/Olympic Movement members. The IOC sessions and general meetings were made public. The IOC implemented new bid procedures aimed at introducing greater transparency and accountability back into the Olympic Movement and specifically into the host city selection.

## A COMPLEX BIDDING PROCESS

An aspiring Olympics host city has to clear many hurdles. For Beijing, it took two bid attempts, one in 1993, and the second successful bid in 2001. With the old lobbying practices now deemed corrupt and unethical, cities had to navigate a complex bureaucratic process set forth in the new "Candidature Acceptance Procedures" adopted by the IOC Executive Board in February 2000.[3]

In Phase I, which lasts about ten months, "applicant cities" compete for the right to make it to the next round, as "candidate cities." Applicant cities must present to the IOC Executive Board, through their respective National Olympic Committees, a completed questionnaire that addresses six themes: motivation and concept, political and public support (including any opposition), general infrastructure, sports infrastructure (including environmental impact), logistics and experience, and financing.

For the 2008 Summer Games, host city hopefuls had to file applications by June 20, 2000. Ten "applicant cities" competed in Phase I: Bangkok, Beijing, Cairo, Havana, Istanbul, Kuala Lumpur, Osaka, Paris, Seville, and Toronto. An IOC Candidature Acceptance Working Group of thirteen IOC members and four outside experts convened to develop technical assessment criteria, a methodology of ranking the cities under a "fuzzy logic" approach. The Working Group examined the data provided by applicant cities, reports of outside experts, and the quality of the information and submitted a report to the IOC Executive Board to determine candidate cities.[4]

In August 2000, the IOC Executive Board named five of these cities as candidate cities: Beijing, Istanbul, Osaka, Paris and Toronto. In Phase II, candidate cities are required to make ten-minute presentations to the IOC Executive Board, submit a candidature file (together with a nonrefundable deposit of US $150,000), and host a four-day site visit by the Evaluation Commission. The candidature file must address eighteen themes and 149 questions. Between mid-February and mid-April 2001, the IOC Evaluation Commission conducted site visits to each of the cities. Based upon review of the candidature files and the report, the IOC Executive Board drew up the final list of candidate cities to be submitted to the IOC Session for election through secret balloting.

The April 3, 2001, IOC Evaluation Commission Report offered this assessment of the Beijing bid:

> "This is a government-driven bid with considerable assistance of the NOC (National Olympic Committee). The combination of a good sports concept with complete Government support results in a high quality bid. The Commission notes the process and pace of change taking place in China and Beijing and the possible challenges caused by population and economic growth in the period leading up to 2008 but is confident that these challenges can be met. There is an environmental challenge but the strong government actions and investment in this area should resolve this and improve the city. It is the Commission's belief that a Beijing Games would leave a unique legacy to China and to sport and the Commission is confident that Beijing could organize excellent Games."[5]

On July 13, 2001, in Moscow, the IOC voted to award China the honor of hosting the 2008 Olympic Games. Despite its failed first Olympics bid in 1993, despite its serious record of ongoing human rights abuses, and despite achieving a top rating in only one out of ten applicant selection categories, Beijing had come from behind to beat Osaka, Paris, Toronto, and Istanbul.

Three days later, on July 16, 2001, Jacques Rogge, a member of the IOC since 1991, was elected the eighth IOC president. Less than three years following a massive IOC corruption scandal, Rogge set three main tasks for the Olympic Movement: the consolidation of the Movement's legacy, the promotion of Olympic values, and the focus on organization of the Olympic Games. The IOC and President Rogge are in for a bumpy ride to Beijing.

## RESPONSIBILITIES OF A HOST CITY

As the host of the 2008 Games, what are Beijing's obligations? What did Beijing promise in order to win the bid? Who is responsible for delivering on these promises? The promises made by Beijing are found in the Beijing bid documents, the Host City Contract (still not public) and the 2002 Action Plan. Immediately following the selection of Beijing, the Host City Contract was signed by the Beijing authorities, the IOC, and China's National Olympic Committee (NOC). Together with China's NOC and the Beijing authorities, the Beijing Organizing Committee for the Olympic Games (BOCOG) is responsible for realizing the obligations set forth in the Host City Contract and the annexes.

While Beijing's actual bid candidature file is not publicly available, the Model IOC candidature file indicates the types of commitments Beijing must have made. These include information, representations, and guarantees regarding:

- the safety and the peaceful operation of the Olympic Games;
- fulfillment of obligations and respect for the Olympic Charter (including the goal of encouraging the establishment of a peaceful society concerned with preservation of human dignity);
- evidence of support of national, regional, and local populations including opinion polls (must be conducted by internationally recognized research agencies or organizations), referendums, awareness campaigns;
- any laws prohibiting or limiting importation of foreign newspapers, periodicals, or other publications;

- economic effect on the city and the region;
- planning, construction and protection of the environment;
- health system, water and air quality, and arrangements for the Games;
- security, including crime rates, risks posed by "activist minorities" (religious, political, ethnic, etc.) or terrorist groups in the country or the region.

Guarantees are required from national, regional, and local authorities, city and other competent authorities.

BOCOG also prepared and released a Beijing Olympic Action Plan (March 2002) that lays out the overall guidelines and plan for the preparations of the Olympics, shaped by the idea of "New Beijing, Great Olympics" with emphasis on "Green Olympics," "High Tech Olympics," and "People's Olympics" as the key to successful Games. The 2002 Olympic Action Plan includes specific standards, such as technical environmental standards, to which Beijing would hold itself accountable in governance, construction of venues and increasing social and economic development.

## SELLING THE "PEOPLE'S OLYMPICS"

A prestigious international team of legal and public relations experts was soon assembled to mount this critical international coming out party for China: in October 2002, Morrison and Foerster LLP was selected as "international legal counsel" to BOCOG, responsible for a wide range of legal advice, including protection of Olympics intellectual property. Prior to securing this lucrative representation, the firm had to unload some inconvenient pro-bono cases—Tibetan asylum clients.[6] In May 2006, BOCOG officially named Hill and Knowlton as its "communications consultant." It too cleared the political litmus test—following the violent 1989 military crackdown on unarmed democracy demonstrators, Beijing hired Hill and Knowlton to help deal with its public relations image "problem." In April 2006, Steven Spielberg joined the team to design the opening and closing ceremonies with Chinese director Zhang Yimou. The director of *Schindler's List*—a moving portrayal of human courage in the face of evil—was thus paired with the director of *Hero*, a controversial film about ruthless empire-building.[7]

Two foreign companies were selected to provide key technological support:

- The French company Atos Origin was awarded the contract to design, build and operate the information technology infrastructure. The Atos IT system, consisting of more than 900 servers, 7,000 PCs and 1,000 network and security devices, links the more than sixty competition and non-competition venues.

- EADS, based in the Netherlands and Germany, was awarded the Phase-3 project of the Beijing Government Shared TETRA Network, a central communications tool for the agencies of the Beijing Municipal government. The project will double the current digital-trunking network size, both in terms of capacity and number of users (increasing from over 40,000 to 90,000). The network aims to provide seamless, secure radio communication for its users in Beijing, including all Olympic venues and sites as well as main highways.

The one-year countdown in August 2007 was marked by protests, open letters, and human rights reports by domestic and international activists and groups. Human Rights Watch and Amnesty International released reports on China's human rights situation. More than forty prominent mainland activists and intellectuals, including Ding Zilin, Liu Xiaobo and Bao Tong, released an open letter, addressed to Chinese leaders and the international community: "'One World, One Dream' and Universal Human Rights." The open letter called for the return of exiles, greater press freedom and protection of residents evicted from their homes to make way for Olympics construction. They link these recommendations with not only the Universal Declaration of Human Rights, but China's own constitution.[8] IOC President Jacques Rogge received open letters from Reporters Without Borders and Students for a Free Tibet. The Fair Labor Association reported on the use of prison labor to manufacture Olympic merchandise. The International Campaign for Tibet launched its "Beijing 2008: Race for Tibet" campaign with the ultimate objective of "ending human rights abuses in Tibet." In a daring action orchestrated by Students for a Free Tibet, six activists scaled the Great Wall of China and unfurled a banner proclaiming the group's slogan, "One World, One Dream, Free Tibet"— a clever expropriation of the official Olympic slogan "One World, One Dream." The six activists were promptly detained and deported to Hong Kong.

In September 2007, Human Rights in China sent an open letter to President Rogge requesting the IOC make public the Host City Contract with Beijing.[9] Earlier in 2002, the Free Tibet campaign and Norwegian Tibet Committee had requested access to the contract and specifically information about human rights provisions. Rogge reportedly rejected these requests based upon claims of commercial confidentiality. However, since the bribery scandal and fallout from the Salt Lake City bid in 1998, other host cities— Atlanta (1996), Sydney (2000), Salt Lake City (2002), and Athens (2004)—have all made their host city contracts publicly available.

Without transparency and disclosure of the key document that sets out the legal, commercial and financial rights and obligations of the IOC and the Beijing Organizing Committee for the Olympic Games, the ability of Chinese citizens and the international community to monitor and promote compliance is completely undermined. On October 22, 2007, Human Rights in China received a letter from the IOC stating the IOC's hope that "organized sport can help bring positive developments from within Olympic Games host countries," but neglecting to make any mention of the Host City Contract or address HRIC's request for its release.

## WHAT WORLD, WHOSE DREAM?

Despite the government's promises to host an Olympics that will promote and help the development of human rights, the Games are instead being used as a justification for further violations, including forced evictions, closure of migrants, schools, crackdowns on lawyers and tightened media controls. Yet the 2008 Games could still leverage the Chinese government's own assurances to improve human rights. This all depends upon the effectiveness of the campaigns and actions of domestic and international media, activists, and civil society, as well as the political will and actions of the actors that should be more concerned— Beijing, the IOC and corporate sponsors. The stakes are high.

Estimated originally at US $1.65 billion, the cost of Olympics preparations has risen over the few years to more than US $2.1 billion, not including the US $35–40 billion spent on upgrading infrastructure and environmental improvements.[10] However, with Olympics investment predominantly focused in Beijing, most of the country will not be seeing any direct benefits. An Internet essay in 2004, entitled "Beware of the Gold Medal Ruse," detailed a shocking figure for the 'cost' of a single gold medal: 700 million *yuan* (approximately $87 million). The author based his figures on the annual budget of China's General Administration of Sports and the number of gold medals won by the Chinese team in Athens. Although his figures were challenged, official numbers still revealed exorbitant Olympic-related expenditures that are being diverted from more pressing public needs.[11]

The construction of Olympic venues has had not only a steep financial price but also a heavy social cost. Migrant labor has been crucial in building Olympic sites. Chinese officials say 4 million migrant workers live in Beijing,[12] but since the total number of migrant workers in cities across China is estimated at 120–140 million, this figure for Beijing is disputed and probably undercounted.

The Geneva-based Center on Housing Rights and Evictions estimates that 1.5 million Beijing residents will be displaced because of the Olympics.[13] Official pronouncements and the "Olympics clean-up" campaign have made it clear that petitioners and migrants will be increasingly targeted in efforts to maintain order before and during the Olympics. In a recent study by the Chinese Academy of Social Sciences, more than 80 percent of petitioners surveyed said they would continue to petition despite the obstacles and the poor results, and this has no doubt contributed to official worries and concerns. Beijing will most likely use the same methods they use currently to handle petitioners, including harassment, forcible removal, detentions, and roundups. They may also use local public security bureaus to control movement of local populations to ensure that they do not "disrupt" the Games.

However, these forced relocations to make room for the Olympic venues in Beijing and Qingdao, for example, have also been met with criticism and protests. A July 2007 article by Wang Daming ("Residents Driven Into Cow Pens as CCTV Claims Land for Olympic Project Sites") in HRIC's electronic weekly newsletter, *Huaxia Dianziba,* described the relocation of residents in Beijing's Zhaoyang district to make way for the construction of CCTV "Olympic project sites." One resident was quoted by Wang as saying, "If the cost of hosting the Olympics is tears, blood, lives and the eviction of people from their homes, then we would rather not have these Olympics."

In Qingdao, which will host the Olympic sailing competition, nearly one hundred relocated residents unfurled a banner, protesting the compensation given them. They gathered in front of the district government's offices in July 2007, demanding that government officials come out to speak with them (they did not).[14] Many of the relocations in Qingdao were done in the name of "beautifying the city."

## VOICES OF DISSENT

Many in China have joined the growing chorus of domestic criticism, often at great personal risk. In June 2007, over 10,000 people, mostly farmers in Fujin City, Heilongjiang Province, signed a petition proclaiming "We want human rights, not the Olympics."[15] Yang Chunlin, a land-rights activist who helped gather the signatures, was detained in July 2007 on charges of subverting state power. According to relatives, he was tortured and denied access to a lawyer while awaiting trial in Heilongjiang Province.[16] On March 24, 2008, Yang received the maximum sentence of five years in prison.

The Internet is also increasingly used as a tool to express dissent. In August 2007, an anonymous blog called "Beijing Olympics: I don't support it" was posted on Bullog, a popular discussion site. The blog received many supporting comments and criticism about the lack of public discussion over the Olympics.[17] It was later revealed that the anonymous poster was the Chinese *Sports Illustrated* reporter Guan Jun (a.k.a. Gua Erjia), who said he started the blog "to let the outside world know that China does not only just have one voice." His blog was shut down.[18]

Disabled persons have also courageously voiced criticism of the Beijing Olympics. On August 7, 2007, more than sixty disabled persons reportedly attempted to present a petition protesting the Beijing government's violations of disabled people's rights in the name of the Olympics. The organizers and demonstrators included Li Zhixin, a blind man who had founded the Miaosen Cultural Center which was demolished in 2002 to make way for the Olympics. Qi Zhiyong, who lost his left leg in the June 4, 1989 crackdown, was wearing a shirt that said "1989 Tiananmen, 2008 Olympics." That same day, Qi Zhiyong gave a phone interview to a German TV station during which he criticized China's human rights situation. The next day, police were stationed in front of his home, barring him from leaving.

Even Chinese artist Ai Weiwei, who worked with Swiss architects Herzog & de Meuron to design the Olympic stadium, has said, "I hate the kind of feeling stirred up by promotion or propaganda. It's the kind of sentiment when you don't stick to the facts, but try to make up something, to mislead people away from a true discussion. It is not good for anyone."[19]

## THE MARATHON BEYOND 2008

Will the Olympics be a force for greater openness and reforms? What will be left behind when the estimated 30,000 journalists, 17,000 athletes and officials, along with the projected 550,000 foreign visitors pack up and go home? In the final countdown to the Games, clouds are gathering on the horizon—and not the officially announced artificial rain-inducing phenomenon. China is juggling a difficult balancing act of maintaining domestic control while simultaneously putting on an open face to welcome the foreigners.

In 2001, while visiting Beijing for the first time, IOC president Jacques Rogge stated that the International Olympic Committee would not monitor China's human rights record or relations with Taiwan in the run-up to the 2008 Olympic Games. "The International Olympic Committee is not a political body, it is a sports organization, so we will not be involved in politics," said Rogge, restating the message several times at a press conference in Beijing. "The IOC is, of course, in favor of the best possible situation for human rights in all countries in the world," he said. "But it is not the task of the International Olympic Committee to get involved in monitoring and/or lobbying and/or influencing." These disclaimers are not persuasive. Throughout the modern Olympic era, the IOC has had to navigate the historical challenges of each Olympiad, including fascist dictatorship, terrorism, violence, and Cold War politics. Having awarded the 2008 Games to Beijing, what will it do with this historic opportunity? Its choices will affect whether it can reclaim the high ideals of promoting peace and preserving human dignity enshrined in the Olympic Charter.

In the past, China has also played a different tune than its current the-Games-are-about-sports refrain: China withdrew from the 1956 Melbourne Games after the IOC recognized Taiwan, and continued to snub the Olympics until it emerged from the Cultural Revolution in 1980.

The struggle for advancing human rights in China is a marathon—one that will last well beyond 2008. The international community should do whatever it can to urge the Chinese government to act like the world leader it wants to be—respected and legitimate not only due to its economic clout but because of its respect for human rights at home and abroad. Beijing can advance this process by really listening to the voices of its own people. This will be good for China's future, for the region, for the world. By demonstrating tolerance for critical and necessary voices, China would truly be bringing home the spirit of Olympic gold.

# CHAPTER 4

# The Ghosts of Olympics Past

### BY DAVE ZIRIN

*Pierre de Coubertin, the founder of the modern Olympics as the nineteenth century came to a close, defined the Games as "the quadrennial celebration of the springtime of humanity." However, the 1936 Berlin Games, 1968 Mexico City Games and 1972 Munich Games evoke less the "springtime of humanity" than the violence of the twentieth century.* DAVE ZIRIN *is a sports writer and the author of* Welcome to the Terrordome: The Pain, Politics and Promise of Sports *(2007). A contributor to* SportsIllustrated.com, *the* Los Angeles Times, *the* Nation, *and* National Public Radio, *Zirin is the author of the forthcoming* People's History of Sports *in the United States.*

As the Olympics descend upon China, the critiques have begun. Already we are hearing stories of more than 1.5 million "displacements" to clear space for Olympic facilities, reports of human rights abuses, sweatshop labor, and Olympics-related graft. The spotlight will naturally be on China, but China is only part of the story. The modern Olympic Movement itself has been highly controversial—and far from the "above politics" Olympian level that some would have us believe.

Under this more skeptical view of the Olympics, the modern Olympic Games began in Athens in 1896 as a place for imperial rivals—then in the process of carving up the world from Cuba to

Congo to the Philippines—to spur nationalist frenzies through sports. Over the years, critics would have reason to conclude that little has changed. During the Cold War, the Games helped to fix ideas of the enemy in the minds of the East and West. Today, the enormous marketing and other monies to be made have led to shocking examples of graft.

For more than a century, the Olympics have been run by the International Olympic Committee, which some would say has changed little from its founding by a club for fossilized aristocrats with nostalgia for epaulets. When French Baron Pierre de Coubertin launched the IOC at the end of the nineteenth century, its membership comprised five European nobles, two generals, and nine leading industrialists. Between 1894 and the turn of the century, de Coubertin added ten more barons, princes, and counts. Indeed, the days of de Coubertin are never far off—the committee has remained elitist and out of touch with the athletes it claims to represent.

## OLYMPIAN BACKING FOR HITLER

Following the 1917 Russian Revolution, when the threatened leisure class found comfort in the politics of fascism, the IOC became a place where the most reactionary could feel at home. The dominant Olympic figure of the twentieth century was not Jesse Owens, Carl Lewis, or Mark Spitz, but Avery Brundage, for many years the IOC president. In 1936, when the Olympics were to be staged in Hitler's Germany, Brundage—then merely the president of the United States Olympic Committee—personally set out to quash a rising din of protest. He met with Hitler in Berlin, where they shared smiles and handshakes for the cameras. Brundage returned to the United States with tales of how the new Germany treated Jews and other national minorities with exceptional care. He dismissed the anti-Hitler rumblings as the work of a Communist conspiracy.

Brundage's steadfast support of Hitler earned him the respect of the other members of the International Olympic Committee. They voted to have him brought into the club, replacing American Ernest Lee Jahnke, who had called for a Berlin boycott. Unlike other prominent Nazi sympathizers like Henry Ford and Joseph Kennedy, Brundage never apologized for his Hitler leanings. As late as 1941, he praised the Third Reich at a Madison Square Garden rally for America First, an organization that opposed American involvement in World War II. Brundage's refusal to distance himself from Hitler would eventually get him expelled even from the America First committee.

Despite the cloud of controversy that surrounded him, Brundage somehow remained chief of the IOC until 1972. Over the years, he used his position to speak out against women competing at the Olympics, continuously denigrating their contributions to sport. He strongly opposed the exclusion of apartheid-ruled Rhodesia and South Africa from the Games. Despite this, he tried to position the Olympics as pure, commenting, "The Olympic Movement is a 20th century religion, where there is no injustice of caste, of race, of family, of wealth."

This would explain why, when Black Americans attempted to organize their own boycott of the Mexico City Olympics in 1968, the removal of Brundage was one of their primary demands. The genesis of the famed black-gloved salute of 200-meter gold and bronze medalists Tommie Smith and John Carlos was tangentially connected to Brundage, as African-American athletes brought the gloves because they didn't want to have to actually touch Brundage's skin if they needed to shake hands with him.

Brundage is perhaps most notorious for his decisions surrounding the 1972 Summer Olympics in Munich, Germany. On September 5, a Palestinian group called Black September took eleven Israeli athletes hostage. Brundage insisted that the Olympics continue while negotiations were taking place for their release. Even after all the athletes were killed in a botched rescue attempt, Brundage announced that the Games would not be halted. Overwhelming outside pressure forced the IOC to interrupt competition for one day and hold a memorial service attended by 80,000 spectators and 3,000 athletes in the Olympic Stadium. When Brundage spoke, he shocked observers by making no reference at all to the slain athletes, praising instead the strength of the Olympic Movement. His position was that "the Games must go on," a stance endorsed by the Israeli government. Not everyone agreed, though, and many countries dropped out of the Games in protest. American marathon runner Kenny Moore, who wrote about the incident for *Sports Illustrated*, quoted a Dutch athlete's simple explanation: "You give a party, and someone is killed at the party, you don't continue the party, you go home. That's what I'm doing."

In a subsequent speech, Brundage stated that Rhodesia, despite its apartheid policies, should never have been excluded from the Games. He then said that the massacre of the Israeli athletes and the barring of the Rhodesian team were crimes of equal weight—a comparison which sparked such widespread outrage that he later apologized.[1] Clearly Brundage, after standing astride the Olympics for most of the century, had become a liability.

Yet when the IOC finally put Brundage out to pasture, they settled on a replacement—after a brief interlude with a man named Lord Killanin—who proved as controversial as Brundage: Juan Antonio Samaranch of Spain. When appointed head of the IOC in 1980, Samaranch was already viewed as a fascist sympathizer in his native Spain. Born in 1920 to a wealthy factory owner in Barcelona, Juan Antonio was already an active youth fascist organizer and professional strikebreaker by the time he was a teenager, when General Francisco Franco's fascists fought the Spanish Republicans during the 1936 Spanish Civil War.

Samaranch was appointed as the government secretary for

sports by Franco in 1966, and also became the president of the Spanish National Olympic Committee and a member of the IOC. Up until the dictator's death in 1975, Samaranch proclaimed himself "one hundred percent Francoist." As a sportsman, Samaranch believed in the Brundage ideal of the Olympics as a celebration of nationalism and power.

As journalist Andrew Jennings wrote in 1992 in his book *Lord of the Rings*, Samaranch schemed for years to be appointed to the Olympic Committee, sending unsolicited letters to its president, Avery Brundage, eulogizing in one of them the American's "intelligence, laboriousness and love for [the] Olympic idea" and promising in another, "I will entirely devote myself to go with your personality and prominent work."

Jennings also observed of Samaranch, "Three decades of devotion to fascism had taught Samaranch a peculiar language. All the institutions in Spain—the monarchy, politics, the church, industry and its workers—were forced into slavish obedience; the dictator and his mouthpieces called it 'sacred unity.' This has been one of Samaranch's contributions to Olympic jargon. He calls frequently for the 'unity' of the Olympic movement and hails the 'sacred unity' of the committee, the international sports barons and the national Olympic committees around the world; all of course under his leadership."[2]

Samaranch also oversaw the transformation of the Olympics from a Cold War spectacle to a corporate bonanza of privatization and fees. After findings of vote-buying and graft in Salt Lake City's bid for the 2002 Winter Olympics, several IOC members were expelled for accepting bribes. Like Brundage, Samaranch had a titanic ego and loved issuing platitudes suitable for fortune cookies. Read today, they are delicious in their irony: for example, "We shall serve sport, not use it. Money generated by sport shall benefit sport." In the peculiar language of Olympic-ese, "sport" is a synonym for "graft." This heartless plundering has in the post–

Cold War era become the Olympic ideal. It is not "Faster, Higher, Stronger." It is "We'll make you an offer you can't refuse." But refuse, by any means necessary, is exactly what cities contemplating the hosting of Olympic Games should do.

## BURDEN FOR HOST CITIES

While Beijing views its choice to host the games as a great achievement, many cities have experienced hosting the Games as an exercise in costly expenditures. As *Sports Illustrated*'s Michael Fish has written, "You stage a two-week athletic carnival and, if things go well, pray the local municipality isn't sent into financial ruin." The 1976 Olympics in Montreal, which featured Nadia Comaneci, the young Romanian gymnast who stole so many hearts, is an example in point. Three decades later, the people of Montreal are still paying for their Summer Games, even though at the time one official said, "Olympics cause deficits as often as men have babies." More recently, the 2004 Summer Games in Athens gutted the Greek economy. In 1997, when Athens was awarded the Games, city leaders and the International Olympic Committee estimated their cost at US $1.3 billion. When the actual detailed planning was done, the price had jumped to US $5.3 billion. By the time the Games were over, Greece had spent some US $14.2 billion, pushing the country's budget deficit to record levels.

This is why, in 2005, activists in New York City organized to keep the 2012 Games out. In a city defined by stark inequalities and a police force ready to enforce them, the prospect of a local Olympics was chilling to many New Yorkers. More than 20 percent of the city's residents live below the poverty line. More than 50 percent of African-American youth in Harlem are unemployed. Losing the Olympics saved thousands of residents from being caught in the web of the criminal justice system. New York City's loss was a bitter pill for Senator Hillary Clinton. She had alluded—shamelessly in the view of some observers—to the terrorist attacks of 9/11 in making the case for a share of Olympic manna. Perhaps the most dispiriting sight was that of the great Muhammad Ali shilling for the New York bid. New York City's mayor, billionaire Michael Bloomberg, called Ali the bid campaign's "secret weapon," as he led the largely incapacitated former boxing champion from photo-op to photo-op.

Remembering the Ali of 1960 paints the scene in even more tragic colors. That Ali, then eighteen and known as Cassius Clay, won Olympic boxing gold in Greece only to be turned away from a white-only restaurant in his hometown of Louisville, despite the medal swinging from his proud neck. The young Clay then took his medallion of gold and, as he said, "gave it a home at the bottom of the Ohio river." Cities should take his lead and jettison the Olympics. The people of New York won a victory in keeping the Olympics out. But their gain was London's loss.

## BLAIR'S OLYMPIAD

Upon finding out that the Olympics will be marching into New Britannia, London organizer Katie Andrews expressed both shock and anger. "There was no plebiscite. No vote. Now we have these Games being shoved down our throats." In an upset, the IOC awarded London the 2012 Games over heavily favored frontrunner Paris. French president Jacques Chirac had spent more than US $30 million on various inducements—otherwise known as graft—to lure the Olympics to France. Victory seemed assured, and Chirac had already lit a cigar, claiming that "the only contribution London has made to European agriculture is Mad Cow Disease." But beneath Chirac's snippy jingoism, a larger drama was playing out on the board of the IOC.

Avery Brundage once said famously, "The cardinal rule of the Olympics is no politics," which is like saying the cardinal rule of boxing is no punching. Fearful not to get their piece of the Iraqi pie, the French government has been a thorn in the side of the United States' imperial objectives in the Middle East. Britain, meanwhile, has been only too happy to yip at the feet around the US dinner table, hoping to be thrown a crust and maybe earn a pat on the head. France, which has been an Olympic bridesmaid three times in the last twenty years, stands humiliated while the UK gets the gold.

The question now is whether the British Left—which responded so brilliantly to the Iraq invasion with mass antiwar demonstrations—can mount a defense against the Olympic leviathan. To do so, they will need to break with Labour politicians who are dressing the Olympic rings in populist garb. Chief among them has been London mayor Ken Livingstone, who in another life, was known as "Red Ken." Livingstone has been a major player in whipping up public support—which currently stands in London at over 50 percent—for the Games. He has been quick to point out, in the words of one observer, that "anyone who is against the Olympics is against the investment and infrastructure and jobs which will help the poor." Yes, "Red Ken" has turned the Olympics into a social-welfare program. But in between cheers, Livingstone has also announced that each London Council taxpayer will have to pay £20 a year for twelve years (in other words, £240), even if the Games do not make a loss, which is about as likely as seeing the Queen wear leather pants. Already in London, property prices have started to rise. If there is anything we can count on, it's that the wealthy of Britain will make out like bandits, the poor will be squeezed, and Big Ben will end up in the back of a Lausanne pawnshop.

Tony Blair told the IOC, "My promise to you is we will be your very best partners. The entire government are united behind this bid. . . . It is the nation's bid." Is it? It probably won't feel like the bid of those caught in the web of temporary martial law that accompanies many Olympics. Already in Britain, and in Beijing as they prepare for the 2008 Games, we are seeing a familiar script replayed every four years, with only the accents changing. Political leaders start by saying that a city must be made "presentable for an international audience." Then the police and security forces get the green light to round up "undesirables."

## OLYMPIC SWEEPS

In 1984, Los Angeles Police Chief Daryl Gates oversaw the jailing of thousands of young Black men in the infamous "Olympic gang sweeps." As Mike Davis has written, it took the reinstatement of the 1916 Anti-Syndicalism Act, a law aimed at the revolutionary union, the Industrial Workers of the World, to make these Stalinesque jailings a reality. The 1916 bill forbade hand signals and modes of dress that implied IWW membership. The LA politicos of the 1980s modernized the bill to include high fives and bandanas, making the case that Blood and Crip Joe Hills were overrunning the city. It was in the Gates sweeps that the seeds for the LA Rebellion of 1992, as well as the first music video by a fledging rap group called N.W.A., were planted.

The Atlanta Games in 1996 were no different. These games were supposed to demonstrate what President Clinton called "the New South," but the New South ended up looking a lot like the old one, as officials razed African American–occupied public housing to make way for Olympic facilities.

Repression followed the Olympic rings to Greece in 2004. Psychiatric hospitals were compelled by the government to lock up the homeless, the mentally ill, and those who suffered from drug dependency. In addition Greece actually overrode its own constitution by "allowing" thousands of armed-to-the-teeth paramilitary troops from the US, Britain, and Israel to police the Games.

But the most heartless example of Olympic repression came in

1968 in Mexico City, where hundreds of Mexican students and workers occupying the National University were slaughtered in the Plaza de las Tres Culturas in Tlatelolco.

## THE GHOSTS OF TLATELOLCO SQUARE

*"There was one Mexico before 1968 and one Mexico afterward. Tlatelolco was the dividing line."*—LUIS GONZALEZ DE ALBA

There was never a year when the worlds of sports and politics collided so breathlessly as 1968. It was the year Muhammad Ali, stripped of his heavyweight title for resisting the draft, spoke on 200 college campuses and asked the question, "Can they take my title without me being whupped?" It was the year Bill Russell's Boston Celtics became champions once again, yet the player-coach saw his house vandalized by bigots. This led Russell to call the city of Boston a "flea market of racism" and say "I am a Celtic, not a *Boston* Celtic." It was the year the Detroit Tigers won the World Series, playing in a city preoccupied by the specter of insurrection, with riots in the hood, snipers on the roofs, wildcat strikes in the auto plants, and Martha and the Vandellas' "Dancing in the Streets" ringing throughout the projects.

And most famously, it was the year that Tommie Smith and John Carlos took the 200-meter medal stand at the Mexico City Olympics to raise their black-gloved fists in a demonstration of pride, power, and politics. Smith and Carlos were part of the Olympic Project for Human Rights, and they made their stand because of what was happening outside the stadium: the assassination of Dr. Martin Luther King, the growth of the Black Panthers, the May strikes in France, and most recently in their thoughts, the slaughter of hundreds in the country where they were being feted with gold.

On October 2, 1968, right before the start of the games, Mexican police murdered as many as 500 students and workers at

Plaza de las Tres Culturas in Tlatelolco, Mexico City. The families of those murdered in 1968 may finally be finding justice. In June 2006, Mexican prosecutors announced that they were finally acceding to a four-decades-long campaign, filing charges against former president Luis Echeverría for ordering the Tlatelolco killings. Echeverría was interior minister and head of national security at the time of the massacre. "It has been almost thirty-seven years of impunity and justice denied," prosecutor Ignacio Carrillo told Reuters. "Now for the first time it is possible that the justice system may perform its duty." On June 30, 2006, Echeverría was placed under house arrest for the duration of the investigation.

The Tlatelolco killings were fatally intertwined with the oncoming Olympics. Student strikes had rocked Mexico throughout the year. This was a time of mass struggle from the Yucatán to Tijuana. But students and their supporters, despite previous clashes with the state police, could not have foreseen the fanatical desire of Mexico to "make their country secure" for the coming Olympic Games. Echeverría's Olympic clean-up, not the actions of panicked police, rogue officers, or indiscriminate trigger-happy shooters, were responsible for the deaths. Recently declassified documents paint a picture of a massacre as cold and methodical—to put it mildly—as Echeverría's instructions. On August 22, Echeverría said, "The government is most willing to meet with the representatives of teachers and students . . . connected with the present problems." But despite this "willingness," in October, Echeverría unleashed hell.

As Kate Doyle, director of the Mexico Documentation Project, describes,

> When the shooting stopped, hundreds of people lay dead or wounded, as army and police forces seized surviving protesters and dragged them away. Although months of

nationwide student strikes had prompted an increasingly hard-line response, no one was prepared for the bloodbath that Tlatelolco became. More shocking still was the cover-up that kicked in as soon as the smoke cleared. Eyewitnesses to the killings pointed to the President's "security" forces, who entered the plaza bristling with weapons, backed by armored vehicles. But the government pointed back, claiming that extremists and communist agitators had initiated the violence. Who was responsible for Tlatelolco? The Mexican people have been demanding an answer ever since.[3]

Thousands of people have marched in the streets every year demanding justice for what is seen as Mexico's Tiananmen Square. And while it is certainly welcome to see Echeverría doddering in cuffs, this arrest should not be seen only as an epilogue of the past but a warning for the future.

The Beijing Olympics in 2008 and the British Olympics of 2012 both hold the potential for significant crackdowns. Openly criticizing the government in China will earn you jail time and independent trade-union organizing is verboten. The authorities will at the very least use the Olympics to crush even mild dissent. In a state like China with a centralized government that leaves little to chance, one that has shown in the recent past that it is willing to violently quell dissent, it is particularly dangerous.

A new Olympic Project for Human Rights is necessary so people in China who want to resist state repression, which trails after the Olympics like so much detritus, have the political space to do so. It would be a true, living justice if the martyrs of 1968 can be resurrected to haunt a new generation of Echeverrías planning security operations in Beijing and beyond.

# CHAPTER 5

# Olympian Changes: Seoul and Beijing

## BY RICHARD POUND

*In 2008, China will become only the third Asian country after Japan and South Korea to host the Olympics in the modern era that began with the 1896 Athens Games. The 1988 Seoul Games made a lasting mark on Asia's political landscape. A wave of political demonstrations in mid-1987 seemed to jeopardize Seoul's ability to host the 1988 Games and contributed to the historic declaration of June 29, 1987, when the military government leader President Chun Doo Hwan agreed to step down and hold direct elections in December 1987, paving the way for democracy in South Korea. Today the most optimistic advocates of political reform in China harbor hopes the Beijing Olympics could lead to similar reform opportunities. RICHARD POUND has been a member of the International Olympic Committee for almost thirty years. He is a past president of the Canadian Olympic Committee and is the founding chairman of the World Anti-Doping Agency. He is the author of numerous books including* Five Rings over Korea *(1994), about the 1988 Seoul Games, and* Inside the Olympics *(2004).*

Few have serious doubts about China's ability to organize first-class Olympic Games in 2008. While the scale of the infrastructure challenges in Beijing is extraordinary, the changes are for the most part both overdue and much needed. Some attract more media attention than others, particularly when they involve relocations of people or industry. Many of the changes are lumped together as "Olympic" costs, leading to predictable mutterings about how expensive it is to host the Games and that perhaps some new solution for this quadrennial problem should be found. The most persistent suggestion is that Greece be designated as the permanent host of the Summer Games, with dedicated facilities located in the Olympic peninsula near ancient Olympia. This is a wholly unrealistic solution and it is certain that the International Olympic Committee will continue to move the Games around the world.

If China faces a debilitating problem regarding the 2008 Games, it will likely fall into one of two categories. Either the political, media and human rights portfolios will be mismanaged, or there will be some form of pandemic. The pandemic scare was not fully developed when China launched its first bid for the 2000 Games during the 1991–1993 period. The concern on the part of those IOC members who voted for Sydney instead of Beijing in the final round arose instead from the then relatively recent events in Tiananmen Square. The balance to be weighed was that awarding the Games to Beijing on that occasion would carry with it an exceptionally high reward for the Olympic Movement were the Games to be a success, but that such a decision would also be accompanied by very high risks. The Chinese bidding committee had not been comfortable in its dealings with the predominantly western IOC. In its dealings with the Western media, it had risen like trout to any politically charged questions, so much so that questions entirely unrelated to the Olympic bid were posed, solely for the purpose of generating the stock doctrinaire responses. China was unable on that occasion to project the level of organizational confidence that would convince an undecided IOC member. On September 23, 1993, in Monte Carlo, China lost to Australia by only two votes in an election that had its share of questionable tactics on both sides.

China returned to bid for the 2008 Games in 2001, this time

with a much more media-savvy team. This team was confident that Games with a Chinese flavor would be possible, but was also aware of the need to make the case that the world's most populous country was ready to host the world's most important international sporting event. At the IOC session held in Moscow in 2001, Beijing easily beat out the other contenders.

Part of its presentation to the IOC members was an acknowledgment of the concerns expressed in many parts of the world regarding its record on human rights, coupled with a preemptive suggestion that the IOC could help increase progress on such matters by awarding the Games to China, since this decision would result in even more media attention to the issue and likely faster evolution. It was an all-but-irresistible prospect for the IOC. The Games will begin on what is an auspicious date for the Chinese, the eighth day of the eighth month of the eighth year of the century. Media and political attention, in consequence, increasingly focus on the implications of Olympic Games to be hosted in China.

## THE PRECEDENT OF THE 1988 SEOUL GAMES

The last Summer Games held in Asia were the 1988 Seoul Games, awarded by the IOC at its session in Baden Baden in 1981. Seoul had been an unlikely choice, considering there were only two candidates, both from Asia—the other being Nagoya, Japan: Seoul's bid had reflected a bold South Korean challenge to Japan, then recognized as the dominant Asian tiger, as well as essential denial of South Korea's own domestic political problems, coming off a presidential assassination and a military coup. For most of the world, with the exception of a hazy recollection of the so-called Korean War in the early 1950s, Korea tended to be a footnote on the international scene, a small, but insoluble problem in which, apart from reflecting the polarization of the Cold War, there was little interest. The Republic of Korea (South Korea) was also still technically at war with the Democratic People's Republic of Korea (DPRK) and was burdened with an uneasy truce and a line of military demarcation at latitude 38° north.

On the other side of the line was a heavily armed and unstable enemy. That practical reality aside, it was an essential political mantra on both sides of the line that reunification of the Korean peninsula would some day occur. Until the late 1990s, endless meetings between both sides produced posturing, diatribe, accusations, denials and no significant progress toward the stated goal. More recently, a flurry of activities has given greater grounds for cautious optimism, such as the Kaesong Industrial Complex, the Diamond Mountain tour project and increased South Korean aid to the DPRK. Tensions have eased to the degree that the two Koreas are now even discussing joint fishing zones across a contested sea border. Perhaps the one-step-forward, one-step-backward nature of the relationship may evolve in the apparent new climate of cooperation, in which the two leaders have been willing to be seen together. The usual Olympic negotiations are under way to see whether the two Koreas can agree on a single Olympic team, this time for the Beijing Games.

As it approached the 1988 Olympic Games, South Korea was in an evident state of political transition. This transition was not apparent when the campaign for the Games began or when they were awarded. A presidential assassination and a subsequent military coup had intervened in the process. These events, violent as they were, may nevertheless be seen in retrospect as preliminary symptoms of that transition. In the years leading up to the Games, there had been astonishing economic progress in South Korea.

With the exception of pro-democracy university students and intellectuals—many of whom were arrested and imprisoned for their expressed views—it seemed that the populace was generally content to trade some political freedom, even significant freedom, for increases in the standard of living. Even the rapidly growing middle class, growing as a consequence of the economic development, fell into this category. There appeared to be a certain Confucian sense of national harmony and purpose that existed under the strong and hierarchical leadership. That philosophical tendency, whatever its strength in the community at large may have been, was also reinforced by the military, which was powerful, disciplined and conservative.

On the other hand, increased economic prosperity, coupled with the broad base of education in South Korea, had brought the inevitable desire for more freedom of expression, whether of thought, economic activity or political action. The seeds of change were sown and it was only a matter of time before they germinated and eventually flowered. The political leadership was not unaware of this pressure for change, but was intensely concerned about its pace and direction. Despite its military origins, the political leadership was not completely opposed to change, but did not want it to be undisciplined or precipitous. Indeed, the military branches were known to be prepared to intervene with such force as might be necessary to prevent it. By the time Seoul was awarded the 1988 Olympic Games by the IOC in late 1981, the presidency was held by Chun Doo Hwan, a former army general who had seized power following the assassination of Park Chung Hee, himself a military figure, in a coup that involved its own share of bloodshed.

## CHUN'S IRON GRIP

In that respect, there had not been much to distinguish the Chun regime from many other military governments, even though Chun went through the ritual cleansing—retiring from the military before assuming the political office of president. Few believed, however, that he threw out all his uniforms when he became president, nor that behind his civilian presidency the military from which he had come had an entirely benign disinterest in matters political. The combination of his Confucian mental set and military conservatism made Chun an unapproachable figure, unattractive to the population at large. Coupled with the muscular legal framework that made full political expression in Korea difficult and even dangerous for those who opposed government policy, the Chun government was regarded with both distaste and fear.

Change was nevertheless in the wind and in some respects this was appreciated as much by the military as any segment of Korean society. As noted above, the military's preoccupations were not so much with the idea of change, but rather with its management, together with an overriding concern, bordering on paranoia, that whatever change might occur, accomplished without exposing South Korea to adventurism on the part of the DPRK. With something on the order of one million armed troops along the borders of the two Koreas, the possibility of misadventure was considerable, and the history of the DPRK gave little reason for relaxing vigilance in the slightest. As a priority, therefore, the military was prepared to intervene in civil matters if the process of change were to get out of control or expose South Korea to a military intervention from the DPRK. This imperative was known by the political leaders on all sides. Its full implications were not always appreciated by student leaders, traditionally important agents of change in Asia, who, with the energy of youth unsupported by experience, occasionally pushed too far, too fast, with an all-too-predictable reaction.

Chun had said that he would leave office at the end of his term, a promise that Koreans greeted with a certain cynicism. He had, with occasional lapses, indicated that he would condone the amendment of the constitution, if the ruling Democratic Justice Party (of which he was part) and the opposition parties could agree on the amendments. Chun had not gone as far as giving up the built-in advantage of the ruling party's ability to load the National Assembly with its own appointees, but a change in this direction was only a matter of time. Nor had he agreed to direct presidential elections, since this squandered the same built-in advantage his party already enjoyed. But this aspect, too, was inevitable and the hand-picked candidate to succeed him, Roh Tae Woo, another former army general, had conceded this within two weeks of being confirmed as his party's candidate in the presidential elections. Chun endorsed this decision and may well have known that the concession would be forthcoming at the time of choosing his successor. Roh benefited from his voluntary and public recognition of the current political reality as well as from the political immaturity of the opposition parties, which fragmented prior to the national elections and allowed him to emerge through the middle as the presidential winner, in effect by default.

## POLITICAL REFORM UNDER THE WORLD'S SPOTLIGHT

There can be little doubt that the new spotlight shining on South Korea in the period leading up to the Seoul Games had an important effect on the speed with which the South Korean leadership was willing to move in the direction of political reform. The media attention on the country was unprecedented and was almost universally supportive of direct presidential elections and of some degree of reduction in the ability of the ruling party to stack the National Assembly. Roh Tae Woo was seen as a much milder and personable form of Chun Doo Hwan. Other political leaders who had been harassed or imprisoned, such as Kim Young Sam and Kim Dae Jung, were free to lead parties in the elections, and each of them later was elected president of the country. Once Roh Tae Woo was president, it was possible for the IOC to meet with the leaders of the opposition parties (such meetings were not possible while Chun Doo Hwan had been president) and they were all invited to dine with the IOC at the Olympic Village. Despite the occasional temptation to use the Games for their political advantage (for which they were severely criticized in the South Korean media), each of the opposition leaders eventually threw the support of their parties behind the Games. The transition to direct presidential elections and reforms in the election of members of the National Assembly were given strong encouragement by the United States and other Western countries, linked, in the case of the United States, to publicly announce increased military presence in Asia during the period of the Games.

The Kafkaesque negotiations regarding possible (but never remotely likely) "cohosting" of the Games with the DPRK conducted under the aegis of the IOC also provided opportunities for the South Koreans to extend their own network of contacts, business, consular and political. Few, if any, of such initiatives could have occurred in the normal course of political push and shove between the two major powers of the day, each with its own acolytes, absent the hugely important Olympic Games. There was general boycott fatigue after Montreal, Moscow and Los Angeles, especially among the Warsaw Pact countries, which had let it be known to the Soviet Union in 1984 that they had no interest in supporting any further Olympic boycotts on a Soviet pretext.

The basis for the Soviet-led boycott of the 1984 Summer Olympics in Los Angeles had been its expressed concern over security, known by all as a false issue, the real one being nothing more than a retaliation for the US-led boycott of the Moscow Games four years earlier. The 1984 boycott had been masterminded by Andrei Gromyko, an experienced cold warrior of the old guard and currently minister of foreign affairs, who controlled the weak and compliant general secretary of the Communist Party, Konstantin Chernenko. Had Chernenko's predecessor, Yuri Andropov, not died earlier in 1984, it is entirely likely that the Soviet Union and those of its allies it was able to persuade or force to boycott would not have engaged in that tactic. In the event, it was a political disaster for the Soviet Union, which could not even hold all of the Warsaw Pact countries together, to which embarrassment was added the highly popular participation of China at the Games. The Soviet allies demonstrated their irritation with the Soviet Union by willingness to develop trade and other relationships with South Korea leading up to 1988. For that matter, the Soviets themselves established their first consular mission in Seoul once it was clear that the Games would be held as planned.

These developments did not of themselves add to the forces leading in the direction of internal political reform, but the resultant lessening of international tensions focused on South Korea made it easier for the domestic evolution to occur more rapidly in the lead-up to the Games. This was especially so once it was clear that China and the Soviet Union, each in its own interests, would not support any disruptive military action by the DPRK in relation to the Games. Neither wanted war with the United States. They would have been placed in a particularly difficult position were the DPRK to have become involved in any significant military activity in South Korea, since there was no doubt that the United States, with some 40,000 troops in South Korea at the time, would immediately have been engaged and would have been required to accelerate such engagement as much as necessary to protect its troops and interests in Korea. For many reasons affecting its Asian policy, the US would have had no alternative but to commit to such action. There was, therefore, a complete congruence of national interests among the three superpowers to prevent any incidents on the Korean peninsula. There can be little doubt that the appropriate messages were conveyed both by China and the Soviet Union to the DPRK in their roles as allies. However unpalatable these may have been to the DPRK, they appear to have been both received and understood.

Perhaps most important of all, however, was that South Korea wanted and was ready for such political change. It must have been a matter of some comfort to the public at large that the desired changes and resulting freedoms were proposed by one of the military politicians and approved by a military president. The risk of attempting to accelerate the process would have been appreciably greater without the backdrop of this particular element, since it was clear that the military was ready and willing to act in circumstances not to its liking. Encouragement from its own allies and the restraints imposed on the DPRK by its protectors, the desire to demonstrate Korean maturity to the world as part of its economic surge, the international lift expected from the Olympic Games and a fortuitous choice of the replacement of Chun Doo Hwan combined to accelerate the change beyond what most observers might have expected, all with remarkably little dissention and social upheaval. The Games did not, of course, solve all of the political problems in South Korea and there was continual pressure for expansion of political and human rights during the presidency of Roh Tae Woo, still perceived as a leader with a military background and the (occasional) authoritarian reflex. On the other hand, demonstrations were not prevented, reforms continued, a civilian president was elected in 1992, and history will probably show that Roh had far more to do with the peaceful progression in South Korea than has as yet been acknowledged. Roh's relative openness to change was ultimately as important as the original decision to allow Seoul to stage the 1988 Games.

## A DIFFERENT OUTLOOK FOR THE BEIJING GAMES

Could the same form of political development occur in China in the context of the 2008 Games? The short answer is no. At least not in the same form.

Not enough of the same parallels exist. The Chinese government is not in a state of visible transition and there seems to be little widespread popular demand for such change, notwithstanding the strong governmental control over almost all aspects of Chinese society. It is true that China is enjoying (and wrestling with) extraordinary economic growth and increasing numbers of well-off citizenry, but this has not yet manifested itself in demands for greater freedom or structural changes in government. Provided government is adroit enough to stay out of the way of the developing business economy in the country, its existence may be ignored or perhaps tolerated as a necessary, but largely irrelevant, cost of doing business. The rate of increased communication will continue to accelerate. It is clear that despite some efforts to attempt to regulate the Internet and the unlimited access to unfiltered information it provides, China will no longer be isolated, even if it does not fully emerge from its traditional isolation. It is too soon to measure the long-term impact of such changes, but not too soon to conclude that no major changes will occur prior to the 2008 Games.

From the perspective of government, unlike the case of South Korea leading up to 1988, China does not consider that it has anything to prove. It is quite content with the raw economic power that it possesses, both as exporter and desirable market for foreign goods and services. It is equally content to exercise that power to further its particular political and other interests. It sees no need to demonstrate that its goods are equal to or better than Japanese goods, a challenge faced by the emerging South Korea in the early 1980s, although a number of recent events have demonstrated that the need for quality control cannot be dismissed as a consideration even with its enormous power. Nor is the Chinese government beholden to its allies for security or dependent upon the conduct of others to ensure a peaceful celebration of the Games, as had been South Korea. It can make its own way in Asia, with virtually no credible security threat. Its internal Games issues are almost entirely logistical. None of these can be considered a driver toward political change from—or reform within—a single-party system of government.

Progress in matters of human rights has probably not been as profound or as quick as observers might have hoped, especially given China's invitation to the IOC in 2001 to consider how hosting the Games could have an impact. Constant pressure will, however, have beneficial results, since the Chinese are not insensitive to international opinion on the question, provided internal stability is not threatened. It can do no harm to remind China of its implied promise in 2001 and to encourage greater progress. It would be unrealistic to expect that the Games, symbolically important as they may be for China, can provide greater political leverage than that provided by the combined efforts of many governments and other international organizations over many years. Patience is required and the Olympic Games are no panacea for the ills of the world. The era of Olympic boycotts on such issues is past. It would be a brave government that would declare itself to be completely without sin in matters of human rights and so offended by conditions in China that it would prohibit its citizens from participating in Games to be held there. In addition, experience has shown that Olympic boycotts harm the boycotters far more than the intended target country.

The period before and after the Games in Beijing will undoubtedly be marked by controversy and criticism. That is one of the prices of being an Olympic host, especially if the host country happens to be a major power, with all of the political baggage coming with that status. Chinese involvement on the international scene and many of its alliances (some of which, like those of other major powers, are inevitably problematic) will be highlighted and used by some as a reason to withdraw the Games from Beijing.

It would be wrong to conclude that the Chinese government does not care what the world thinks about it. On the contrary, as it plays a greater part on the Asian and world stages, it cares very much about public opinion, as can be seen from its reactions to criticisms and to support of its positions. Recent evolution in its public support of Myanmar is tangible evidence, as is cooperation with the public authorities in the United States in Operation Raw Deal, in which evidence has pointed to China as the source of massive amounts of performance-enhancing drugs. In the months leading up to the Games, it is likely that more steps will be made in the direction of expanded rights. China is nothing if not adept and nuanced at sending signals and making political gestures to achieve political and other objectives.

It would be equally wrong to conclude that, because of the Games, China will abandon any of its present core policies, whether internal or foreign. Those stakes are regarded by the Chinese as too important to be allowed to change in any precipitate manner. The Korean parallel would be the concern of the military that political change had the possibility to get out of control and lead to encroachment by the DPRK. China looked into that chasm of uncontrolled change—and over its shoulder at the rapid disintegration of the former Soviet Union—at the time of Tiananmen Square.

On the other hand, no host country of the Olympic Games has ever been the same after the Games as it had been before, especially countries that had been closed or particularly authoritarian. China will not be unaffected by the opening up of the country to the world in 2008. Its size and present governance may mean that the change does not occur as quickly as it might in other countries. Its lack of transparency may also mean that the elements of change are not easily apparent, which will not mean that they are not occurring. Patience and firmness on the part of the international community can be effective catalysts. As can the Olympic Games.

PART II

# HUMAN RIGHTS ABUSES
# EXPOSED IN THE OLYMPIC FLAME

# CHAPTER 6

# Five Olympic Rings, Thousands of Handcuffs

BY WANG DAN

*The Beijing Olympic Games have not one but five mascots—a panda, a fish, an antelope and a swallow, as well as the Olympic flame itself. Symbolizing the five Olympic rings, these mascots are meant to convey to the world a message of friendship and peace. However, the reality in China is more complex: thousands of ordinary citizens languish in prisons for having dared to press for freedom.* WANG DAN, *a leading student organizer of the 1989 Tiananmen democracy movement, was imprisoned twice for his democracy advocacy, spending nearly seven years in a prison in Liaoning Province. In 1998 he left prison for the United States, earning a master's degree in East Asian Studies (2001) at Harvard University, where he is currently pursuing a PhD. He is a visiting scholar at the University of California, Los Angeles, and chairs the Chinese Constitutional Reform Association.*

Chinese citizens who have been arbitrarily arrested without breaking any laws should be allowed to enjoy the Olympics along with the rest of China. The world should press Beijing to rid them of their shackles to enjoy the Games with dignity. When the French press freedom group Reporters Without Borders launched its Olympics campaign, the organization chose a powerful symbol: the familiar five-ring Olympics logo—with five handcuffs instead of rings.

Such initiatives are designed to shock, and may well anger the Chinese authorities and even some Chinese people. But China jails more journalists than any country in the world, and so relations with press-freedom organizations have obviously been poor. Ironically, press freedom was one of the most publicized pledges Chinese government officials made to the International Olympic Committee and the world to secure the Games.

## CHINA'S "CATCH AND RELEASE" PROGRAM

In 1993, I was one of twenty high-profile dissidents released from prison as part of China's first charm offensive to secure the Olympics. I was released one month before the International Olympic Committee came to Beijing for an inspection tour. I publicly supported China's bid then and again in 2001, because I believe the Games should be a boost to China, a chance for Chinese people to be in touch with the world. Obviously, I was glad to be free, but I also recognized that I was being used as a bargaining chip. Though I was released, I was also aware that many others remained in prison for peacefully expressing their beliefs.

At the same time, I said publicly that I supported China being awarded the Olympic Games. This is because I believe China must develop a strong civil society, and one way to do that would be to have the international community come to China and engage with our people.

As my own case shows, the Olympics provide us with a rare opportunity to secure the release of the many dissidents still under detention. But after China's first Olympic bid failed, I was arrested again and sentenced to return to prison on charges of "subversion." The evidence against me included the fact that I had enrolled in a history correspondence course offered by the University of California.

In 1998, I was finally exiled to the United States along with fellow dissident Wang Juntao, in another bid to manipulate public opinion before President Clinton's visit to China for a major summit. During both of China's Olympic bids, my central hope was that the Games would have a catalytic effect on the paralyzed political environment in China.

## THE CHINESE PEOPLE AND THE CHINESE GOVERNMENT

The Chinese people are not their government. Since 1989, my country, China, and its people, have changed much. But the government has changed remarkably little. The many dissidents still behind bars today are a national tragedy as well as a political humiliation. The Chinese government, when bidding for the Olympics both times, solemnly vowed before the world to improve its human rights conditions. Yet the autocrats who control the Chinese Communist Party—the only political force allowed to operate in the country since 1949—continue to ignore and abuse the rights of their own citizens, cracking down on any voices asking for the most basic human rights.

Instead of the reforms to rejoin the world I had hoped for, we see that the persecution of dissidents and religious believers by the Chinese government continues unabated.

To distract from this record of repression, today the Chinese government is attempting to use the Olympic Games to once again propagate a new economic "leap forward" model, with narrow-minded nationalism as its flag. I fear that the generation that came of age during the Cultural Revolution has lost the ability to understand what it truly means to be patriotic and to love the country. Nationalism is no substitute for an open, transparent, and democratic system of government.

## HANDCUFFED CIVIL SOCIETY

There are many people in China today serving long prison terms for activities that would be considered normal political engagement in most of the rest of the world. China's prisons still hold thousands of political prisoners. The exact number is not known because the government does not provide official figures. John Kamm—the head of Dui Hua and an expert on this subject—has estimated that some 3,000 people are in prison on charges of "endangering state security." This charge is commonly used to target political activists. Moreover, an estimated 300,000 Chinese citizens have been sent to reeducation-through-labor camps across China, often for political activities.

Well-known legal activists, including Guo Feixiong and Chen Guangcheng, remain in prison where they reportedly have been tortured. Chen Guangcheng, a blind activist who was sentenced to four years in prison in 2006 after documenting cases of forced abortions and other rights violations in Shandong Province, was awarded a prestigious Magsaysay Award—Asia's equivalent of the Nobel Prize—for his courageous work. In August 2007, his wife was detained at Beijing Airport as she tried to fly to Manila to accept the award on his behalf. And in June 2007, police in several Chinese cities arrested members of the Pan-Blue Coalition of China for offenses such as displaying the flag of the Kuomintang, the main political party in Taiwan. Thus the disturbing handcuff image used by Reporters Without Borders is a grim but accurate reminder that while the Chinese government actively prepares to host the Olympic Games and show the world a polished, happy face, it also relentlessly continues to crush all forms of dissent. The handcuff image can also be seen to symbolize the worst types of labor abuses, amounting in some cases to modern slavery. The image should remind us of China's Shanxi brick kilns. In twenty-first-century China, we see child slavery and government cover-ups. In June 2007, it was revealed that hundreds of workers, including dozens who were underage, were forced to work in Shanxi's brick kilns. Many were beaten, abused and deprived of pay. Even after these revelations, the Shanxi authorities were negligent in rescuing the enslaved workers, fueling suspicion that they fabricated rescue information and engineered the disappearance of some "rescued" workers from government premises.

In the same month, other distressing news on child labor trickled out of Chinese provinces: a fourteen-year-old boy was killed in an explosion at a chemical factory near Nanjing. A fifteen-year-old boy was crushed to death by a cotton gin in Nanchang. Young girls work grueling sixteen-hour shifts at a grape-processing plant in Ningbo.

## A SHACKLED MEDIA

Moreover, the Chinese government is cracking down on conventional as well as online media outlets in an effort to keep such stories hidden. Two separate reports by Human Rights Watch and the Committee to Protect Journalists in August 2007, one year before the launch of the Beijing Olympics, painted a dire picture of the harassment, intimidation and censorship of Chinese journalists.

Where I once had hoped that the Olympics might help the Chinese government wake up to the reality that it must actively improve its human rights conditions, instead the leaders in Beijing are suppressing information about how bad things are.

With such a disappointing track record, the international community should do much more to promote reform before the launch of the Beijing Olympic Games. History points to the need for vigilance. The 1936 Berlin Games provided Hitler with a prominent stage for the glorification of the Nazi regime and they remain a disgrace in Olympic history. The 1980 Moscow Olympics were held amid the gunfire of the Soviet Union's invasion of Afghanistan, and were no credit to Olympic history.

The Olympics were awarded to China by the International Olympic Committee, but it is the international community that is responsible to use this moment in history to urge Beijing to improve human rights. Will the world stand by to watch another stain on Olympic history?

## AN "OLYMPIC AMNESTY"

The Olympic Games should be a celebration of peace and harmony for all mankind. Instead of jailing more critics such as human rights advocate Hu Jia, the Chinese government should declare an "Olympic Amnesty" for all political prisoners, and also allow all exiled dissidents to return to China. All Chinese citizens who were arbitrarily arrested without breaking any laws should be released and be able to enjoy the Olympics along with billions of people throughout the world. They have the right to be freed from their shackles and to enjoy with dignity the peace and happiness which are ostensibly part of the Olympic spirit. Only in a China that is free of handcuffs can the Beijing Olympics truly live up to their motto, "One World, One Dream."

As the Olympic Charter puts it, the Olympic Games should serve "the harmonious development of man, with a view to promoting a peaceful society concerned with the preservation of human dignity." Now is the moment for national Olympic committees, governments of participating nations, human rights groups, media organizations, athletes and sports fans throughout the world to forcefully voice their concerns about human rights to the Chinese government. Beijing needs to fulfill its promises if the Chinese people are to emerge as the true winners of the 2008 Summer Games.

# CHAPTER 7

# Physical Strength, Moral Poverty

BY JIMMY LAI

*The Beijing Games are designed to showcase a powerful yet peace-loving China. The People's Liberation Army is the world's largest standing army with 2.2 million soldiers, and with an annual growth rate estimated at close to 10 percent, China's economic power is also growing. However, China lacks one type of power that tanks cannot provide and money cannot buy: "soft power," the ability to influence people and nations through inspiration and the upholding of moral values.* JIMMY LAI *is the founder of Next Media, the largest listed media company in Hong Kong and the publisher of leading newspapers and magazines in Hong Kong and Taiwan, including* Apple Daily *and* Next Magazine. *Born in Guangdong province, he smuggled himself to Hong Kong on a boat at the age of twelve, and was a child laborer in a garment factory before becoming one of greater China's best-known clothing and media entrepreneurs.*

When the Olympic Games begin in Beijing, China will show the world its physical strength, but also its moral poverty. This is unavoidable because the Olympics are more than just a sporting event; they are an expression of the human drive for greatness in all pursuits. They are about aspirations and human faith in the value of pursuing those aspirations. That faith gives the Games a moral dimension that, despite all the gold medals won by authoritarian regimes in the modern era of the Olympics, remains incompatible with dictatorship.

China cannot be a truly good host for the Games. On the mainland, the pursuit of one's aspirations remains extremely limited. Ever since the market liberalization initiated by Deng Xiaoping in the late 1970s, the Chinese government has opened its markets to the world's goods and technology but has kept the social and political spheres tightly sealed. The gradual opening of the Chinese market has led to an influx of foreign business and investment, thereby lifting hundreds of millions of people out of poverty. But because the Communist Party has impeded the development of civil society and democratic institutions, this new affluence has not led to a renaissance in culture or morality. When the intense spotlight of the Olympics shines on China, I believe that this emptiness will become apparent to the world.

Yet despite my skepticism about Beijing's ability to turn the Olympics into the public relations success story it so strongly seeks, I remain optimistic about China in the long term. I even dare to hope that the clash of values that will inevitably be on display at the Olympics will play some role in breaking Beijing's stranglehold on people's minds. The reactions of the half million or so foreigners thronging into China to watch the Games, as well as the billions more who will watch via television throughout the world, could be a huge wake-up call to China. The realization that the rest of the world will not swallow the myth of a "harmonious society" propagated by the Communist Party will unleash a healthy round of soul-searching.

The Chinese people's moral consciousness has been awakening, but the changes have been slow and hard to see. This is not surprising. When changes begin, they evolve very slowly until they gather enough momentum. When their development reaches the "knee of the curve"—the point beyond which a nearly flat curve begins to soar upwards—then the growth explodes into an exponential trend.

## THE PARABLE OF THE LAKE OWNER

The nature of exponential growth after it reaches this "knee of the curve"—the stage at which a trend goes from insignificant to overwhelming—can be illustrated by a simple parable.

A lake owner wants to stay at home to tend to the lake's fish and make certain that the lake will not become covered with lily pads, the number of which doubles every few days. Month after month, he patiently waits, yet only tiny patches of lily pads can be discerned and they do not seem to be expanding in any noticeable way. With the lily pads covering less than 1 percent of the lake, the owner finally assumes that it is safe to take a vacation and leaves with his family. When he returns a few weeks later, he is shocked to discover that the entire lake has become covered with the pads, and his fish have perished. By doubling their number every few days, the last seven doublings were sufficient to extend the pads' coverage to the entire lake.

Human society evolves in a similar fashion. China's moral and political changes have also been largely imperceptible, though long subjected to value inducement through information from the outside world that slipped past the control of the government through the open marketplace, the Internet and other media. Will the reactions of Olympics tourists and audiences stimulate these changes to help our country reach the "knee of the curve"?

It is possible, and I certainly hope they will.

China's focus on economic expansion alone at the expense of the development of civil institutions has created serious moral problems. Prosperity gives people the ability to aspire to a higher purpose than just survival, but if they are constrained then they will begin to perceive that their lives are empty. China is ignoring its institutional development and its moral problems at its peril.

Make no mistake, I believe that a free market is good for society, and the market opening has been good for China. But the market is just a single part of a human society, one that cannot exist in isolation. If a government focuses on economic expansion alone—as Beijing has done, considering this its primary mandate to rule—the market will eventually become pathological and a threat to life itself. China's constant struggle with contaminated food, fake medicines and faulty goods are cases in point. Freedom in its true sense derives from ordered liberty, a freedom whose roots are in moral and ethical values of trust, honesty and integrity. China needs the complementary development of civil institutions and moral infrastructure, so that the market can play its proper role.

As a result of its fast economic growth in the last two decades, China's clout in the world has risen, but its national prestige has not. In its single-minded focus on efficient economic development, the government has relied on political repression to achieve its ends. For instance, when the government needs land for development or for building roads, it just takes over people's farmland or demolishes their homes, with very little compensation to the owners. While such actions betray a callous indifference toward the well being of its own people, the government can also show a ruthless side in dealing with individuals who are seen as having damaged China's image among business and consumer circles abroad.

In 2007, reports that Chinese companies had repeatedly shipped contaminated food abroad were threatening to seriously damage the reputation of the country's exports. Beijing stunned observers by executing Zheng Xiaoyu, the former head of the Chinese Food and Drug Administration who had been convicted of bribery charges. Many foreign commentators saw Zheng as a scapegoat for the government's own failures, but Beijing felt it could show the mortified populace at home and abroad a bloody head on the spike and get on with business. Perhaps some people like doing business in China for this reason, but actually it is a stain on the country's honor.

## CHINA'S LACK OF "SOFT POWER"

In recent decades, China has been focusing on the development of its economic power, in parallel with the expansion of its military power. However it has neglected to cultivate its "soft power," the more subtle means of influence described by Harvard University professor Joseph Nye in his book, *Soft Power: The Means to Success in World Politics*. Soft power, contrasted with the coercive "hard power" of military action or the economic power of the marketplace, refers to the ability of a government to wield influence in a more indirect and positive fashion, through the appeal of values or its culture.

Many observers tend to exaggerate China's rising influence, because they focus solely on its military might or economic expansion, ignoring its lack of soft power—a result of its moral poverty. Soft power is not about what businesspeople or their governments think, but about what a country is perceived as standing for. Astute observers know that there is more to China than just its gross domestic product growth. They know also that Beijing at this writing holds some 3,900 political prisoners[1] and 29 journalists in prison,[2] more than any other country, and that the government censors the press and Internet with extraordinary efficiency. They know that such behavior is not only wrong and deeply immoral, but also cancerous within the state organism since in the long term, freedom of ideas and expression is as important as freedom of markets. The collapse of the Soviet Union showed that a society that is not free, however powerful it may be in military or economic terms, risks imploding in the long term because its citizens yearn to live freely and with basic human rights. Such aspirations also triggered the successful democracy movements in Eastern and Central Europe following the break-up of the Soviet Union.

The 2008 Olympics will take place in Beijing and a number of other Chinese cities: Shanghai, Hong Kong, Qingdao, Tianjin, Shenyang and Qinhuangdao. Visitors will presumably experience China's dismal environmental record firsthand. Sixteen of the world's twenty most polluted cities are in China, which has overtaken the United States as the world's largest source of carbon dioxide emissions.[3] China's environmental problem is not just a symptom of regulatory laxity, but another symptom of China's moral disease. When a government focuses on rapid economic expansion regardless of the human cost to its own people, how much would it care for the air, the water, the forests and the animals?

## A HISTORIC OPPORTUNITY

Despite its increasing economic clout and influence, China is still seen as a pariah state. And despite an economic boom that has lifted millions of people out of poverty, people are still not happy with the current situation. In 2005, there were nearly 80,000 social uprisings of varying scales throughout the country,[4] and the gap between the poor and the rich was still widening despite—or maybe as a result of—the swift economic growth. The main reason is simple: because economic development is driven and directed from the top, the people in power retain most of the benefit. The 1 percent of people at the top of China's economic pyramid control 60 percent of the country's domestic wealth.[5] It is obvious that in such a moral vacuum, China is struggling to find the truly sound solutions required by its emerging social problems. It becomes clearer every day that social changes are urgently needed. Can the Olympic Games help break this logjam?

They just might. The fact that China's society currently evolves in a moral vacuum also means that there are no entrenched intermediate institutions; people are less inhibited and can accept new ideas and values with greater ease and speed. The current isolation of Chinese society from the system of democratic values shared by an ever larger part of the outside world is possible only as long as the workability of the economic-expansion-alone-is-enough paradigm is taken for granted. But if this paradigm is impeded by the incompatibility of its current solutions to emerging problems, coupled with a desire for more democratic values spurred by the interaction with the outside world on the occasion of the Olympics, it could disintegrate and give rise to people's awareness of the need for a new set of alternative solutions.

The Olympic Games will provide a unique opportunity to deliver a strong message to Beijing: in the long term, China cannot expect to be a major player in the global market without being a respected member of the world community. And to be part of the world community, China must embrace the world's shared values and build a firm foundation based on democratic values, healthy civil institutions and basic protections of human rights for its citizens.

# CHAPTER 8

# A Gold Medal in Media Censorship

## BY PHELIM KINE

*The Olympic Charter describes Olympism as a philosophy which "seeks to create a way of life based on the joy of effort, the educational value of good example and respect for universal fundamental ethical principles." An obvious ethical principle is freedom of expression. Although the Chinese government has temporarily loosened some regulations that have long restricted the freedom of journalists, in line with pledges made while bidding for the 2008 Olympics, Chinese authorities have yet to honor their promises in deed as well as word.* PHELIM KINE, *a researcher in Human Rights Watch's Asia Division, is a former journalist with more than a decade of experience reporting from Greater China and Southeast Asia.*

> "We will give the media complete freedom to report when they come to China."
> —WANG WEI, SECRETARY GENERAL OF THE BEIJING OLYMPIC BID COMMITTEE, IN 2001

If media censorship were an Olympic competition, China's prowess at smothering some reportage would give it the dubious honor of a gold medal. The Committee to Protect Journalists (CPJ) annually tracks reporters imprisoned across the world. In 2007—for the ninth consecutive year—China was named as the world's leading jailer of journalists, with twenty-nine imprisoned.

The global competition is not even close, with China far ahead of silver medalist Cuba and bronze medalist Eritrea, jailers of respectively twenty-four and fourteen journalists. Moreover, the longest sentences in CPJ's census were those served by the Chinese journalists Chen Renjie and Lin Youping, in jail since July 1983 for having published a pamphlet titled *Ziyou Bao* (Freedom Report). Codefendant Chen Biling was later executed.[1]

China's ubiquitous government censors and state controls on news content can't and don't completely eradicate the reporting freedom of the country's thousands of newspapers and Web sites. China's media, except the main government mouthpieces such as the *People's Daily* newspaper, People's Radio and China Central Television, enjoy relatively wide discretion in their ability to report on topics, including sports, entertainment, consumer lifestyle and local news safely denuded of any overtly political undertones. But China's media remain hamstrung by prohibitions against reporting anything which falls under the government's vast rubric of "sensitive" topics, which include anything unflattering about the government, the Chinese Communist Party and events of the day, which might prompt doubt about the stability of the country and the wisdom and benevolence of its leaders.

The Chinese government's failure to fully respect press freedom was no obstacle to the International Olympic Committee awarding the 2008 Summer Games to Beijing. But removing restrictions on reporters was one of the specific promises China's leadership made to the world and to the International Olympic Committee to win the privilege to host the Games. That commitment to wider media freedom was in line with the obligation of Olympic host cities to comply with Article 51 of the International Olympic Committee Charter, which stipulates that the IOC should take "all necessary steps in order to ensure the fullest coverage by the different media and the widest possible audience in the world for the Olympic Games." Yet in clear violation of its promise to loosen its reflexive stranglehold on the media, the Chinese government has continued to harass, intimidate and detain local and foreign journalists in the run-up to the Beijing Games.

Today in China, even some nonpolitical events such as industrial or engineering accidents are deemed unmentionable, since thorough investigations might shed light on official corruption or incompetence. In August 2007, sixty-four people were killed in a deadly bridge collapse in central China's Hunan province. What followed was depressingly familiar. A group of unidentified thugs interrupted five Chinese journalists interviewing relatives of the victims of the Fenghuang bridge collapse. The journalists, including even a reporter from the government's *People's Daily*, were kicked and punched. When police finally arrived on the scene, they didn't arrest the assailants—they arrested the journalists. The incident, far from uncommon, is emblematic of how the Chinese government's commitment to media freedom, enshrined in both the country's constitution and international agreements, as well as its pledges to the International Olympic Committee, are routinely violated or ignored by state security forces and anonymous thugs who appear to operate at official behest. Not that any such reminder was really necessary.

For decades, the Chinese government and Chinese Communist Party have exercised strict control over domestic media, effectively turning the bulk of China's press into components of a vast national propaganda system. Mostly untouched by the "reform and opening" initiated by Deng Xiaoping in 1978, domestic news in China is painstakingly filtered through outright censorship of material deemed objectionable by the Communist Party and a web of rules and regulations that strictly limit the reporting scope of journalists.[2] While China's constitution nominally guarantees "publishing freedom," an array of national media regulations with vague and sweeping prohibitions on the publication of material that "harms the honor or the interests of the nation," "spreads rumors," or "harms the credibility of a government agency," are implicit threats to Chinese and international journalists who pursue stories deemed sensitive by the government.

New temporary regulations in place from January 1, 2007 to October 17, 2008, as part of the government's media freedom commitments to the IOC were designed to at least loosen a few of the buckles on the straitjacket of official controls. The new rules are detailed in a "Service Guide for Foreign Media."3 The guide states that "the regulations on reporting activities by foreign journalists shall apply to the coverage of the Beijing Olympic Games and the preparation, as well as political, economic, social and cultural matters of China by foreign journalists in conformity with Chinese laws and regulations." Those regulations appeared to remove long-standing handcuffs requiring foreign correspondents to get foreign ministry permission for interviews. But in practice the freedoms enshrined in the regulations have been routinely ignored if not willfully flouted. Some reporters say that the temporary regulations finally make it possible to access certain high-profile dissidents, but other foreign correspondents in China are still routinely subjected to harassment, detention and intimidation in the course of simply trying to do their jobs. Indeed, a survey by the Foreign Correspondents Club of China found that in 2007—the first year of the temporary regulations' implementation—there were more than 180 incidents of intimidation of sources, detentions, surveillance, official reprimands, and even violence against staff and sources.

In addition, the 2007 temporary Olympics regulations that should free the press to report explicitly exclude Chinese journalists and Chinese nationals who are assistants, researchers, translators, or sources for foreign news organizations or correspondents.

## HIGH RISKS FOR CHINESE JOURNALISTS

That exclusion highlights the much higher risks Chinese journalists face compared to their foreign counterparts. While the worst official reprisal a foreign correspondent may face in China for unfavorable reporting is refusal to grant or renew a visa, Chinese journalists face arrest and imprisonment for incurring the anger of the Chinese government. Chinese reporters are closely monitored by state security agencies to ensure that their reporting doesn't stray from that of the official propaganda line or touch on taboo topics affecting "social stability," such as unrest in Tibet and the Muslim Uighur region of Xinjiang, or coverage of Taiwan or prominent dissidents. Chinese reporters are also subject to penalties ranging from dismissal to prosecution for violating vaguely worded regulations against "spreading rumors" or violations of "news discipline," which are prone to arbitrary interpretation by police and the judiciary.

Indeed, in China, the editorial content of Chinese language print, radio, and television media is dictated by weekly faxes from the government's official Publicity Department (formerly titled the Propaganda Department in English), which explicitly sets out which topics are taboo. Many Chinese journalists have paid a heavy price for venturing outside the strictly delineated areas deemed acceptable for news coverage. Wang Daqi, editor of the magazine *Ecology*, was jailed for a year in January 2003 for "incitement to overthrow the government" after publishing articles about the Cultural Revolution. Zan Aizong, a journalist for the *Haoyang Bao* in Zhejiang province, was detained for a week in August 2006 on charges of "spreading rumors harmful to society" for reporting on the demolition of a Protestant church, and subsequently lost his job.

Chinese journalists are particularly vulnerable to official

reprisals in advance of political events or anniversaries deemed "sensitive" by the government. Chinese journalists are acutely aware of the heightened scrutiny of official censors and security agencies ahead of each anniversary of the June 4, 1989, Tiananmen Square Massacre or of high-level meetings meetings of the Chinese Communist Party and the country's rubber-stamp parliament, the National People's Congress.

Ahead of every Chinese Communist Party Congress, the government routinely intensifies its already carefully stage-managed news coverage. That clampdown is part of the tightened security precautions and heightened official concerns about potential threats to "social stability" that occur ahead of and during each Party Congress, held every five years, due to their importance as the forum where the future leadership of the party is unveiled. Official efforts to script the media's message before the 2007 congress went so far as to echo those of the era of Chairman Mao Zedong, with five newspapers, the *People's Daily*, *Guangming Daily*, *Economic Daily*, *People's Liberation Army Daily* and the *Beijing Daily* all running near-identical front pages on August 19, 2007.

Pre–Party Congress media control efforts also include a crackdown on "fake news" and "illegal news coverage." While fake news reports and individuals who impersonate journalists for personal financial gain are a legitimate concern in China, one highlighted by the uproar over falsified stories about food safety threats, the government's main objective appears to be using such vaguely worded directives to punish journalists who publish factual reports of scandal, disaster and official malfeasance.

The Chinese government has apparently forgotten that it was a similar directive that prompted the initial cover-up of the early stages of the SARS outbreak in Guangdong province in late 2002. That decision allowed the illness to spread, and within months it had spilled over China's borders, eventually killing more than 700 people in nine countries.

## INTIMIDATION OF CHINESE ASSISTANTS TO FOREIGN JOURNALISTS

The Chinese assistants, researchers, and translators for foreign correspondents are uniquely vulnerable to reprisals from official and non-official agents. Because their work involves the pursuit of stories that are often classified as off-limits for domestic journalists, work on those topics often attracts the interest of state security officials who regularly interrogate them or their employers.

A potent lesson of the dangers faced by Chinese assistants to foreign correspondents is the case of Zhao Yan, the news researcher for the *New York Times* in Beijing who served three years in prison after being accused of fraud and leaking state secrets. Zhao was detained in September 2004 in connection with a *New York Times* article correctly predicting a reshuffle of top leadership positions in the Communist Party of China. His case was marred by multiple violations of due process including the refusal of the court to allow his lawyers to call witnesses on his behalf. When he was finally released in September 2007, Bill Keller, the *Times* executive editor, pointed out that "Zhao Yan is an honorable, hardworking reporter whose only offense seems to have been practicing journalism."

In an incident typical for Chinese assistants, researchers and translators, one local assistant of a Beijing-based foreign correspondent had become the target of tightening surveillance and pressure from at least two security organs of the Chinese government, the Public Security Bureau and the State Security Bureau, following the publication of a story about dissident couple Hu Jia and Zeng Jinyan. Agents of the two bureaus monitoring the assistant openly argued in his presence about which agency should have jurisdiction in his case. Pressure from those agencies even extended to members of the assistant's family, as explained by the foreign correspondent: "Several times the security agents asked [the assistant] for lunch, for coffee, for tea. The security agents were friendly, not threatening, and said, 'It's your responsibility to let us know if you and you boss do [coverage of] anything sensitive.' They kept calling him back for meetings . . . then they started calling his family, his parents . . . and asked for his registration information, confirmed where he lives and informed him of the job he does. After that, he became very upset."[4]

The security forces did not make any explicit threats to the family of the correspondent's assistant, but a call from such agencies to a family carries a heavy implicit warning of potential legal troubles. The correspondent said that his assistant naturally became extremely sensitive to any perceived surveillance, electronic or otherwise, of his movements and his news gathering activities by the security agencies. The assistant also asked to be allowed to avoid doing stories that might involve potential violent demonstrations.

## HARASSMENT OF FOREIGN JOURNALISTS

In the first half of 2007, at least seven foreign journalists were called in for meetings at the Ministry of Foreign Affairs in Beijing to receive what the correspondents said were implicit warnings about the tone or content of recent reporting. In one case, officials demanded changes to overseas coverage of what they labeled as a "sensitive" topic. While correspondents uniformly describe foreign ministry reprimands as perfunctory, tightly scripted encounters, their implicit threat value is extremely high. Foreign journalists are acutely aware that their annual work-permit renewals are at the ministry's discretion.

Human Rights Watch has documented numerous examples of harassment of foreign journalists. One Canadian correspondent was called in to face Ministry of Foreign Affairs complaints about an article he had written about the lawyer of Canadian religious leader Huseyin Celil, who had been sentenced to life imprisonment in China on terrorism charges. The Ministry of Foreign Affairs also expressed concerns about a story the correspondent had written about a nongovernmental organization's report on the systemic discrimination and poverty afflicting China's ethnic minorities, especially Tibetans and the Uighur Muslim minority in Xinjiang. The correspondent explained, "There are certain red lines [on news coverage] like 'terrorism' in Xinjiang . . . and anyone who covers those stories and strays from the official line attracts attention. [The encounter] was ritualistic, but it was a warning."[5]

Both the Committee to Protect Journalists and Human Rights Watch issued critical reports on media freedom restrictions in China on August 8, 2007,[6] to mark the one-year countdown to the launch of the Games. Even with the negative spotlight from these reports, police later that month prevented a group of seven foreign journalists from visiting Yuan Weijing, the wife of jailed human rights defender Chen Guangcheng, prior to her scheduled flight to Manila to receive an international human rights award on her husband's behalf. The police on duty outside Yuan's Beijing residence forced the journalists to accompany them to the neighborhood police post, where they were subjected to a lengthy "registration" process in order to get access to the residence. After the authorities barred Yuan from leaving China, the Associated Press reported that a group of "government workers" abducted Yuan from a Beijing-bound bus on August 31 and then forced her back to Shandong province.

## AN OLYMPIAN INFORMATION CHALLENGE

Notwithstanding Chinese officials' hollow guarantees, genuine media freedom will only be achieved once the government lifts restrictions on the reporting of subjects now deemed as taboo, ceases to stifle access to dissidents or any ordinary citizen whose opinions might not stick to the party line, and allows unfettered reporting from all areas, including Xianjiang and the Tibet

Autonomous Region. For the long-term benefit and welfare of its citizens, senior Chinese officials should end the surveillance, harassment, and intimidation of journalists across the country, both Chinese and foreign.

The International Olympic Committee, world leaders and government officials planning to attend the Olympics can and should seize the historic opportunity provided by the Beijing Games to urge the Chinese government to make media freedom a permanent component of Chinese law for both foreign and Chinese journalists beyond the October 17, 2008, expiration of the temporary regulations for foreign correspondents. By using its leverage this way, the IOC would truly fulfill what may be the most important part of its mission as described in the Olympic Charter: to "promote a positive legacy from the Olympic Games to the host cities and host countries."

Despite the political pressures of the 2008 Beijing Olympics, the Chinese government must realize that the lack of free media poses a far greater danger to the country's safety than press reports that shine an unflattering light on the complex realities of modern China. The truths of corruption, public health scandals, environmental crises, and abusive local authorities may be inconvenient. Yet the impulse to smother the reporting of these truths has contributed measurably to other global debacles, including recalls of tainted food, toys, and tires. This has caused international confidence in Chinese producers to plummet, and worsened situations in which transparency and honesty might have mitigated much of the negative consequences of such incidents.

Ultimately, stifling political dissent is destabilizing and leads to deeper political and ethnic polarization. China's stable development as a rising global power may ultimately hinge on its government's willingness to unshackle its media to allow greater transparency and honesty in reporting the country's realities.

# CHAPTER 9

# High Hurdles to Health in China

BY JOSEPH AMON

*The official website of the Beijing Olympics proclaims that the Games—described as the "People's Olympics"—will provide the opportunity to "promote healthy interaction between individuals and society and to foster mental and physical health." This admirable pronouncement is at odds with the experience of the vast majority of China's 1.3 billion citizens, whose fundamental right to health is frequently violated by their own government. The "right to health" is often understood as a right of individuals to access health care, but it also encompasses the right to simply seek, impart and receive information on health matters.* JOSEPH AMON *is an epidemiologist and molecular biologist by training. He joined Human Rights Watch as Director of the HIV/AIDS Program in 2005, after conducting research and designing public health programs in countries around the world. He addresses how China's general disregard for human rights has constrained its response to emerging infectious diseases and other health risks.*

Just as governments struggle with how to respond to political protest and unrest, they often grapple with how to react to public health threats, particularly the emergence of new and scary infectious diseases.

Is the most effective response a repressive one? Quarantine those suspected of being infected or even whole neighborhoods or cities where the disease has emerged? Limit the spread of information on the disease and cover up reports which could damage the country's reputation, business or tourism? Or should the response be to disseminate information openly and widely, collaborate with nongovernmental organizations and encourage less restrictive, voluntary compliance with public health measures?

While every disease threat has to be evaluated individually, global authorities such as the World Health Organization (WHO) have long recognized that public health interventions are most effective if they also succeed in respecting, protecting, and fulfilling human rights.[1] The WHO has also found that repressive responses to disease threats can backfire. Quarantines can push people who are infected or suspect they may be infected *away* from health care, as they seek to avoid restrictions on their freedom or the stigmatization and discrimination which can come from being identified as diseased. Quarantines are also rarely perfect—leading to a false sense of security for those outside the quarantine zone.

Efforts to limit information are also usually imperfect, allowing rumors to spread and undermining the credibility of all government statements as information slowly leaks out. In addition, governments often have little access to certain populations. For example, ethnic minorities, migrant workers, sex workers, men who have sex with men, and injection drug users may be difficult to reach by government services and distrustful of government information, yet remain particularly vulnerable to emerging diseases.

The Chinese government's response to public health threats has been characterized by limiting information and restricting freedoms. More recently, China has taken some positive steps toward transparency, and has acknowledged the need for greater collaboration with nongovernmental organizations. The Chinese government's response to HIV/AIDS, SARS, counterfeit drugs, and the risk of pandemic and avian influenza highlight some of the hurdles to health and accountability in China. To differing degrees, the emergence of each of these health threats elicited initially repressive responses before the Chinese government adopted more effective and rights-respecting approaches. However, the tensions which mediate Chinese government response to health threats—tensions between central and provincial governments and state security and public health officials—persist, and China's next health crisis will surely see another close competition between respecting rights and adopting repressive approaches.

## DENYING THE HIV/AIDS CRISIS

*"Some government leaders do not understand the potential for the further spread of HIV and its consequences for China . . . [they] conceal the true situation and block measures to prevent HIV."*
—ZHENG XIWEN, NATIONAL AIDS PREVENTION AND CONTROL CENTER, JULY 2001

Like nearly everywhere, HIV/AIDS was first noted in China among foreigners and those who had traveled abroad. As such it was easy to ignore and the Chinese government assumed that the epidemic could be prevented by banning HIV-infected persons from entering the country. Then, in the late eighties and early nineties, China's AIDS epidemic began in earnest among injecting heroin users, at first centered in Yunnan Province, on the largely unregulated Burma border. Just as the emergence of AIDS among foreigners and foreign travelers had allowed the Chinese government to consider AIDS a disease of "others," the spread of HIV among injection drug users in Yunnan shaped the initial understanding and response to the disease. Since the largest concentration of China's ethnic minorities live in Yunnan, many felt that AIDS was a problem only for stigmatized "tribal" peoples.

Again the Chinese government's response was to restrict the movement of those infected. The Chinese passed legislation in 1989 that declared AIDS to be a notifiable disease and specified that AIDS patients must be quarantined for a period of time dependent on medical examination.[2] The government also began returning HIV-positive migrants, under armed guard, to their home provinces. During this period the Chinese government did little to educate the general population or those at highest risk about HIV. A study conducted in 1994 in Yunnan among Dai villagers found that only 18 percent had ever heard of AIDS. Even among those who had heard of AIDS, little specific information was known and myths and misconceptions were common. A second study done at the same time in eighty-two villages in Longchuan (Yunnan) among young men similarly found very low knowledge of HIV transmission and prevention. Unsurprisingly, the study found little use of condoms and high rates of needle sharing among injecting drug users.

## HENAN'S BLOOD SCANDAL

As HIV spread in Yunnan, and along drug-smuggling routes north to Xinjiang and east to Guangdong, a second focus of the epidemic was quietly underway in Henan province.[3] About a million persons in Henan, mostly poor farmers trying to supplement their incomes, regularly sold their blood plasma at legal and illegal blood-donation stations. These stations, promoted and sometimes run by local government health officials, blithely ignored basic tenets of blood-borne disease prevention. Tubes used to collect blood were reused. Sometimes officials pooled the red cells from different donors and reinjected the pooled blood into each person. Donors sold blood frequently, even daily, and local governments saw the blood stations as an important source of revenue. Once HIV was introduced into Henan, it spread quickly, and in a number of villages the majority of the population became infected. The problems were not limited to Henan, and HIV cases related to blood donation were reported from Shanxi, Shaanxi, Hebei, Gansu, and Hubei provinces.

Another factor that encouraged the spread of HIV in the 1990s was the reuse of needles in health care settings—due to both corruption and the lack of knowledge about HIV/AIDS among health care providers. Even as late as 1999, a survey by the Ministry of Health in Hubei Province found that 88 percent of injections were unsafe. A 2001 report in a Chengdu newspaper found that local hospitals were selling unsterilized, used medical waste, including disposable syringes, disposable transfusion equipment and disposable blood containers for reuse.

By 1996, all but one province in China had reported AIDS cases. But it was not until 2001, when the Chinese government reported a 58 percent increase in the annual number of reported AIDS cases, that it acknowledged the seriousness of the AIDS epidemic. The government finally admitted that illegal blood-collection centers had facilitated the spread of HIV, and that local government officials had been complicit in their operations. Yet the government did little to help those infected and hesitated to act decisively to ensure a safe blood supply or to increase knowledge about HIV.[4] The Chinese authorities continued to refuse to provide those at highest risk of HIV with access to proven, effective means of preventing the spread of the disease. By 2008, nearly one million people were believed to be living with HIV/AIDS.

## SWEEPING SARS UNDER THE RUG

*"If the world had known about SARS in November of 2002, it might have been able to prevent its spread to the rest of the world."*
—DAVID L. HEYMANN, WHO'S EXECUTIVE DIRECTOR OF COMMUNICABLE DISEASES

In November and December 2002 there was an outbreak of a mysterious new disease in Guangdong Province. By January, local doctors were investigating what they thought was a kind of "atypical pneumonia."[5] But no information was spread publicly by the Chinese government and little information seeped to the outside world. The timing of the outbreak was inconvenient—just before the central handover of power from Jiang Zemin to Hu Jintao. Just as with the onset of AIDS, the Chinese government's response was to treat the health information as "top secret" and to limit information about the illness. However, unlike a decade earlier, controlling news about the new disease in the era of mobile phones and the Internet proved to be difficult. Word of the disease gradually, and then explosively, emerged.

On February 8, 2003, a mobile-phone text message that read "There is a fatal flu in Guangzhou" was sent 40 million times. The next day it was sent 41 million times and the following day it was sent 45 million times. The same news spread rapidly through e-mail and Internet chat rooms, ahead of government efforts to block messages containing the word "flu." Despite government restrictions on publishing information, journalists in Guangzhou printed stories about the outbreak starting on February 9.

For a time, the government struggled to maintain control over the information or tried to release positive reports of government steps to control the outbreak. The government's propaganda department ordered public reporting on the disease to be halted in order to "ensure the smoothness" of the National People's Congress meeting planned for March. China also continued to maintain that the outbreak was due to "atypical pneumonia" but came under increasing pressure from WHO to acknowledge that the outbreak was in fact another disease—Severe Acute Respiratory Syndrome, or SARS.

On March 16, 2003, the World Health Organization issued a report on SARS, listing cases and fatalities from Vietnam, Hong Kong, Singapore, Thailand, Canada, Philippines, Indonesia, and Germany, but reported only about China that "an epidemic of atypical pneumonia had previously been reported by the Chinese government starting in November 2002 in Guangdong Province. This epidemic is reported to be under control." A week later, mounting international pressure led the Chinese to concede that the pneumonia outbreak was "linked geographically and by timing" to the SARS outbreak being seen globally. China finally requested assistance from WHO.

After being forced to acknowledge the outbreak, the Chinese government continued to downplay and cover up its scope. In April, the Chinese health minister claimed that the outbreak was under control—even as the WHO issued an unusual worldwide warning against non-essential travel to Guangdong province and Hong Kong. The government also hid SARS patients in Beijing— moving them from isolation wards being visited by WHO teams to hospital beds elsewhere. Only on April 18, as information about the extent of the outbreak continued to leak out of China, did the leaders of China's Communist Party finally get serious about fighting SARS. According to the *Washington Post*, the Party's leaders "declared a nationwide war on the SARS virus and ordered officials to stop covering up." Government leaders warned that local officials would be held accountable for the SARS situation in their respective jurisdictions.

On April 20, 2003, Chinese President Hu Jintao encouraged medical researchers to be confident of winning the war on SARS through a combination of "high technology and persistent effort." The minister of health and mayor of Beijing were removed from their posts, and the government promised "honest reporting" of SARS cases. The number of confirmed SARS cases in Beijing abruptly jumped from thirty-seven to 346. A day later, China reported another 109 SARS cases in Beijing, and the secretary of Beijing's Communist Party issued an apology for the mishandling of the epidemic. By mid-May 2003, the Ministry of Health issued regulations holding officials legally accountable for delays in reporting health emergencies and requiring rapid public disclosure of health threats. The regulations also stipulated penalties ranging from ten years in prison to death for individuals intentionally spreading SARS. Although many Chinese continued to distrust their government's response, the *People's Daily* newspaper stated that "the people have become more trusting and supportive of the party and government."[6]

## BATTLING NONGOVERNMENTAL ORGANIZATIONS AND ACTIVISTS INSTEAD OF DISEASES

*We should mobilize all the partners in the society to participate in the fight against HIV/AIDS. We need to improve our policies and strategies to build a better environment for all the forces in the society to participate in the response, and try our best to facilitate the involvement of all sectors.*
—VICE PREMIER AND MINISTER OF HEALTH WU YI, 2004

China's disastrous and deadly experience with SARS influenced its approach to public health more generally. The Chinese government began to acknowledge the importance of nongovernmental organizations in the fight against disease outbreaks and to lift some of its tight restrictions on the country's civil society. Senior Chinese officials have shown a growing awareness about the need to mobilize civil society in order to combat a range of social problems, ranging from humanitarian relief to environmental protection and education. As a result, many nongovernmental organizations (NGOs), grassroots groups, and nonprofit websites have sprung up around the country.

In April 2004, speaking with the World Health Organization on the occasion of the launch of a new AIDS program that planned to include NGOs, Hao Yang, a senior Ministry of Health official, pledged that the Chinese government would strengthen cooperation with NGOs, would provide financial support to them, and would begin encouraging more NGOs to participate in AIDS prevention and control work. Roughly 30,000 nongovernmental organizations have legal recognition in China—meaning that they have the required government sponsor and have cleared various bureaucratic hurdles. But perhaps as many as three million unrecognized NGOs are operating in China, to varying degrees of efficiency and functionality. The Chinese state remains deeply ambivalent about these groups, as it does of any institution that is outside of direct state control. Continuing restrictions on civil society, free expression and free association, along with a general lack of accountability for government officials, have hindered the growth of mature, effective grassroots groups.

Local activists and NGOs are also hampered by the Chinese government's sporadic harassment and detention of activists whose public criticism threatens the interest of some segments of the government.[7] Even as NGO activity generally increases, activists and NGO staff continue to report constant state surveillance, a web of bureaucratic obstacles, and even open harassment in the course of doing their daily work. The government frequently imposes travel bans and house arrest on NGO leaders to control criticism and dissent. House arrest in particular is common, because it sidesteps having to formally charge and prosecute under Chinese law, and because it draws less attention and condemnation from the international community.

In early 2007, HIV/AIDS activist Dr. Gao Yaojie, eighty, who became well-known in the 1990s when she helped expose the blood-donation scandal that led to an HIV/AIDS crisis, was placed under house arrest and banned from going to the United States to receive a human rights award. International uproar over her case, including a letter from Senator Hillary Clinton, led the Chinese government to allow her to travel to the US and accept the award. In the US she refuted the Chinese government's suggestions that the delay in her travel had been due to poor health, and she charged the government with continuing to allow unsafe blood donations and transfusions, and condemned what she felt was a continued complacency by the government toward the AIDS crisis.

Similarly, HIV/AIDS and human rights-activist couple Hu Jia

and Zeng Jinyan have been repeatedly put under house arrest and prevented from traveling abroad. In May 2007, the couple was barred from leaving for a two-month trip to Europe where they were to screen their documentary, *Prisoner in Freedom City*, about the 214-day house arrest Hu faced in 2006. In late December 2007, Hu was arrested for "inciting subversion." His wife and infant were prevented from leaving their home, and Hu's lawyers were denied access to their client because the case allegedly involved "state secrets." On April 3, 2008, Hu was sentenced to three and a half years in prison.

Even when HIV/AIDS activists are not put under house arrest they are intimidated and denied the opportunity to speak out. In July 2007, a conference on AIDS sponsored by two NGOs was canceled by the Guangzhou Public Security Bureau and the head of one of the organizations was detained. In mid-August, security agents canceled a meeting sponsored by the China Network of People Living with HIV and AIDS (Beijing), in collaboration with an organization of people living with HIV/AIDS based in Henan. Shortly thereafter, the police shut down two offices of an NGO working with children affected by AIDS in Henan Province. NGOs working in Beijing with sex workers and men who have sex with men have also reported increased police scrutiny and harassment.

## PUNISHING THE MESSENGERS

Yet another example of how civil society has been prevented from playing a role in protecting public health is the Chinese government's treatment of whistleblowers. In 2001, Zhou Huanxi accused her employer, a pharmaceutical company in Hangzhou, of using fake ingredients in a product for pregnant women. A subsequent investigation led to a recall and the company was fined. But Zhou was also harshly punished. She was sentenced to three years in prison on extortion charges. In 2003, Gao Jingde, purchasing manager for Shanghai Litian Pharmaceutical, exposed how the company repackaged another company's drug and sold it at a price eight times higher. The company reduced the price; Gao was fired. Tang Zhixiong, a cardiologist at Eastern Hospital in Shanghai, accused fellow doctors of conducting unethical transplant surgery. Tang received numerous threats, was fired, and then accused by the hospital of overcharging his own patients.

Even more outrageous is the case of Zhang Shijuan. In the spring of 2006 an essay alleging that the former head of China's Food and Drug agency had colluded with pharmaceutical companies to approve counterfeit medicines circulated on the Internet. The essay said that Zheng Xiaoyu took bribes from eight companies in exchange for approving fake medicines. In response to these allegations against Zheng, law enforcement responded by targeting and arresting whistleblowers. Zhang Shijuan was jailed for nine months simply for copying and pasting the essay onto another bulletin board. A year later, after a tidal wave of international criticism over increasing evidence of Chinese counterfeit medicines, the government conducted an aggressive investigation, and subsequent prosecution of Zheng, finding that he had accepted more than US $800,000 in bribes in return for approving fake drugs. To demonstrate—belatedly—concern about the counterfeit medicines crisis, China executed Zheng in July 2007.[8]

## HEALTH HURDLES FOR CHINA

HIV/AIDS continues to be of major public health concern in China. Since emerging in Yunnan and Henan provinces, the disease has spread, increasingly through sexual transmission. But injecting drug use continues to be an important means of HIV transmission in China and the fight against AIDS among drug users provides a useful example of how the tension between

respecting, protecting and fulfilling human rights and China's traditional pattern of restricting information and repressing
freedoms are felt.

In China, drug possession is illegal but is considered a violation of administrative law rather than criminal law, and the
accompanying punishments are less severe than those for drug
trafficking. There are more than one million registered drug users
in China, and more than 280,000 drug users are believed to be
infected with HIV. Chinese law dictates that "drug takers must be
rehabilitated," and those arrested for drug possession and use are
put into mandatory drug detoxification.

There are some 700 mandatory drug detoxification centers in
China, and in 2005, 298,000 people were confined to these centers, with approximately 70,000 more consigned to forced labor
in reeducation-through-labor centers (RELCs), officially for having
relapsed after detoxification. Ostensibly the Chinese government
puts people into detoxification centers and RELCs to help them
quit drugs, however neither provide behavioral or substitution
therapy to facilitate treatment. The centers do provide moral education, where intravenous drug users are forced to repeat slogans
such as, "Drug use is bad, I am bad." It is estimated that the rate
of successful treatment in both centers is negligible and thought
that drug use continues during detention, which without access to
clean needles or syringes leads to the further spread of HIV.

The Chinese government introduced methadone therapy in
2004, recognizing it as an effective approach to treating drug
addiction and addressing the AIDS epidemic among drug users.
However, despite what has been justifiably called—and internationally hailed—as a "rapid" scale-up of methadone treatment, by
the end of 2006 only 37,000 patients or about 2 percent of drug
users have access to it. Plans to have 200,000 patients in treatment by 2010 would still represent only 10 percent of opiate users
in the country.[9]

Despite the government's efforts to reach out to intravenous drug users with methadone therapy, China continues to stigmatize and abuse them. Most drug users are afraid to seek help or information openly. Broad police sweeps as well as specific targeting of injection drug users accessing methadone centers and pharmacies, deter drug users from seeking treatment or clean needles. Police also pay "commissions" to informants from fines collected from drug users in order to fill arrest quotas. The few Chinese nongovernmental organizations that risk working directly with drug users have inadequate resources to provide outreach and education.

Speaking of HIV and China in September 2007, Peter Piot, the director of the United Nations AIDS Program said: "I know of no country that has been successful in its fight against AIDS without a vibrant civil society." Particularly to reach populations such as injecting drug users, China needs to recognize and support NGOs and adopt pragmatic policies which ensure access to information, prevention and treatment.

Another looming concern is the global threat of avian and human pandemic influenza. Since 2003, avian flu, a type of influenza virus typically found in birds but capable of infecting humans, has spread throughout Asia, Europe, the Middle East, and Africa. As of February 2006, WHO confirmed 170 human cases of which ninety-two people died. On January 18, 2006, Chinese Premier Wen Jiabao spoke at the opening session of the Ministerial Meeting of the International Pledging Conference on Avian and Human Pandemic Influenza, where he touted China's response to avian flu. As part of its response, China created an avian-flu command center, developed emergency management plans, and reiterated its obligations to report outbreaks to international health organizations in a timely manner. Premier Wen Jiabao also pledged US $10 million for the prevention and control of avian flu.

China has been forthcoming and proactive in its response to avian flu, especially when compared to its past responses to health crises, including HIV/AIDS and SARS. However, its efforts are mired by the same past challenges, including local protectionism, bureaucratic deadlock, and the lack of a free media that could call officials to account. While the Chinese government's preparation for pandemic flu has emphasized transparency and participation, the real test will come when cases emerge in the thousands (or hundreds of thousands or millions). Only then will it truly be seen if the lessons of past epidemics will be applied to future ones.[10]

## WHAT THE FUTURE HOLDS

*"More than ever, sport can be a catalyst in our society to improve quality of life and human well-being. Because the prevention of and fight against discrimination are the two fields in which sport can clearly make a difference . . . the sports movement has decided to join the world campaign against the HIV/AIDS epidemic."*
—INTERNATIONAL OLYMPIC COMMITTEE PRESIDENT JACQUES ROGGE, SEPTEMBER 2007

The Chinese basketball player Yao Ming has been an eloquent spokesman against AIDS discrimination. Yao has spoken publicly about AIDS and the need for support for China's AIDS orphans, inviting them to watch the 2008 Olympics with him. However, what is needed in the fight against the AIDS epidemic in China—or any emerging infectious disease epidemic—is not simply addressing the public stigma and bias against those who are infected with the virus, but also the systematic abuses of human rights perpetuated by the government. Effective public health programs can only be conducted with transparency, accountability, participation of civil society, and by adopting pragmatic measures which do not sacrifice health concerns to criminal justice. China is not alone in struggling with this tension. Worldwide, the response to infectious disease epidemics is often influenced to the detriment of the public health by the level of social opprobrium against the populations affected, social discomfort with the means of transmission implicated (such as drug use or sex), and by fear and ignorance surrounding the disease or its means of transmission. Health officials and law enforcement officials often differ in their response to disease outbreaks, and while politicians may consult health experts, their decisions are not always guided by their advice.

For China in the future, the most important hurdles will not be health hurdles but human rights hurdles. The extent to which the government adopts health policies that respect rights will ultimately determine if it can succeed and win the race against fast-paced infectious diseases.

# CHAPTER 10

# Worship Beyond the Gods of Victory

BY MICKEY SPIEGEL

*The ancient Olympics, dating back to at least 776 BC, were a religious festival honoring Zeus, the supreme Greek god, who along with the other principal gods called Mount Olympus home. Winning athletes, it was said, owed their success, at least in part, to Zeus's intervention. The fifth Fundamental Principle of Olympism, from the Olympic Charter, states that "any form of discrimination with regard to a country or a person on grounds of race, religion, politics, gender or otherwise is incompatible with belonging to the Olympic Movement." Although incidents of religious persecution in China are less frequent since the adoption of more moderate policies in 1982, freedom to worship as one chooses remains a challenge in China today.* MICKEY SPIEGEL, *who holds a Masters of Philosophy degree in anthropology from Columbia University, is a senior researcher in the Asia Division of Human Rights Watch.*

China's leaders, although dedicated to the eradication of religion, recognize it will take decades, if not longer, to accomplish. In the interim, they guarantee China's citizens "freedom of religious belief."[1] But that guarantee, enshrined in article 36 of China's constitution, and since October 21, 2007, in the Constitution of the Communist Party of China,[2] comes with caveats, as visitors to Beijing for the 2008 Olympic Games will quickly discover. Olympic athletes will be able to worship in a planned "Olympic chapel" and spectators will be able to visit

approved houses of worship, but no Olympic volunteer will conduct a tour of the many religious sites that function without
official approval or introduce visitors to any of the thousands who
worship secretly to escape persecution.

Since the founding of the People's Republic of China in 1949,
China's leaders have viewed religious practice as a threat to the
Chinese Communist Party's hold on political power. Nevertheless,
a quarter of a century ago, in an accommodation to the demonstrated strength of religious belief, official attitudes shifted from
unmitigated and active hostility to a suspicious and grudging
acceptance. The change came on the heels of the 1966–1976 Cultural Revolution, after a vicious campaign—imprisonment and
execution of clergy, destruction of artifacts and worship sites, and
humiliation of believers—attempted, without success, to eradicate
every last vestige of religious belief and practice. Obviously, a new
policy, new strategies, and new tactics had to be devised.

The official party line, that "religion will eventually disappear
from human history," remains.[3] But until then, the autonomy of
religious communities must be limited through policies set by
senior party leaders and by regulations governing belief, rituals,
and activities that are devised and implemented by the State
Administration for Religious Affairs, its local chapters, and the
so-called patriotic associations which mediate between the government and party and religious organizations.

## THE CHINESE GOVERNMENT'S FEAR OF RELIGION

The change in attitude—and the accompanying change in tactics—are reflected in the fundamental religious paradox evident in
today's China: explosive growth in the number of believers amidst
ongoing repression. In 1982, the party made clear its readiness to
accommodate religion so long as there would be no threat to its
political rule—a threat the late paramount leader Deng Xiaoping

called the "Polish disease" in reference to the alliance of religion and independent social forces, which in Poland empowered the trade union Solidarity in opposing the Communist-led government. The bargain was simple: if you stay within the boundaries of state-controlled religion and away from politics, you will have progressively more space and more freedom for prayer, religious activities, and controlled exchanges with your overseas counterparts. If you stray, repression remains the rule.

As China's leaders came to understand, outlawing religion might be partially successful in eliminating competition with the party for political power and ideological legitimacy, but it risked driving organizational efforts underground where they would be less amenable to control. The party compromised. In two 1982 documents, the "Constitution of the People's Republic of China" and "The Basic Viewpoint and Policy on the Religious Question during Our Country's Socialist Period," the latter usually referred to as Document 19, it laid out a pair of policy initiatives. Although modified over the years, these two policies—tolerating belief but controlling public activity, and favoring coercion based on law rather than on some official's whim—still hold.

What has also held is a third 1982 policy decision, the absolute prohibition against foreign domination of religion. The key words governing all religious organizations' relationships with their foreign counterparts remain self-administration, self-support, and self-propagation.

## CONSTRAINTS ON RELIGION

The first policy compromise offered tolerance for privately held religious belief in exchange for stringent control of communal expressions of faith and, in particular, of activities which sustained and supported that faith. Article 36 of China's constitution then codified the distinction between belief and action, theoretically guaranteeing the former, but protecting only "normal" religious activities. According to the article, religion may not disrupt public order, impair the health of citizens or interfere with the educational system of the state." Beyond these broad exclusions, the word "normal" has never been officially defined.

To ensure only "normalcy," all religious organizations and meeting sites must be officially approved and registered—a protracted process requiring proof that among other restrictions "there is a need to carry out collective religious activities."[4] Unregistered temples, churches, monasteries, and mosques are, by definition, illegal. Although the reality differs from province to province and county to county, all Chinese worshippers at such sites risk harassment, fines, and imprisonment.

The second policy compromise traded physical coercion initiated by local officials for reliance on law-based directives encapsulated in a series of detailed regulations dating from 1991 and extending into the present. They cover all organizational aspects, including where a worship site might be established, what texts are acceptable, who qualifies as clergy, and when new construction is permissible. At the time the regulations were consolidated in March 2005—as the "Regulations on Religious Affairs"—official announcements made clear that the objective was to curb the power of local officials accustomed to implementing policy as they saw fit. Although the reported incidence of beatings and torture diminished, a degree of arbitrariness remains. Local public security officers still resort to excessive force when they rely on their own interpretation of loosely worded regulations to break up an "illegal" meeting, close down an "illegal" worship site, or destroy a mosque, a church, or a religious statue.

Even freedom of belief is not, as Chinese officials imply, absolute. Document 19 recognizes only five world religions, Buddhism, Daoism, Islam, Catholicism, and a version of Protestantism, labeled Christianity. The Chinese version of Protestantism melds an assortment of doctrinal beliefs, rituals, and theological underpinnings into one "post-denomination" structure easier for China's religious bureaucracy to control and administer. Protestant congregations which refuse to be bound by the Chinese version of Protestant orthodoxy or whose members travel throughout China to convert others, are refused registration along with other religious groups that resist regulation. Some such congregations, which the government considers heterodox cults, are vigorously persecuted. The South Church was one such congregation. Its charismatic leader received a death sentence, later commuted to life in prison, for "undermining the law."

Although official recognition is withheld, other world religions, such as Eastern Orthodoxy, Judaism, and Hinduism, all of which have few Chinese adherents and which do not actively proselytize, are not perceived as threats to party power, and thus are tolerated. For example, such congregations may be denied the right to hire professional clergy or to obtain a permit to build a religious structure, but they are permitted to hold religious services. There is also room for Chinese followers of what is usually labeled popular or folk religion, a catchall phrase referring to the idiosyncratic religious practices of the largest group of believers in China, those who pay homage to a vast array of gods and goddesses, some narrowly local, some revered more widely. The acceptance comes despite the state's view of popular religion's associated rituals and beliefs as superstitious, unscientific, and antimodern—images China's leadership expects to counter through cutting-edge Olympic facilities, a renovated Beijing skyline and transportation system, and well-modulated (and controlled) worship sites.

## OSTENSIBLE OPENNESS PROMOTED BY OLYMPIC ORGANIZERS

China's usual religious policy is to strictly prohibit non-sanctioned relationships between Chinese and foreign religious believers.

However, Beijing's Olympic bureaucracy promotes the image of a nation where freedom of religious belief and practice thrive and where Chinese and foreign worshippers may easily mingle. "Beijing 2008," the official website of the 2008 Olympic Games, not only explicitly states that "China is a country with religious freedom and respects every religion," but it invites visits to religious venues in Beijing, including four Buddhist temples, five Catholic churches, one Protestant church, one mosque, and one lamasery. (The Chinese government refers to Tibetan Buddhism as Lamaism.)[5] However, it is unclear whether foreign visitors may attend regular worship services at the listed sites.

A similar impression, that China welcomes religious observance, was conveyed by a September 2007 announcement by Liu Bainian, vice chairman of the party-controlled Chinese Catholic Patriotic Association. He said that, with regard to accommodating religious worship during the Olympics, "all will be arranged in accordance with the practices adopted by other Olympic host cities."[6] But, unlike the usual briefings by the Beijing Organizing Committee for the Olympic Games, details were sparse. The announcement referred only to an accommodation for athletes, an Olympic Village multifaith religious service staffed by professional religious personnel to "meet the needs (including dietary restrictions) of athletes from various religious convictions." But, the notice added, there would have to be "a limit to the number of religions that can be catered to."[7]

In October 2007, Ye Xiaowen, director of the State Administration of Religious Affairs, affirmed that "a large number of religious faithful will be arriving for the Games . . . Our religious facilities will be up to previous (Olympic) standards."[8] In its commentary, Xinhua, China's official news agency, noted, "As the host country of the 2008 Summer Olympic Games, China has pledged to offer religious services for foreigners arriving for the Games."[9]

Such seeming openness may convince some visitors that China's religious policy is more maligned than malignant. They may be impressed by the splendor of the listed official sites and by the size of the congregations. Should Olympic visitors travel in China they will be able to visit Buddhist monasteries and Daoist temples, perhaps without realizing that many monasteries and temples have become more tourist site than religious institution.

## FIVE TARGETED GROUPS

Indeed, Olympic visitors may remain largely ignorant of the dangers faced by five targeted groups: evangelical "house church" Protestants, so-called underground Catholics, Tibetan Buddhists, Uighur Muslims, and Falun Gong practitioners. These groups risk illegality rather than cede control over the choice of their leaders, their teachers, their texts, and their freedom to meet with co-religionists or preach outside their home bases. Should foreigners try to meet with such groups, not only do they risk interrogation and expulsion, they expose group members to severe government retaliation.

Although there are commonalities, the problematic issues and the control mechanisms employed by the Chinese government differ for each of the five targeted groups. In all cases, the government and party emphasis is on keeping membership small and groups discrete. In four of the five groups—Falun Gong is the exception—officials have limited the growth in the number of Chinese citizens who count themselves believers by restricting children's access to the religious teachings, rituals, and congregant activities of their parents, and by systematic failure to permit appropriate education for a would-be new generation of teachers and leaders. By arbitrarily interpreting religious regulations, the criminal code, rules applicable to the formation of civil-society organizations, and property law, among others, the government is not only able to restrict religious practice but can further its claim that it is adhering to a strict "rule of law."

## CLAMPDOWN ON EVANGELICAL PROTESTANTS

Evangelical Protestant congregations are often inaccurately termed "house churches," as if the term referred only to small groups of believers meeting at a member's home to pray and study. More commonly, house churches are organized in intricate hierarchies beginning at the village level and moving upward through counties and provinces. Some are organized by foreigners, some by indigenous leaders. Many make no secret of their mission to convert tens of thousands of Chinese citizens to their particular belief structure. Such congregations are most vulnerable to repression in that, by and large, they have refused or been refused registrations, hence are operating illegally. Additionally, contrary to regulations, they make use of foreign missionaries to recruit new members, train leaders, and educate their youth. Some such missionaries are caught, fined, maybe physically abused, and expelled, including more than a hundred rounded up during a crackdown that began in July 2007.

Over the past two years, some house churches reported that public security raids targeted large-scale leadership training sessions led by missionaries or local religious authorities, bible-study sessions, and youth services. Although the comprehensive "Regulations on Religious Affairs" does not specifically prohibit such meetings, it does mandate advance permission for so-called "large-scale activity" and for meetings that draw participants from more than one locale. In cases like these, where terms such as "large-scale" are not precisely defined, authorities are able to claim that believers are punished, often on criminal charges, not for their religious activities but for breaking the law. For example, Pastor Cai Zhuohua spent three years in prison, not for distributing bibles but for doing so without a business license.

## DELICATE BALANCING ACT FOR CHINESE CATHOLICS

The divide among Catholics is not, as sometimes described, a total schism pitting congregations belonging to the so-called underground church, whose first loyalty is to the pope and the universal church, against those official Chinese Catholic congregations whose first allegiance is to the Chinese government. The reality is more complicated. At least half the Chinese bishops, priests, and lay members have managed to accommodate to the official Chinese religious structure—and to find comfort there—while remaining firmly committed to the unity of the church and the spiritual authority of the pope. Most Chinese bishops, theoretically elected by the priests of their respective dioceses, have sought and received Vatican approval, as have the priests themselves. In a few contentious cases, approval has been withheld and questions of legitimacy have surfaced.

Although the Chinese government and the Holy See have yet to find a formula that will ease each party's political, religious, and practical concerns, both China and the Holy See have, to some extent, adapted to the reality of Catholicism in China. But bishops or priests who publicly refuse to accept the official Chinese version of Catholicism are still isolated from their congregations, sometimes for years, and subjected to reeducation sessions in an attempt to impose at least a public display of accommodation to the official church. Bishop Han Dingxiang was one such prelate. He died on September 9, 2007, after almost eight continuous years in some form of house arrest. In all, Bishop Han spent thirty-five of his seventy-one years in custody.

## TWO-PRONGED CRACKDOWN ON TIBETAN BUDDHISTS

*As this book went to press in March 2008, Tibetans throughout the Tibet Autonomous Region and adjacent Chinese provinces mounted the largest protests in twenty years against China's policies in Tibetan areas. The Chinese government responded with violence, large-scale arrests, and a ban on foreign reporting from the affected areas.*

In recognition of the crucial role religion plays in supporting the cultural identity and nationalist aspirations of Tibetan Buddhists and Muslim Uighurs, the Chinese government has systematically moved to control all aspects of religious expression among these two ethnic constituencies.

In the Tibetan Autonomous Region and other Tibetan areas in China, the crackdown has been essentially two-pronged. One prong is denigration of the religious legitimacy of the Dalai Lama—whom Chinese authorities have called "a false religious leader"—coupled with harsh treatment, including long prison sentences, for anyone who dares express support for him. The other is suffocating control of all religious institutions, personnel, and publications, as well as rites and rituals. Tenzin Delek, a locally respected lama who had long angered local officials through his support for the Dalai Lama, escaped death when his original sentence, imposed during a trial replete with legal irregularities, was commuted to a life sentence. He had been charged with "causing explosions [and] inciting the separation of the state."[10] And it is not just the religious community that is targeted. Government employees are denied the right to religious belief and practice.

In an audacious move which took effect on September 1, 2007, the State Administration for Religious Affairs issued the "Measures on the Management of the Reincarnation of Living Buddhas in Tibetan Buddhism," stipulating that without government approval, no reincarnation is valid. Buddhism, like other religions nurtured within Indian civilization, believes that all beings are on a round of birth, life, death and rebirth. Tibetan Buddhism has institutionalized this so that those who are thought to be accomplished spiritual teachers are sought out as children in order to continue their work and to maintain continuity within Tibet's various religious communities. The Chinese directive obliterates centuries of Tibetan religious continuity and tradition by placing the future direction of Tibetan Buddhism in government hands. From its inception, a secular religious bureaucracy will control the choice of all recognized reincarnated Tibetan Buddhist teachers who are seated in monasteries. The choice of the next Dalai Lama, or even whether further reincarnations of the Dalai Lama will be officially allowed, will rest with China's leaders, not with Tibetans trying to exercise their rights to religious freedom.

In addition to this startling innovation, the religious bureaucracy in China decides on the number of permitted Tibetan Buddhist monasteries and nunneries, as well as the number of monks and nuns in each. It vets all candidate monks and nuns for patriotism and is responsible for the patriotic education campaign within the monasteries, during which monks and nuns must refute their allegiance to the Dalai Lama or face expulsion. Children under eighteen may no longer enter monasteries (although some do unofficially) and school children must be careful not to show enthusiasm for religious practice if they wish to advance their secular education. Buddhist education is further corrupted by a dearth of competent teachers, regulations banning monks from going abroad to study particular aspects of Buddhism, and rules prohibiting students from traveling within China to meet with expert teachers outside their home locales.

## UNDERMINING UIGHUR MUSLIMS

In the Xinjiang-Uighur Autonomous Region in northwest China, Uighurs face similar restrictions on religious practice, characterized by government officials as necessary to rid the region of "terrorism, separatism, and religious extremists," all allegedly supported by religious adherence. Major campaigns have changed the status of imams. Not only are they "reeducated" in patriotism and expected to adhere to local religious affairs bureaus' suggested sermon topics, but they are paid by the state and required to renew their licenses yearly. Informal rules penalize Uighurs, particularly teachers and government employees, who honor their religion through observation of religious holidays, such as Ramadan, through daily prayers, or through their personal grooming. They may be denied promotion, demoted, or even lose their jobs.

Harsh restrictions extend to Uighur children who are kept from entering mosques and cautioned against an interest in religious belief and practice. There have been reports that "government officials, state employees (on active duty or retired), Communist Party members, and youth league members" in certain parts of Xinjiang also have been warned against entering mosques.[11] Local officials control the number of mosques permitted to operate in a given area; and government authorities have moved to take firm control of yearly preparations for Muslims planning to make the hajj, a sacred journey to Mecca in Saudi Arabia. Starting in 2007, Chinese pilgrims will not be allowed into Saudi Arabia unless they have a permit issued by China's Islam Patriotic Association.

The family of Rebiya Kadeer, a Uighur businesswoman who before her arrest and imprisonment in 1999 used her accumulated wealth to help create economic and educational opportunities for her fellow Uighurs, has been penalized for her leadership role in bringing to light human rights abuses in Xinjiang. When she was released from prison and exiled to the United States in March 2005, prison officials warned that if she spoke out, her adult children would suffer and the family business would be ruined. Today, two of her children are imprisoned, other family members are under constant surveillance, and the family businesses are bankrupt.

## PERSECUTION OF FALUN GONG

In August 1999, the Chinese Ministry of Foreign Affairs characterized Falun Gong, a variant of the ancient exercise and meditation practices collectively known as *qi gong*, as "an anti-human, anti-social, anti-government and illegal organization with all the characteristics of an evil religion." By then the central government, alarmed by evidence of Falun Gong's organizational talents and technical sophistication, had instituted measures to completely eradicate it as an organization and to eliminate all individual practice.[12] Anticult legislation was quickly drafted, Falun Gong was declared a heretical cult, and arrests of thousands of believers began.[13]

Leaders and those who produced Falun Gong literature are still serving long prison sentences. According to unverifiable reports by practitioners and spokespersons, many of those imprisoned were subject to severe torture, brainwashing, and intense pressure to recant. Some died. Practitioners who escaped imprisonment lost their jobs after special security forces compelled employers to rid their enterprises of all adherents. Family members and friends were pressured to expose practitioners. The numbers of those affected by the crackdown may never be known.

Falun Gong is still totally banned in China and practitioners there still risk severe punishment should they publicly promote the practice or should their private practice come to light. Bu Dongwei, a staff member at the Asia Foundation, is serving two-and-a-half years in a reeducation-through-labor camp for "resisting the implementation of national laws" and "disturbing social order." A search of his home had uncovered Falun Gong materials.

## A "HARMONIOUS SOCIETY"?

For China's persecuted believers, the Beijing Olympics present a painful dilemma: the need to balance protection of their communities against the need to expose the persecution. Should they believe that official celebrations of religious tolerance signal a policy change? Should they risk ferocious repression by attempting to meet with foreigners, many of them sympathetic missionaries who have already announced their intention of using the Olympics to focus attention on the true extent of religious repression in China? Should they gamble that celebrating their religious faith will not exclude them from participation in China's "harmonious society" to be?

In October 2006, the Central Committee of the Chinese Communist Party called for establishing China as a "harmonious society," shorthand for redressing economic imbalances and enhancing social stability. Religion, the party postulated, could make a major contribution through the "mutual adaptation" of religion and socialism and by enhancing ethnic unity. Unfortunately, adaptation has come to mean that the government and the party make the rules, and religious organizations and believers adapt.

International law demands the contrary: protection of the right to believe and to manifest that belief in private or public, individual or communal "worship, observance, practice, and teaching."[14]

In accordance with traditional Chinese folk beliefs, Chinese leaders have chosen the date and time of the opening of Beijing's Olympics, August 8, 2008, at 8:08 p.m., for its auspicious properties. It could also be an auspicious moment for the government to advance its goal of a "harmonious society." One way to do so would be to end the pretense that religious freedom exists in China and to dismantle the structures that have held it hostage to power and ideology.

# CHAPTER 11

# A Slow March to
# Legal Reform

### BY JEROME COHEN

*If legal reform in China were an Olympic event, judicial change could only be called a long march. The criminal justice system is hampered chiefly by the fact that the Communist Party is above the law, along with extrajudicial tools like "reeducation through labor" that are used to repress critical voices. Yet there are grounds for cautious optimism, including recent efforts by the Supreme People's Court to assert authority and bring down the number of state executions.* JEROME ALAN COHEN, *an expert in China's legal system, is a law professor at New York University and an Adjunct Senior Fellow for Asia at the Council on Foreign Relations. He has written and edited several books, includ-ing* China's Legal Tradition, *and frequently works with Chinese criminal defense lawyers in human rights cases.*

Just as the Tokyo and Seoul Olympics respectively focused the world's attention on Japan in 1964 and on South Korea in 1988, the Beijing Olympics of 2008 are meant to showcase the progress of the People's Republic of China (PRC) and confirm its acceptance as a proud and prominent member of the civilized world. Having failed to win the right to host the 2000 Olympics because of the tragic Tiananmen slaughter of June 4, 1989, Chi-nese government negotiators, in order to assure a better outcome for their second effort to host the world's greatest ath-letic spectacle, promised the International Olympic Committee that awarding the torch to Beijing would enhance the country's respect for human rights.

A nation's criminal justice system is, of course, a major index of its civilization. In recent years, influential Chinese legal officials and scholars have privately expressed the belief that China's notoriously deficient criminal justice system would be brought closer to minimal international standards by the time the torch reached Beijing. This was to be accomplished in two ways.

## THE ROAD TO REFORM

The first way would be for the PRC to finally ratify the United Nations International Covenant on Civil and Political Rights (ICCPR), which, among other obligations, commits adhering states to implement the fundamental elements of due process of law when determining criminal punishment. The PRC signed the ICCPR in 1998. Many experts expected PRC ratification of the Covenant, with or without limiting reservations or declarations, by the tenth anniversary of its signature, which coincides with the holding of the Olympics. This was to be an important symbol of China's readiness to assume international responsibilities that go far beyond the sports world.

The second way to assure compliance with minimal international standards was for the National People's Congress (NPC) or its Standing Committee to enact new legislation. This legislation was to revise the Criminal Procedure Law of 1996 by belatedly adopting many of the reforms that had been considered at that time, but were ultimately deferred as too radical.

To be sure, the 1996 Criminal Procedure Law (CPL) made many improvements in principle to China's initial CPL of 1979. For example, it allowed lawyers to interview and advise suspects from the moment of their detention and interrogation by the police and other investigators; it granted the accused the right to confront and cross-examine witnesses who testified at trial; and it required appellate courts generally to hold a formal hearing when reviewing a criminal conviction rather than merely scrutinizing the records and briefs of the original conviction. Unfortunately, such reforms, by and large, have only been haltingly implemented, if at all. Moreover, the 1996 legislation left certain proposed reforms, such as the presumption of innocence, unclarified, and others, such as a suspect's privilege against self-incrimination and even broader right to silence, were actually rejected.

## "REEDUCATION THROUGH LABOR"

The price of winning the acquiescence of police and prosecutors even to those reforms that were adopted in 1996 proved to be very high—legitimating, for example, the power of investigators to detain criminal suspects for as long as thirty-seven days before obtaining the prosecutor's approval of "arrest" that leads to much longer detention pending completion of the investigation. The reformers of 1996 were also unable to restrict the long-standing power of the police to entirely circumvent the Criminal Procedure Law's restraints by imposing "administrative" punishments, especially "Reeducation through Labor," which authorizes the police to send people off to a labor camp for three or four years without the scrutiny of even the prosecutor's office, not to mention that of the courts.

By 2008, ratification of the ICCPR and revision of the Criminal Procedure Law in accordance with the demands of the Covenant were supposed to have significantly improved China's criminal justice. Yet, as of early 2008, it seems unlikely that these maximum expectations will be vindicated. For many years Chinese experts have been carefully studying the difficult issues involved in their government's ratification of the ICCPR. Many academic specialists have favored ratification, but no consensus appears to have emerged among law enforcement agencies, which are fully aware of the profound impact that ratification would have upon the administration of justice.

The Covenant, for example, prohibits governments from sentencing people to criminal-type punishment without the approval of an independent court. Chinese government ratification, in the absence of a reservation that would emasculate this major guarantee of freedom of the person, would therefore create an international obligation to end "Reeducation through Labor." This would reinforce existing provisions of China's constitution and recent legislation that should be construed also to prohibit the extralegal practice. For more than half a century, however, "Reeducation through Labor" has remained a key weapon in the police arsenal employed against political and religious dissidents, hooligans, suspects against whom sufficient evidence is lacking to sustain a criminal conviction and all others whose conduct is deemed to be antisocial but not criminal.

Most influential Chinese scholars would like to terminate the unfettered power of the police to whisk people off to labor camp for several years. Many leading judges and prosecutors agree that the final decision regarding so substantial a deprivation of personal freedom should be the exclusive province of the judiciary, but thus far the political power of the Ministry of Public Security has prevailed.

## POWERFUL MINISTER

After all, for the past five years, it has been Minister of Public Security Zhou Yongkang—not the president of the Supreme Court, the procurator general or the minister of justice—who has served on the Communist Party Politburo, and at the 2007 Party Congress, Minister Zhou was promoted to the Politburo's inner sanctum, its Standing Committee. He is now in charge of the

Central Party Political-Legal Committee that decides all policies relating to the legal system and "coordinates" the operations of the courts, the procuracy, the police, the justice departments and even the nation's lawyers.

Given the leadership's preoccupation with attaining "stability and harmony," Minister Zhou is unlikely to favor ICCPR ratification. It would even cast doubt on the consistency with China's international obligations of the 2005 Law on Public Security Administration Punishments, since the law permits the police alone to punish people with up to twenty days of administrative detention for a broad range of minor offenses too petty to be deemed criminal. Invalidation of the Law on Public Security Administration Punishments for failing to require court approval of its punishments would itself vastly increase the burden on judicial and law enforcement resources because each year perhaps eight times as many people are punished under the Law on Public Security Administration Punishments as are punished under both the Criminal Law and "Reeducation through Labor."

This is undoubtedly why the Law on Public Security Administration Punishments has not been seriously challenged, as it might be, under China's constitution and domestic legislation. Moreover, ICCPR ratification would also highlight other types of detention that are plainly not authorized by law, such as the "shuanggui" imposed on suspects by the Party Discipline and Inspection Commission, and it would affirm the Chinese government's obligation to cease the brutal abuse of human rights lawyers by Chinese police and their hired thugs.

While the ascension of Minister Zhou does not bode well for ICCPR ratification, it does not rule out the possibility that there may well be, prior to the Olympics, new legislation that may effect significant improvements in the criminal process or at least improve the rules to be applied in this process. Indeed, criminal justice experts of the National People's Congress Legislative

Affairs Commission have been working long and hard to prepare draft revisions of the 1996 Criminal Procedure Law.

## FURTHER REFORMS?

Just as NPC legislation recently confirmed interpretations by the Supreme People's Court reclaiming for itself the exclusive power to conduct final review of all death penalty adjudications, it may soon also confirm other reforms initiated by the Supreme People's Court, such as the top court's assertion that criminal convictions should not be based on confessions alone and that coerced confessions and other illegally obtained evidence must be excluded from judicial consideration. The National People's Congress may also clearly endorse the presumption of innocence and, following the Supreme People's Court's lead, eliminate the loopholes in legislation that have permitted prosecutors and judges to keep most witnesses from testifying at trial, thus frustrating a defendant's right to confront and cross-examine accusers.

This widely anticipated next round of Criminal Procedure Law reforms is not likely to do more than give vague lip service to a privilege against self-incrimination, and it is almost certainly not going to endorse an absolute right to silence. These principles do not yet enjoy strong support from Chinese society and officialdom, not only because of deeply held traditional beliefs about the importance of confession but also because of widespread desire not to unduly hamper police efforts to deal with rising crime rates and social instability. In the present conservative Chinese political climate, there also does not appear to be popular support for abolishing "Reeducation through Labor." Draft legislation to abolish it or to significantly "improve" it by giving it a blander name, reducing its duration, diluting its harshness and injecting a few procedural protections, such as a role for defense counsel, has been on the NPC calendar for five years, but enjoys no current momentum. This does not mean that some outrageous "Reeducation through Labor" tragedy resulting in a nationwide scandal could not spark its long-awaited annulment or reform, just as the 2003 killing of university graduate Sun Zhigang in police custody led to the abolition of "Shelter and Repatriation," another of the frequently abused administrative punishments relied on by the police.

## THE DEATH PENALTY

This account of criminal justice at the time of the Party Congress and the Olympics makes clear the major role currently played by the Supreme People's Court. Although the Supreme People's Court has not been allowed to relieve the government's repression of freedoms of expression and organization, it has been permitted to moderate some of the worst aspects of that other principal branch of human rights—the administration of criminal justice. Because the Chinese government's astounding, promiscuous resort to the death penalty is the most prominent symbol of law enforcement that cries out for reform, it is here that the Supreme People's Court has chosen to focus its reformist energy. Although it has faithfully complied with the party's insistence that the number of annual executions remain a state secret—the best evidence of the shame felt by the regime on this score—the SPC in recent years has boldly and consistently tried to bring down the numbers and to increase public confidence in the accuracy of death penalty adjudications.

The Supreme People's Court has frequently admonished the lower courts and local authorities to restrain their zeal for imposing capital punishment, even while the Politburo oscillates between calls to "strike hard against crime" and calls to "combine leniency with suppression." Because the National People's Congress has made little progress in reducing the number of offenses for which the death penalty can be imposed—at last count there were no fewer than sixty-eight—the SPC has been seeking reform on a case-by-case basis by urging the lower courts to sentence defendants to immediate execution only when "absolutely necessary." In effect, it has been pleading with them, in the vague language that so often characterizes China's criminal process, to "kill fewer, kill with restraint," and seriously consider whether it would not be preferable to invoke China's vaunted and unique alternative of sentencing the defendant to death but suspending execution for two years in order to allow the condemned to demonstrate a capacity for rehabilitation. In practice, at the end of the two-year period, virtually all those who receive suspended death sentences have their punishment commuted to life imprisonment or a long, fixed term.

In order to make suspended death sentences more attractive to "hanging judges," Chinese experts are beginning to consider adding to the present panoply of sentencing options a new possibility—"life imprisonment without parole." One of the reasons that Chinese judges frequently opt for immediate execution is their belief that the current punishment of "life imprisonment" does not guarantee that dangerous and heinous criminals will indeed remain behind bars for the rest of their lives. Instead, their original life sentence is often commuted to a term of years that eventually enables them to win their release. Thus, some experts have argued for the addition of "life imprisonment without parole" to the judicial arsenal in an effort to stimulate courts to spare the lives of many offenders who might otherwise be executed. This would be not only a humanitarian measure but also a practical one to prevent the possibility of sending them to a fate that might later be discovered to have been unjust.

The major emphasis of the Supreme People's Court's recent reforms, however, has been on procedure. Reclaiming the exclusive final review power over death sentences has been only the first step in what has become a persistent campaign to improve fairness and accuracy in such cases. How to make this reassertion of judicial power meaningful has itself proved to be a formidable challenge. So huge is the annual number of death sentences that literally hundreds of new judges have had to be recruited to carry out the Supreme People's Court's new duties. It has proved difficult for the court to find a sufficient number of suitable new judges without depriving the provincial high courts and intermediate courts of their best talent. Some able law professors and lawyers have been selected to expand the group. Moreover, once on the scene, the new arrivals have had to be trained in appropriate new review procedures since previous procedures were acknowledged to be inadequate. Yet it has not been easy for reformers to agree on the content of the new procedures.

Should Supreme People's Court review be confined to study of the case records and any written briefs submitted by the prosecution and defense, plus a final private interrogation of the defendant by one or two judges or their staff? Or should the SPC, in addition, grant an opportunity for oral argument by representatives of the parties? Or should it hold a broader hearing to confirm relevant facts that appear to be in doubt, as well as legal issues? If judicial resources are too scarce to allow a fact-based hearing or even oral argument by counsel, how should the SPC's limited scrutiny be conducted? Should it take place in Beijing or in the provincial capital where the high court had affirmed the original sentence? Should SPC judges be stationed in the provinces or regions to promote review efficiency or would efficiency be enhanced by keeping all final reviews under the closer supervision permitted if all reviews are conducted in the capital?

If all final reviews are to be Beijing-based, should the accused be brought to the capital for a last, albeit private, judicial interrogation or should one or two SPC judges handling the case be dispatched to the site of detention? Finally, what standards should the final review judges observe in determining whether the facts and the law are "sufficiently clear" and capital punishment "absolutely necessary" to warrant conviction and immediate execution? This last challenge has already led SPC drafters to develop a list of aggravating and mitigating circumstances that resembles those considerations taken into account by death penalty law in the United States.

The SPC has construed its reformist mandate to go beyond radical revamping of the final review process. It has also revised provincial high court procedures for carrying out the preceding appellate review of the original death penalty trial. Thorough, competent and confidence-inspiring appellate review can do much to ease the Supreme People's Court 's final review burden. Until recently, these provincial high courts generally conducted their appellate scrutiny of death cases on the basis of the trial record and any briefs submitted by prosecution and defense counsel, plus a private interrogation of the condemned person. They seldom granted an oral hearing to fully explore disputed facts or to hear argument about legal issues.

Beginning in 2006, the Supreme People's Court changed this situation by requiring an oral hearing to be held in every death case appellate review. This does not mean, as the foreign media sometimes suggest, that the required hearing will always be open to the public. Hearings allegedly involving "state secrets," a broad and often abused term, as well as certain personal matters, remain closed. But even in such cases there must be a formal, oral hearing in the courtroom that allows an opportunity to confirm the facts and clarify both the application of the law and the appropriateness of the death sentence. Yet this reform at the provincial-court level, like its counterpart at the SPC, poses many new and difficult questions. What should be the scope of the oral review hearing? For example, will important witnesses be required to testify in court so that the accused and counsel are guaranteed the right in practice as well as in principle to confront and cross-examine them? The judges themselves benefit from actually seeing and hearing the witnesses, and even asking them any questions they deem necessary, rather than merely relying on written out-of-court statements that often may be imprecise or mistaken. Should the appellate review consider all the issues that the court believes are involved in the case or only those raised by defense counsel and defendant? How great a role should defense counsel be permitted in the review process?

## A WORK IN PROGRESS

As in the case of final Supreme People's Court review, the answers to such questions are a work in progress. China is a vast, diverse, developing country, and judicial reforms in China have always taken considerable time to implement on a nationwide scale. Yet it seems certain that these changes will make a significant improvement in death penalty review procedures and substantially reduce the number of executions ordered. Indeed, SPC officials have already claimed important, albeit vague, progress in this respect. It also seems certain that judicial reforms in capital cases will not be limited to review by the appellate courts and the Supreme People's Court. The reform process appears to be inexorably marching toward the trial itself and even to the crucial pretrial investigation/interrogation and indictment stages on which trials rest.

These major advances cannot be confined to capital cases but will inevitably extend to all serious criminal cases. Can someone who may be sentenced to life imprisonment or a term of fifteen or twenty years be denied protections that are now recognized as essential to the fair and accurate handling of a death case? Although "death is different" and in every country that retains the death penalty capital cases require special judicial care, most of the reforms that are under way in China's capital cases will soon be required in order to legitimate any serious punishment.

Of course, we must always keep in mind the often gaping chasm between centrally promulgated norms, whether approved by the National People's Congress or the Supreme People's Court, and the realities on the ground. Perhaps the best litmus test of reality in the administration of justice in any country is its treatment of its legal profession. One has to note with both regret and shock that, even under the intense scrutiny to which foreign media are subjecting Chinese government actions in the run-up to the Olympics, China's police—including agents of both the Ministry of Public Security and the Ministry of State Security—continue to restrict, threaten, harass, assault, detain, arrest and recommend prosecution of not only human rights lawyers who dare to defend the accused, but also those who give legal assistance to ordinary people who challenge arbitrary government actions.

Moreover, the Ministry of Justice continues to take away the license to practice law and to close down the law firms of those lawyers who refuse to heed its warnings to cease a broad range of public interest lawyering activities. The prolonged and severe beating of Beijing human rights lawyer Li Heping by a dozen plainclothes police agents, who put a bag over his head, forced him to a remote basement and then assaulted him for hours, with electric cattle prods and other weapons, because of his refusal to follow earlier police "suggestions" to leave Beijing is only one of many recent reminders that central law reform can be accompanied by lawless "law enforcement."

The continuing severe restrictions imposed on the freedom of former Shanghai lawyer Zheng Enchong, after losing his license, serving three years in prison and completing his subsequent one-year deprivation of political rights, is daily public testimony to the fate of lawyers bold enough to help local residents seeking to protest the arbitrary seizure of their homes by corrupt officials in cahoots with real-estate developers. And the sentence to over four years in prison of the blind "Barefoot Lawyer" Chen Guangcheng illustrates the regime's determination to crush even ordinary farmers and other members of the masses who have never formally studied law but who strive to invoke it to end unlawfully imposed abortions and sterilizations, unauthorized taxation, illegal discrimination against disabled people, and repression of local religions.

Nevertheless, although we should not underestimate the possibility that both centrally promulgated legislative and judicial reforms may be frustrated in practice, as the Olympics brings the world to Beijing, there is some ground for hoping that China may gradually, if incompletely, continue the process of introducing international standards concerning the administration of justice. Implementation will inevitably take longer, but law reform is the first step in China's long march toward true criminal justice.

PART III

# POLLUTED AIR, UNCLEAN BUSINESS PRACTICES

# CHAPTER 12

# Building the New Beijing: So Much Work, So Little Time

BY MEI FONG

*China's victorious bid for the 2008 Summer Olympics spawned a colossal build-ing boom, perhaps as ambitious as the construction of the Great Wall undertaken under the Qin Dynasty in the third century BC. In August 2008, Olympic visi-tors will discover thirty-one new Olympic venues, including the Beijing National Stadium, nicknamed the "Bird's Nest," and the Beijing National Aquatics Cen-ter, known as the "Water Cube"—structures built by an invisible army of migrant workers laboring in harsh conditions.* MEI FONG *is a China correspon-dent for the* Wall Street Journal. *"So Much Work, So Little Time" won the 2007 Pulitzer Prize for International Reporting and was originally published by the* Journal *on December 23, 2006. Mei Fong's contribution below gives voice to the many anonymous migrant workers toiling to build the new Beijing.*

About a mile from Tiananmen Square lies a pit from which a twenty-eight-story hotel will rise in a little more than a year. An army of construction workers lives and works at the open site, enduring plunging temperatures and freezing winds.

Some work the midnight hours, while the rest of the city sleeps.

Others rise at dawn. They work fifteen-hour days or longer, seven days a week. When they topple onto their bunk beds, it is twelve to a room. There is no heat.

One of them is Wei Zhongwen. He has more than two decades as a construction worker, and the injuries to prove it: a missing pinkie and a palm-size dent on his head under his neatly cropped hair. In the past decade, the forty-one-year-old has helped build skyscrapers, shopping malls and much else in Beijing and nearby provinces. He hasn't seen his wife or daughter in two years, and because of the press of work ahead of the Beijing Summer Olympics in 2008, he may not see them this year either.

"For me, one of the biggest problems of this job is loneliness," says Mr. Wei, puffing on a cigarette. In his rural hometown, the money Mr. Wei has sent back has built his extended family a five-room house with a thatch roof, a twenty-one-inch color television set and rooms housing a horse and some pigs. The hardship of his work is worth it, Mr. Wei says, to educate his daughter and sustain his family on their farm.

Beijing is in the midst of an enormous building boom—one of the most ambitious construction projects the world has ever seen. Cranes clutter its skyline. At more than 10,000 sites across the city, there is a total of 1.7 billion square feet of floor space under construction—an area that, if laid out, would be nearly three times the size of Manhattan.

## AN INVISIBLE ARMY OF MIGRANT WORKERS

This colossal development is due to the efforts of a nearly invisible army, a group of almost 2 million migrant workers who drift from China's farmlands. Toting their bedrolls from work site to work site, they earn as little as fifty cents an hour. They work in a hazardous profession with practically no workplace protections and little or no medical coverage. Many of the workers live right in the heart of the city, yet few ordinary Beijing residents ever glimpse their crowded barracks, where privacy, cleanliness—even meat—are luxuries.

They often get paid late or not at all. A report this year by the research arm of the State Council, China's highest administrative body, found that in 2004, construction firms in Beijing owed roughly 700,000 of their workers more than $380 million in wages. Mr. Wei is fighting to collect about $400 he says he is owed—half his earnings last year—and he may never see it.

In such an uncertain environment, workers drift from job to job together. They rely on word of mouth to protect themselves against bad bosses. And, in bad times, they rely on each other.

These men—there are few women in their crews—are working against a deadline: December 2007. That is when the bulk of the Olympic construction work must be completed so that Beijing, one of the world's most polluted cities, has time for the air to clear of construction dust before the Games begin.

There is a lot to finish. The Olympics will attract a flood of foreign visitors and unprecedented media attention. Beijing's construction workers are aiming to have built a chunk of a subway system that, when completed, is projected to be the longest in the world, surpassing London's underground. They are erecting an airport terminal bigger than all five at London's Heathrow Airport and about 110 hotels. Including the suburbs of Beijing, the building binge could cost more than $180 billion. Some call it China's most ambitious construction project since the Great Wall.

What happens to these workers after the boom already has become a topic of controversy; Beijing officials have made it clear they want to clear them out ahead of the Olympics. But authorities also fear political instability if so many workers are forced to leave because they may have trouble finding jobs back home.

As it is, the construction workers have a tenuous standing in the city. Lacking the papers to stay in Beijing legally, most work off the books, relying on oral promises instead of contracts. When they are sick, they visit illegal clinics, which are cheap but often dirty and run by unlicensed doctors.

Mr. Wei speaks proudly of his eighteen-year-old daughter Xiaowei, who lives with the rest of his family on a farm in Yushu county, in northeastern Jilin province. He says the girl is a good student and obedient. "We're not that close. I don't know what she likes," he says, awkwardly fingering a bunch of keys on his belt. A badge of prosperity among middle-age Chinese men, Mr. Wei's keys are a small vanity. He says he picked them up on the street. They are keys to things he doesn't have: a car, an apartment.

Like other construction workers, he lives frugally in the city. In his latest job he earns about $300 or so a month, but keeps only about $60 of it. The rest he sends home to the "3861 army"—a term used to describe the women and children left behind in China's interior. (March 8 is China's Women's Day; June 1, Children's Day.)

## BROKEN BONES AND UNPAID WAGES

Next to coal mining, construction work has the highest number of casualties in China, with 2,607 reported fatalities in 2005. Steel-tipped boots are rare. China's workers clamber around in thin canvas shoes, often without safety harnesses, and buy their own work gloves. Many of their hard hats are just thin plastic shells, sold for a dollar apiece.

Wang Qishan, the mayor of Beijing, said in a recent interview that he personally reviews construction accident statistics daily. "I can never be happy when I read such reports," he said. "Beijing can't do without these people." The city tries to provide services such as health care for registered migrant workers, but its resources are overstretched, he said.

Like many other construction workers, Mr. Wei entered the trade because there was little else to do on his family's farm, a small plot where corn and soybeans grow. He left home at seventeen for a province next to Beijing.

When he was in his twenties, Mr. Wei's left little finger was sliced off by an electric saw. In 1994, he was hit on the head by a steel rod, landing him in the hospital for more than a month. He counts himself lucky because his employer paid for his medical bills.

Last year, the owner of an art gallery in Tongzhou, a Beijing suburb, stiffed Mr. Wei and seventy-six crew mates, according to the men and a later court ruling. They had been paid halfway through the project and promised the rest of the pay upon completion. Instead, when they finished they say they were driven from the site by thugs armed with iron staffs and meat cleavers.

China's state-controlled banks have poured credit into real estate, where many companies are politically connected. The easy money often leads to ill-conceived projects that quickly go bust. When financing collapses, construction workers—the ones at the bottom of the totem pole—aren't paid. They find it difficult to claim restitution because they often are employed indirectly through subcontractors.

Mr. Wei and his friends say they had no success appealing to authorities in Tongzhou. About twenty of the workers drifted home, defeated. With no money, Mr. Wei and the remaining workers were forced to make camp in the neighboring province of Hebei, eking out a living with odd jobs. They say they lived on steamed buns, mostly, six for one yuan, or about thirteen cents.

In November 2005, more than fifty of them rose at dawn. They marched for five hours to central Beijing to appeal to authorities there. They wound up at Beijing's Legal Aid office on Qianmen West Street. Wang Xuefa, the center's director, remembers the sight of Mr. Wei and his friends kneeling en masse on the office floor. "It was sad to see men brought so low," he says.

The Intermediate People's Court in Tongzhou ruled in the group's favor on January 6, ordering the Hong Kong developer Lian Ka Fu International to pay more than $30,000 in back wages to the workers. They haven't seen a cent. Lian Ka Fu's proprietor, Wang Xiaohu, told the court she doesn't have the money, says

Chang Mingchuan, a lawyer at Beijing Legal Aid. Ms. Wang couldn't be reached for comment, and her Europe American Art Gallery—a green low-rise with gold Corinthian columns—is now shuttered.

## FROZEN FAMILY LIVES

Going home for Chinese New Year, China's most important holiday, is a ritual for construction workers. It is the only time in the year they see their families. Like returning heroes, they are feted and tell tales of car-choked streets and the towering skyscrapers they helped build. "Some of my neighbors have not even taken a train," Mr. Wei says.

Back home, Mr. Wei is a man of substance. Over the years, his wages, which are higher than average among construction workers because of his bricklaying expertise, have helped his family enjoy some comforts. "We're very well respected in my home," he says. Last January, however, Mr. Wei stayed in a Hebei flophouse instead of returning home for the New Year holiday. Penniless, he and his friends were too ashamed to go. To cheer up, they went to an airfield and watched planes taking off.

"Really, that's the only time I felt like suicide. I thought if a car hit me, at least I can get some compensation," Mr. Wei says.

Reached by telephone, his wife, Ding Guiying, says it is a hard life taking care of Mr. Wei's aged parents, raising her daughter alone and tending the crops. Mr. Wei's wages nowadays go to pay for his daughter's secondary education—which isn't free in China, even at public schools. Ms. Ding says the bill comes to around $1,300 a year. Ms. Ding, forty-two, hopes her husband can come home when their daughter has finished school. "We keep being separated for such a long time, and I can hardly count how many days we've been together in the past nineteen years," she says.

Mr. Wei spent most of this year in Hebei, the province surrounding Beijing. In May, he and his friends found a job at a residential site. Mr. Wei roomed in a wooden shack with ten other workers. The floor was a brick-and-dirt mixture. The only running water was from a sink in the courtyard. The toilet was a shed with wooden planks over a hole. In the kitchen, flies clustered thickly.

In Hebei, as is common on such jobs, Mr. Wei paid his employer about sixty cents daily for three meals, mostly rice and tofu. Meat was rare, but he is a vegetarian. Growing up poor, he never got used to the taste of meat.

One of the crew, Yang Xinguo, fifty-three, injured his leg in a traffic accident and had to stop working in September. After lingering for a while, hoping to get compensation from the art-gallery job, he decided to go home in mid-November. He had a few dollars earned before the accident and $50 or so that Mr. Wei and other friends gave him.

"We will send your pay to you, once we get it," promised Mr. Wei, sitting on Mr. Yang's bed. He offered his departing friend a cigarette. Through the smoke, Mr. Yang's eyes shimmered. "Men don't want to cry, but we have cried many times," he said.

## CRAMMED QUARTERS AND FREEZING TEMPERATURES

By late November, Mr. Wei and his crew had moved back to Beijing. They found better work building the twenty-eight-story, four-star hotel. Conditions are cleaner. Mr. Wei now lives in barracks perched next to the yawning site. He has ten roommates, including some new ones. There is no canteen, so they cook in the room, using a gas ring attached to a five-foot canister next to Mr. Wei's bed. With no heating, they sleep in their jackets, and sometimes hats and gloves, too. Temperatures can drop below zero Fahrenheit in Beijing's winter. Some have electric blankets they bought for about $1.25 each.

They are creative with their limited space, rolling back their bedrolls and using the boards beneath as makeshift tables. The cook, Wen Fenglin, adroitly uses the space to chop cabbages and peel onions, ladling water from an old paint bucket to clean the food and utensils. The fifty-five-year-old used to work on the crew but now is employed by the construction company to cook. "Boss said I have to learn because I'm too old to do heavy work," he says, browning onions for an omelet.

There are no washing facilities, so baths and clean clothes are treats. Mr. Wei remembers taking a bath well more than a month ago at a bathhouse, paying about sixty cents.

With no laundry, Mr. Wei buys secondhand clothes, wearing them until they get too dirty. Currently, his favorite is a gray cotton shirt he bought for a little more than a dollar, which looks as if it once might have belonged to a corporate executive. "I normally throw away the clothes after wearing, but maybe I'll sell this. In about ten days," he says.

Around Beijing's small alleyways, an underground economy caters to construction workers. Vendors often do their business by barter because the workers don't have space to keep much and adopt a throwaway culture. One popular item is underwear with zippered pockets, to keep money and valuables close.

## MODEST WAGES FOR TWENTY-FOUR SHIFTS

Mr. Wei's pace of work is now frenetic. The hotel still is just a big hole in the ground. Under city ordinances, concrete trucks from the hundreds of factories ringing the city are allowed in the city center only after 11 p.m. and on weekends, so he and his friends must work long past midnight curing concrete. Once the hotel's foundation is done, in about two months, Mr. Wei says the plan is to build a floor every five days.

On the next-to-last day of November, Mr. Wei and his comrades crowded into a small postal outlet, their grimy appearance setting them apart from other customers. The air smelled of unwashed clothes, and some people edged away. It was exactly a year since they had made their long march to the Beijing Legal Aid office. Mr. Wei had given up hope of recovering his lost wages, but on this day the mood was celebratory. It was payday, and the men wanted to mail their money home. There was a flurry of bewilderment as they fumbled with forms. Mr. Wei, his eyes red-rimmed after a twenty-four-hour shift, helped some of the workers who can't write well fill out the forms.

Zhang Tao, twenty, in a paint-stained blue sweater and matted hair, slowly scrawled the amount he is sending home: 900 yuan, or about $115. He said he earns 1,000 yuan, or $128, a month.

On another night, Mr. Wei took a walk, wandering around the city's glittering towers and looming cranes. "I have no regrets," he said. "I'm the migrant worker who stays out all year so home is better. I've seen things my neighbors have never imagined—fifty-story buildings, planes so big they can carry hundreds."

He stopped in front of a European five-star hotel near his work site. "I build these things, but I have never been inside," he said.

Timidly, he pushed the swing door and went in.

Authorized reprint from the *Wall Street Journal*.

# CHAPTER 13

# China's Olympic Dream, No Workers' Paradise

BY HAN DONGFANG AND GEOFFREY CROTHALL

*The slogan of the 2008 Beijing Games is "One World, One Dream." The Chinese word used for "One" in the original slogan is "tongyi," which means "the same." This word was chosen because it highlights the idea, as explained on the official Beijing Olympics website, that "the whole mankind lives in the same world and seeks the same dream and ideal." Yet this lofty message is at odds with the harsh conditions for the migrant workers who labored at the construction of the Olympic venues, often for the equivalent of five dollars per day.* HAN DONGFANG *was jailed for nearly two years for his participation in the 1989 Tiananmen democracy movement. In 1994, he founded China Labour Bulletin, a Hong Kong–based group that promotes labor rights and democratic trade unionism in mainland China.* GEOFFREY CROTHALL *is the editor of China Labour Bulletin's English language website. He has reported on China since 1985.*

On August 8, 2008, China will formally announce its emergence on the world stage as a powerful, prosperous and modern nation with a spectacular party attended by representatives from just about every nation on earth. For the Chinese government, the Olympic Games will be the culmination of nearly two decades of work stretching back to the original bid for the Games in the early 1990s. China's current leaders are determined that the political mission initiated by their predecessors, to make the Olympics both an international success and a source of pride for the Chinese nation, will be completed on time and without a hitch. By showcasing breathtaking new venues, Olympic medalists and Beijing's clean streets, the Games will doubtless be a success. But at what cost?

The all-consuming process of gaining, preparing for and hosting the Olympics has become highly politicized. Indeed, the government's mission to demonstrate its greatness through the Games could overshadow and distract from the increasingly serious social and economic problems Chinese workers have to contend with every day of their lives.

Some of these problems, such as the appalling health and safety record of Chinese construction sites, are right under the noses of Beijing's Olympic organizers. The construction workers who built the Olympic stadiums and support facilities, and completely overhauled Beijing's transport system in readiness for the Games, are almost exclusively migrant laborers who work in extremely hazardous conditions, usually have no labor contract, no work-related medical insurance, cannot form a trade union and have no right to collective bargaining.

## OLYMPIC TORCH FAILS TO SHINE ON CONSTRUCTION SITES

In late July 2007, *Sports Pictorial*, a magazine published under the auspices of the Chinese Olympic Committee, interviewed a group of fifty-seven migrant workers on Beijing's Olympic construction sites about their work and living conditions. Most workers earned between forty yuan (about US $5) and sixty yuan a day, although a few earned more than eighty yuan. Many said they did not know how exactly they would be paid, and more than a third said they only got paid at the end of the year and received a small monthly allowance to live on. "I earn more than 1,000 yuan a month and get paid at the end of the year," said twenty-eight-year-old Hu

Yaowu from Hebei "I've been married four years but can't afford to start a family."

Nearly all the interviewees worked ten-hour days, and only took days off if they were sick or had to go home to help with the harvest. They did not get weekends off, certainly no paid vacation, and most had no work contract or medical insurance. All those who suffered from minor injuries or illnesses at work paid for their own over-the-counter medicine or treatment at the local clinic. One worker, Liu Jiafu, who required surgery after incurring serious chest and leg injuries in a work-related accident, did have his medical expenses paid by his boss. However, when Liu, fifty-five, was released from hospital, his boss had vanished and he received no compensation for his disability or loss of work. "Right now, I'm good for nothing," Liu told *Sports Pictorial*.

These problems are by no means confined to the construction industry. Lu Guorong lost her fingers while operating crude machinery at a small factory in a rural town on the Hebei-Shandong border, less than a day's drive from Beijing. Not only did the factory owner refuse to help her, he fired her two days after the accident because without her fingers she could no longer operate the machinery. Lu sought redress at the local labor bureau but in the arbitration hearing her official trade union representative appeared on behalf of the factory owner.

In the metallurgical industry, there has been a spate of accidents over the last few months. Thirty-two workers at a steel plant in Liaoning were killed in April 2007 when nearly thirty tons of molten steel poured onto the shop floor. And in August, fourteen mainly migrant workers died and fifty-nine were injured following an aluminum spill at a factory in Shandong.

Coal mining is probably still the most dangerous profession in China, and one of the most dangerous in the world. The number of accidents and fatalities has decreased from the horrendous highs of 2004 and 2005, when about 6,000 miners died each year, but there were still, according to official statistics, 1,066 accidents and 1,792 fatalities in the first half of 2007 alone. In August 2007, 181 miners died after two coal mines in Xintai, Shandong, flooded following torrential rains mid-month. It is also important to note that the majority of accidents occur in small-scale illegal mines, precisely the kind of operations most likely to conceal accidents. The State Administration of Work Safety claimed on July 14 that it had uncovered forty-six coal mine accident cover-ups in the first half of the year, which suggests many others remain covered up and that the actual death toll is much higher than officially acknowledged.

In factories across China, workers are forced under threat of dismissal to labor in hazardous, even life-threatening conditions. In gemstone-processing factories where dust concentrations exceed permitted levels and visibility is down to one meter, workers must operate equipment without any form of silica dust protection; to complete order contracts, many workers in toy factories are forced to do overtime until they faint at their machines or even die from exhaustion. In these factories, bosses often illegally confiscate identification papers to prevent workers from quitting or running away when they can no longer endure the conditions, and many factories withhold most of workers' monthly wage packets, allowing them only pocket money.

## FAIR PLAY FOR WORKERS?

These conditions are commonplace across China, but the government usually takes action when specific outrages are brought to public attention by an outside agency. When a report by Playfair in June 2007 exposed the use of child labor at factories producing official Olympic merchandise, the Beijing Organizing Committee for the Olympic Games revoked the license of one company and suspended three others. BOCOG's prompt response to the revelation of abusive labor practices at its licensee factories is a good first step, but it is little help to the workers if the government stops there. The workers are out of a job and have no guarantee that even if they find another job their work conditions will be any better. Instead of merely punishing employers caught in the act, the government should give workers the power to protect their own interests by granting them the fundamental freedoms to organize their own unions and the right to strike.

The response by the Beijing Organizing Committee for the Olympic Games to the Playfair exposé is very much in keeping with the government's heavy-handed approach to potentially embarrassing labor issues. On June 29, more than 3,000 workers at the giant Shuangma Cement Plant in Mianyang, Sichuan Province, went on strike to protest against the company's proposed severance package. Shuangma, a former state-owned enterprise, was in the process of restructuring after being acquired in May by the world's leading building materials company, Lafarge. Shuangma's proposed severance package of 1,380 yuan for each year of employment was the equivalent of the average monthly wage in Mianyang and included a clause which meant workers agreed to forgo all other retirement, medical and welfare benefits. When this package was presented to the workers on June 27 as the company's final offer, it was immediately rejected. Nevertheless, management went ahead and attended a planned banquet in Mianyang City with local government officials to celebrate their good fortune after the Lafarge buyout. They had just started the banquet when the strike began. Management and local government officials rushed back to the plant, but instead of addressing the strikers' demands, they sealed off the town, surrounded the plant with police and removed all Internet postings related to the dispute.

Likewise, when news emerged that the entire workforce of the Jinzhou bus company in Liaoning had gone on strike on July 19—

bringing the town to a standstill—the authorities did not address the drivers' concerns over pay and privatization but merely blocked all news related to the strike. By contrast, the rescue of sixty-nine miners from a flooded coal mine in Henan in July 2007 was given extensive national coverage and portrayed in the official media as a miracle, without any analysis of how the miners became trapped in the first place. Blame for the accident was put on nature, rather than the human abuse of it. The August 2007 Xintai mine disaster killed 181 coal miners and was initially given much publicity, as authorities hoped it would provide them with another miraculous rescue story. However, as hopes faded for the trapped miners, we once again saw the usual media clampdown as families of the miners were ordered not to talk to the media. Those journalists who attempted to interview relatives were threatened with violence. After seven days, the government ordered a complete news blackout and all coverage in the official media of what had been a major news story ceased overnight.

## ONE WORLD, ONE DREAM?

The intensification of news management in the run-up to the Olympics has been obvious to all; while foreign journalists have been told they will have unfettered access to all news stories in China during the run-up to the Games, domestic journalists have been warned not to report "false" (bad) stories, their movements have been restricted, and critical blogs and websites taken down. The television journalist who created the infamous "cardboard pork dumpling" story in Beijing, which claimed that vendors were selling dumplings made of pulped cardboard to unsuspecting customers, was jailed for one year and fined 1,000 yuan on August 12, 2007, for faking news reports and "infringing the reputation of commodities." Even the most innocuous criticism has been punished. At the end of July, two high school teachers on

Hainan Island were given fifteen days administrative detention for posting bawdy song lyrics critical of local officials.

All this does not bode well for the Olympics. If, as seems very likely, these domestic controls are maintained, how will petitioners or protestors arriving in Beijing be treated? Will this traditional avenue for seeking redress be allowed any public expression at all in the capital next year? We have already seen an attempted march on Tiananmen Square on August 28, 2007, by 300 migrant workers demanding the payment of their rightful wages broken up by police before it could even begin. What will happen to the millions of migrant workers in Beijing who have no permanent residency? Will they be forced to return to their hometowns? Will other social undesirables, beggars and mentally ill people be removed from the streets too?

It seems from the evidence so far that Beijing is more concerned with image management than dealing with the underlying causes of its problems. We believe, however, that the government should take precisely the opposite approach. Instead of trying to conceal the less flattering side of China in order to protect its own image, the government should grasp the opportunity presented by the international media spotlight to openly discuss the real problems facing the country. If the Chinese people and the global community could better understand these issues, everyone including the government would be in a better position to resolve them.

## CHILD LABOR IN THE SHADOWS

The specter of child labor, which BOCOG sought to exorcise so swiftly after the Playfair 2007 report, is an obvious example. Statistics related to child labor in China are designated "highly secret," and apart from occasional highly publicized crackdowns on employers the government has done little to address the problem. If, however, the use of child labor is brought out in the open and the government encourages the active involvement of all sectors of society in addressing the problem at its root, the greater the chances are that child labor can be checked and reduced in the future. Moreover, the government for its part should take urgent measures to reform the rural education system and provide sufficient funds to ensure that children stay in school, thereby cutting off the supply of child labor at its source. Many primary and middle schools in rural areas are currently funded almost entirely by fees charged to students' parents. And increasingly, these parents are deciding there is little point in them paying out thousands of yuan each year if there is little or no chance of their child going on to high school or university. As such, many children drop out in their second year of middle school (about age fourteen) and go straight to work, even though the legal minimum employment age in China is sixteen. The government could solve this problem by providing enough funding to ensure that the compulsory nine years of schooling in China are free and universally available. However, the government currently only spends about 3 percent of the gross domestic product on education, half the United Nations recommended minimum level of 6 percent.

In addition to the state's chronic underinvestment in education, public health care has declined to the point where millions of ordinary workers' families cannot afford to seek medical treatment or risk crippling debt if they do. In the past, workers' health care was covered by the state-owned enterprises. However, with the break-up of the state-owned enterprise system over the last decade or so, the health care system has broken down too. Many workers laid-off in the privatization process had limited or no health care benefits and were forced to seek work in the private sector where the intense competition for jobs meant that employers could very often set their own terms and conditions of employment. Moreover, the migrant workers who have now replaced state-run enterprise employees as the backbone of China's working class come predominantly from an agricultural background and have never had medical insurance, and are therefore less likely to demand it from their employers in the cities.

## TILTING THE BALANCE OF POWER

Many employers ruthlessly exploit the passivity and stoicism of migrant workers, however many of those migrant workers are now beginning to stand up for their rights and demand not only appropriate wages but decent working conditions and proper health care. China's labor legislation, especially the newly promulgated Labor Contract Law, which gives individual workers a wide range of rights and safeguards, should in theory provide workers with adequate protection from exploitation and abuse. However, as has been demonstrated time and again since the enactment of the Labor Law in 1994, the Chinese government has routinely failed to enforce its own legislation. All the power resides in the hands of the enterprise owners, who in collusion with corrupt government officials (often part-owners themselves) can dictate how hard and for how long their employees have to work and for what reward. In some extreme cases, such as the 2007 Shanxi brick factory scandal in which thousands of workers were forced or abducted into slavery, that reward was imprisonment and physical abuse.

Not only can the government not enforce national labor laws, it cannot even enforce labor-related regulations and directives issued by the country's most senior leaders. In 2003, Prime Minister Wen Jiabao made it his personal mission to resolve the endemic problem of wage arrears in China; however, four years later, migrant workers, school teachers and factory workers across the country are still only receiving a small proportion of their promised salary. Again, following the spate of coal-mining disasters in 2004 and 2005, the prime minister spearheaded a campaign to improve mine safety. While visiting the families of victims of the Chenjiashan Coal Mine disaster of November 2004 in which 166 miners died, Wen Jiabao stated, "We must improve safety in the workplace. We cannot let another tragedy like this happen again. We must take responsibility for our miners." However the economic demand for coal in China combined with local level corruption in the coal fields has meant that production routinely exceeds safe capacity, and thousands of miners continue to die each year.

Given the government's persistent failure to enforce its own laws and regulations, the Chinese government should not merely draft more legislation to plug the gaps but empower the workers to defend their own rights. If workers had the right to organize their own grassroots democratic trade unions and the legal right to strike if necessary, they could literally play a life-saving role in ensuring coal-mine safety. Workers could demand that employers pay collectively negotiated wages in full and on time. Moreover, unions could act as an important facilitator bridging the gap between workers and management so that many of the violent protests that have erupted all over China in the last decade could be resolved or at least addressed through negotiation before protest becomes imperative. However, despite its commitment to "putting people first" and creating a "harmonious society," the Chinese government shows little sign of granting its citizens the rights or the ability to protect themselves. Rather we have seen a disturbing trend in which workers (like miners trapped in flooded coal mines) are portrayed as weak, pitiable and in need of rescue. And of course in this scenario, the only body that can rescue them is the government.

## FLEETING GLORY FOR A FEW

Chinese workers are dying every single day in China, from industrial accidents and work-related illness. Most cannot afford decent medical treatment and have to suffer further from breathing polluted air, drinking polluted water and eating contaminated food. While the supreme health and fitness of the elite will be celebrated during the Olympics, the overall health of the nation is not advancing.

There are state-of-the-art sporting facilities all over China—private gyms, swimming pools, tennis courts and golf courses—but only the very rich can make use of them. The majority of Chinese citizens have limited or no access to such facilities. If the massive sums of money spent over the last two decades on bringing the Olympics to China had been spent on education, health care and sporting facilities accessible to everyone, Chinese people would be in a better position to actually enjoy the Games. And though the money has already been spent, there is still a chance that the international exposure brought by the Olympics will have a positive effect on workers' rights, which would indeed provide some lasting benefit to the country as a whole.

The opening date of the Olympics on the eighth day of the eight month of the eighth year of this millennium should signify good fortune for the people of China as a whole and not just the privileged few. Thus far, however, the Olympics have failed to inspire even those ordinary workers closest to the project. Indeed, for many migrant workers interviewed at the city's Olympic construction sites, their contribution to China's Olympic dream is just another job.

"We don't need to know what these buildings are for. As long as we do the work and get paid, that's fine," a nineteen-year-old migrant worker named Dai told the *Sports Pictorial*. One quarter of the migrant workers interviewed by *Sports Pictorial* said they did not know exactly what they were working on and less than a third could correctly identify the opening date of the Games. The majority of interviewees had no interest in the opening ceremony or who would light the Olympic torch. Eight workers thought President Hu Jintao would light the torch, others nominated themselves, their work mates or famous movie stars such as Chow Yun-Fat. Many workers had no idea if they would still be in Beijing during the Olympics, most said they would go wherever the work was. For those who were confident they would still be in the capital, most did not think they would ever be able to enter the facilities they had built. "Attending the Olympics? That is for rich people! We can watch it on television, we can't expect any more than that," said thirty-year-old Zhu Wanming from Sichuan.

Zhu Wanming and hundreds of millions like him will be faced with great hardships for a long time after the Olympic closing ceremony, and it is the Chinese government's responsibility not only to ease those hardships but to give ordinary workers the power and the right and the ability to improve their own lives.

# PHOTO ESSAY
## **MIGRANT WORKERS** RACE THE CLOCK
Photos by Kadir van Lohuizen

The Olympic slogan "One World, One Dream" might apply to the athletes who will break records in Beijing, or to the thousands of visitors who will be staying in the capital's new five star hotels. But the theme is hollow for countless Chinese citizens behind the curtain of the Olympic extravaganza—migrant workers racing the clock to finish key infrastructure before the opening ceremony, rural petitioners whose temporary housing in Beijing was demolished soon after the one-year countdown began in August 2007, or residents being unjustly evicted from their homes to make way for Olympic venues.

**Kadir van Lohuizen** is a Dutch photographer who has documented human rights abuses in Asia, Africa and the Middle East, and most recently received a fellowship to capture the aftermath of Hurricane Katrina in the United States. He has won numerous awards for his photographs, which have been featured in solo exhibits and published worldwide. The photographs on the following pages, taken in August 2007, show facets of Beijing Olympic organizers would prefer to conceal.

**MIGRANT WORKERS** BUILD
BEIJING'S OLYMPIC DREAM

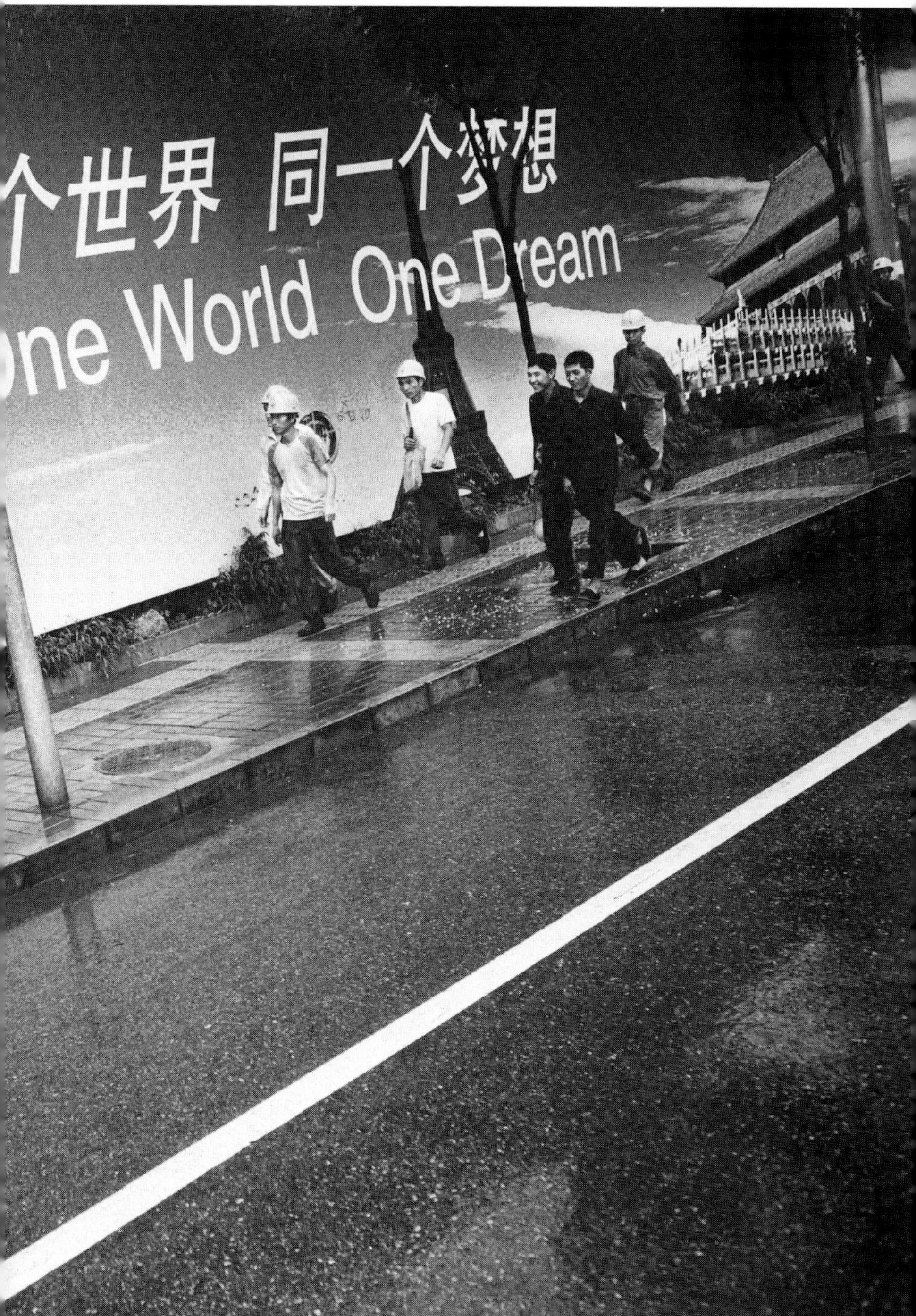
个世界 同一个梦想
ne World One Dream

Previous page:
Migrant construction workers walk past a billboard advertising the 2008 Beijing Olympics. Migrant workers are laborers who have moved from China's rural areas to its cities in search of work. A conservative estimate of migrant workers across the country is 150 million.

Top right:
Migrant construction workers walk past a billboard depicting the new Beijing which they are building, often under harsh conditions and brutal wage exploitation. These workers constitute 25% of all migrant workers in Beijing, a number officially estimated at 4 million but which may be higher.

Bottom right:
Many migrant workers live in overcrowded, makeshift shelters near the construction sites. Washing facilities are a rarity. Workers are often obliged to go to a public bathhouse to pay for the privilege of cleaning themselves.

**Above:**
Other migrant workers live in dingy dormitories such as this one near the Olympic village in Beijing. The rooms are generally unheated, and many are crammed with a dozen bunk beds.

**Top right:**
Migrant workers wait for buses to transport them to construction sites. The work is often dangerous, as many workers lack basic safety training and equipment needed to protect them from injury in one of China's most dangerous industries. The Chinese government has confirmed at least six workers died and four were injured building the National Stadium and other Olympic sites.

**Bottom right:**
The buses are crowded with men who generally rarely see their families. Like Wei Zhongwen, the worker profiled in Mei Fong's chapter, many only return to their home towns or villages once a year for the Chinese New Year's holiday.

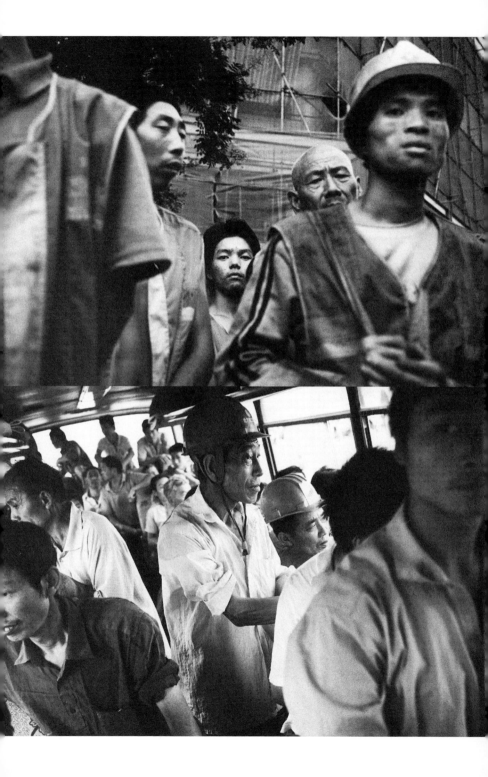

Top left:
Migrant workers at the construction site of Beijing's new National Stadium, also known as "the Bird's Nest," where the opening ceremony of the Beijing Games will take place on August 8, 2008. The stadium was designed by the Chinese artist Ai Weiwei, in collaboration with the Swiss firm Herzog & de Meuron. Ai has said he would not attend the opening ceremony, explaining that he rejects the "tendency to use culture for the purpose of propaganda."

Bottom left:
Migrant workers at a construction site near the Olympic stadium "Bird's Nest." They are racing against the clock to meet the deadline of the Beijing Games' opening ceremony. In October 2007, Sun Weijia, an official at the Beijing Organizing Committee for the Olympic Games, assured journalists that "It can be done... The workers labor in shifts around the clock, seven days per week."

Above:
Migrant worker walking home to his dormitory, carrying a young child. The skyline reflects Beijing's building boom —it is estimated that more than 10,000 sites are currently undergoing construction or renovation in the capital, contributing to the intense pollution described in Christine Loh's chapter.

DEMOLITION
OF THE *HUTONGS*

Previous page:
Demolition of a *hutong* in central Beijing. *Hutongs* are traditional Chinese neighborhoods, though the term can also refer to narrow alleys within these neighborhoods. Many *hutongs* are being demolished to make way for high-end residential communities, shopping malls, golf courses and, more recently, Olympic venues, with many of their residents evicted without consultation or fair compensation.

Top right:
Residents of a *hutong* undergoing demolition. In violation of official regulations, the amount of compensation is sometimes decided unilaterally by the developers or demolition companies, and is far less than the actual market value. Evicted residents have limited means of redress.

Bottom right:
A *hutong* resident contemplating debris from the demolition. Although development companies are required by law to pay the evictees compensation equal to the full market value of their properties, as well as additional compensation for business loss in the case of non-residential properties, this requirement is often ignored. On some occasions, compensation is paid to the local authorities instead of the evictees.

UNDESIRABLE
**PETITIONERS**

Previous page:
Petitioners hold letters
of complaint (*xinfang*) in
the so-called "Petitioners'
Village" in Beijing's Fengtai
district. The petitioning
system in theory enables
citizens across China to
contest official decisions
or air grievances over
corruption. Petitioning has
historic roots: Qing dynasty
petitioners waited on their
knees at the gates of the
emperor's palace to present
appeals. Chinese citizens
seeking redress today hold
signs, stage sit-ins, and
try to push petitions into
Beijing leaders' limousines.

Above:
The "Petitioners' Village"
in Beijing's Fengtai district.
The Chinese government's
efforts to rid Beijing of
"undesirables" ahead of
the 2008 Olympics have
accelerated the eviction of
petitioners. In September
2007, the Beijing municipal
government began the
demolition of the settlement
in Fengtai district, which
housed up to 4,000
petitioners; the demolition
was completed in October.

# CHAPTER 14

# The Race for Profits

### BY ARVIND GANESAN

*On the eve of the one-year countdown to the Beijing Games, International Olympic Committee president Jacques Rogge hosted a grand dinner for the sixty-four worldwide corporate sponsors of the Games, with Wang Qishan, mayor of Beijing and president of the Beijing Organizing Committee for the Olympic Games attending. Rogge expressed his appreciation for the support of the Olympic corporate sponsors, describing it as a crucial guarantee for the long-term development of the Olympic movement, and as a positive contribution to the Olympic spirit. But today many people around the world also expect companies to use their influence in positive ways to demonstrate "corporate social responsibility" by acting on human rights violations ranging from abuses in Darfur to media censorship and labor abuses in China.* **ARVIND GANESAN** *is the director of the Business and Human Rights Program at Human Rights Watch. He works with companies, governments and multilateral organizations to promote respect for human rights in business practices throughout the world. He has authored reports on numerous topics, including child labor in India and the complicity of major corporations such as Enron in human rights violations.*

The Olympics have long been at the center of geopolitics and often a focus of human rights disputes. But the 2008 Beijing Games are unique because they will be held at a time of heightened scrutiny of human rights, combined with scrutiny of China's human rights record and the Games themselves. The Beijing Games corporate sponsors will likely face more pressure to be responsible companies than the sponsors and supporters of prior

Olympics, and they will find it hard to separate themselves from human rights issues surrounding them. From Jesse Owens's four gold medals at the 1936 Olympics in Berlin to the United States leading a sixty-two-country boycott of the 1980 Moscow Games, politics have played a key role in the Games. Prior Olympics focused on the role of governments in political and human rights disputes, but the 2008 Beijing Olympics have added a new element to Olympic politics: the role of corporations. The added focus on corporate sponsors is the culmination of three key trends since the Olympics were first awarded to Beijing in July 2001.

First, there has been a growing recognition in the last decade that corporations have human rights responsibilities, an ethos embraced at least rhetorically by some Olympics sponsors. Since the Beijing Games are the first Olympics held in an undemocratic country since the 1984 Winter Games in Sarajevo, corporations sponsoring the games in such an environment will find it hard to avoid questions related to corporate social responsibility. Not only is the Chinese government's overall human rights record within its own borders poor, but it has also been a supporter of some of the worst regimes abroad, including Sudan, North Korea and Burma. This has brought heightened scrutiny and criticism of the country's foreign policy because of the scale of the atrocities in Darfur and Chinese investment in Sudan's oil sector, the principal source of revenue for the Sudanese government. China is a key arms supplier and trading partner to the Burmese military regime, which brutally suppressed peaceful protests in September 2007 led by Buddhist monks and civilians who were demonstrating against economic mismanagement and other excesses by the government, and confined the country's democratically elected leader Aung San Suu Kyi to house arrest. During the latest crisis in Burma, at least twenty people were killed, including a Japanese photojournalist, and perhaps hundreds more arrested. China refused to allow harsher measures, such as sanctions, to condemn these acts, in part because of its economic interests in the country.

Second, the Beijing Olympics coincide with China's dramatic economic growth, and are viewed by the government as a chance to showcase China's emergence as a global power. In 2001, China's gross domestic product was approximately US $1.1 trillion. By 2007, it had tripled to an estimated US $3.3 trillion, making the Chinese economy the fourth largest in the world. The economic boom has also brought its share of problems domestically, most notably widespread corruption, massive environmental degradation, and abuses against workers needed to fuel the country's growth. Foreign corporations, eager to tap into this huge market, can no longer hope to do so without having to answer some hard questions from consumers and shareholders who are concerned with the social and environmental costs of such investments.

Finally, without corporations such as the broadcast media and high-level sponsors, the Olympics probably would not be the global event that it is today.

## LOFTY PRINCIPLES AND SKY-HIGH BROADCAST AND MARKETING FEES

The Olympic Charter espouses lofty principles, stating at the outset that "Olympism seeks to create a way of life based on the joy of effort, the educational value of good example and respect for universal fundamental ethical principles."

In fact, today the Olympics are much more of a money-driven marketing vehicle than pure expression of a moral philosophy. The Olympic Games can be a huge money-making machine, though ticket sales are not the main source of revenue and have actually declined in the last few years as more viewers follow sports on television sets and computer screens.[1]

Most of the Olympics revenue is derived from corporations, largely in the form of broadcast rights and corporate sponsorships. Since 1993, Olympic revenue has steadily grown, with the bulk of new revenue coming from corporations. According to the Olympics quadrennial reviews, some 78 percent of the US $2.63 billion in Olympics revenue came from broadcasting fees and sponsorships from 1993 to 1996. Between 2001 and 2004, 87 percent of revenue came from broadcasting and sponsorships. This amount included approximately US $2.6 billion in broadcasting fees, and US $603 million in sponsorships by the companies that are members of The Olympic Partner program, the highest level of corporate sponsorship for the Olympics; the companies that participate in it are known as the "TOP" sponsors. TOP sponsors pay for the exclusive use of the Olympics brand, and receive preferred access to the Games for marketing purposes and other privileges. Revenue from broadcast fees and TOP program sponsors accounted for about 70 percent of the overall Olympics revenue from 2001 to 2004.

Given both the economic realities and the sensitive political context of the Beijing Games, corporate sponsors and broadcasters cannot avoid questions about human rights issues related to China. This is particularly true of corporations which present themselves, in their annual reports or on their websites, as "socially responsible" companies. For the 2008 Beijing Olympics, the twelve TOP sponsors are Atos Origin, Coca-Cola, General Electric, Johnson & Johnson, Kodak, Lenovo, John Hancock (Manulife), McDonald's, Omega, Panasonic, Samsung and Visa. In some instances, corporations have spent more than US $80 million on sponsorship rights. Between April 2006 and February 2008, Olympic sponsors spent more than US $4.1 billion on advertising in China.[2]

NBC owns the broadcasting rights in the United States for the Beijing Games as part of a multibillion dollar broadcasting package for multiple Olympic Games through 2012. The company reportedly paid US $894 million for the Beijing broadcast rights alone. NBC is also a subsidiary of General Electric, a TOP sponsor. In total, the International Olympic Committee expects to earn approximately US $1.7 billion in broadcasting fees for the Beijing Olympics.

## THE THORNY ISSUE OF INTERNET AND MEDIA FREEDOM

Broadcasting is inextricably intertwined with human rights issues, since the lack of media freedom is a major problem for the Beijing Games. In 2001, the Chinese government assured the IOC that it would ease restrictions on the media if it were awarded the 2008 Games. In 2006, it even issued temporary regulations that apparently allowed foreign correspondents to conduct interviews with any consenting Chinese organizations or citizens between January 1, 2007, and October 17, 2008. However, those commitments did not actually stop censorship or the routine harassment of foreign journalists trying to do their jobs. Local journalists and media have a much harder time than foreign reporters, since the temporarily loosened regulations do not even apply to them.

Internet communications have also been subject to new restrictions, compounding the existing censorship of search engines, blogs, and Internet news services. In 2006, companies such as Yahoo!, Google, and Microsoft have faced much criticism of their operations in China. Yahoo! turned over information about Shi Tao, a journalist who used his Yahoo! e-mail account to disclose the government's strategy to spin the anniversary of the 1989 Tiananmen Square protests and massacre. Afterward, Chinese authorities imprisoned him for ten years for "leaking state secrets." Microsoft—which in June 2007 announced the appointment of Microsoft China as "System Software and Support Supplier" for the Beijing Games—eliminated blogs critical of the government. Those activities led to hearings in Congress, reports by human rights organizations, and legislation and the development of voluntary standards by industry, academics, and human rights groups that perhaps could curtail that conduct.

Those events have led to efforts to try to address these human rights issues through a combination of voluntary and potentially mandatory standards that would apply to companies operating in China or other countries in which governments try to censor information or punish users for exercising their rights to expression. However, those efforts are still under development at this writing, and the process could take years to complete.

The Chinese government, however, was unmoved by these controversies. Their new efforts to censor were partly in anticipation of the 17th Congress of the Chinese Communist Party, which opened on October 15, 2007. On August 31, the government ordered domestic search engines, such as those operated by Yahoo! China, Google China and Baidu.com to remove "illegal and unhealthy content" within a week and without specifying what constituted such content or the penalties for noncompliance. The government also closed many Internet data centers, ostensibly to make it more difficult for certain websites, blogs, and other Internet forums to operate.

In a sign that corporations realize the potential for true human rights and public relations catastrophes around the Games in China, a number of unnamed companies are working with a leading US law firm on a "crisis management" strategy that is apparently aimed to counter criticism stemming from the Beijing Olympics, according to the *Wall Street Journal*.[3] Instead of investing resources in a public relations campaign, companies would be much better served by ensuring that their own operations respect human rights. These companies should also ensure that the Chinese government fully understands that its conduct is an issue for Olympics sponsors and broadcasters.

## CORPORATE SOCIAL RESPONSIBILITY

It is widely recognized by many companies, governments, and nongovernmental organizations that corporations have human rights responsibilities and need to take them into account during their operations. Broadly speaking, companies must ensure that they respect the rights of their employees by adhering to internationally recognized labor standards, ensure respect for these rights throughout their supply chain of subcontractors and other business partners, and ensure that their operations do not have adverse human rights impact in the surrounding communities where they operate. However, in countries with very poor human rights records, such as China, companies face further scrutiny about their operations because the government's conduct makes it so difficult for even a responsible company to meet its obligations.

China does not allow free and independent trade unions, and working conditions in the country are poor. The authorities do not tolerate political dissent, and they censor and restrict the free flow of information. But China is also one of the world's largest economies and a highly sought-after destination for investment and trade. Historically, companies and pro-business constituencies have argued that the best way to improve human rights in China is to allow more foreign investment and trade, as if somehow by osmosis, human rights would improve. By now, it is clear that unless companies and governments forcefully respect and promote human rights, protection of these rights will not just improve simply because an economy grows.

The Olympics are in some ways the symbolic culmination of "constructive engagement" with China. They are a symbol of the country's rise on the world stage as an economic and political power. But so far, companies and even the IOC have not been willing to address human rights directly tied to the Beijing Olympics, such as forced evictions in Beijing and labor rights abuses in the run-up to the Games. As reported by Human Rights Watch and other groups, thousands of people have been forcibly evicted in order to make room for Olympic venues. At least one million migrant workers have been employed by construction firms on the building of these venues; in many cases these workers do not receive legally required pay and benefits, and must do dangerous work without adequate protection. The IOC and companies should at least pledge to respect workers rights and ensure that they are not parties to such abuses during construction for the Olympics.

China clearly does not follow one of the Olympic Charter's fundamental principles, which states that "any form of discrimination with regard to a country or a person on grounds of race, religion, politics, gender or otherwise is incompatible with belonging to the Olympic Movement." Instead, the Chinese government regularly discriminates against and represses ethnic minorities. Dissident Uighurs (a Turkic-speaking Muslim group) who express "separatist" leanings are routinely arrested and sentenced in quick secret trials. The death penalty is a common form of punishment. In Tibet, the government views the exiled Dalai Lama as a separatist leader and routinely imprisons Tibetans suspected of "separatism." It has forcibly relocated at least 700,000 Tibetan herders in an ill-conceived and abusive urbanization program. China does not respect religious freedom and only recognizes state-controlled entities while denouncing some religions outside of their control as "cults." Political dissent is punished.

As the financial engine for the Olympics, it would seem that companies, particularly broadcasters and major sponsors, would have an interest in ensuring that the Beijing Games do not become a byword for human rights abuses and would presumably want to show that they represent the progressive end of responsible companies on human rights. Yet only two TOP sponsors, Coca-Cola and General Electric, have explicitly expressed support for human rights in public policy statements. General Electric has a human rights policy while Coke has joined the Business Leaders Initiative for Human Rights, an effort involving fourteen multinational companies to "find practical ways of applying the aspirations of the Universal Declaration of Human Rights within a business context and to inspire other businesses to do likewise." The other TOP sponsors have varying degrees of corporate responsibility policies, including some which address labor-rights issues, but they do not explicitly make reference to human rights.

## WHAT CAN CORPORATE SPONSORS DO?

There are several steps that all corporate sponsors could take to help ensure that human rights abuses do not further taint the Beijing Olympics. Sponsors could publicly embrace human rights policies and pledge that their operations in China will be conducted so that they respect human rights. A starting point would be to articulate clear human rights policies, detail how they will be implemented and allow for independent monitoring of their implementation. They could also make it clear to the Chinese government that media and Internet censorship, forced evictions, labor rights abuses, state controls on religious freedom, and repression of ethnic minorities violate the very spirit of the Olympic Games. As Olympic sponsors, they should publicly emphasize that they expect the IOC and the government to respect and uphold key elements of the Olympic Charter, particularly those that acknowledge human rights, such as the principle that "any form of discrimination with regard to a country or a person on grounds of race, religion, politics, gender or otherwise is incompatible with belonging to the Olympic Movement." The combined effect of major sponsors and other key actors speaking out about such abuses would increase the pressure on the government to improve its practices that would also mitigate the reputational damage on the Games that such abuses create.

Companies should also focus on specific issues, depending on how their operations intersect with abuses tied to the Beijing Games. For example, broadcasters and sponsors involved in the Olympics telecommunications or computer infrastructure have a responsibility to address freedom of expression and censorship. NBC and computer manufacturer Lenovo, a TOP sponsor, should forcefully speak up about these issues because they are respectively broadcasting the Games and providing the computer infrastructure. NBC News could test the government's stated media openness for foreign journalists by reporting on human rights issues during the Beijing Games, and it should publicly ask the Chinese government to make media freedom a permanent component of law for both foreign and Chinese journalists.

Lenovo is providing approximately 14,000 pieces of equipment for the Games, and it designed the Beijing Olympics' torch. Since it is providing the means for people to access the Internet and to manage information, the company should speak publicly about the issue of censorship in China and should categorically state how it plans to protect freedom of expression during the Beijing Olympics. Microsoft, although not a TOP sponsor, is nonetheless a supplier for the Games and should be aggressive about stopping censorship, given its role as an Olympic supplier and its past history of censoring blogs in China. If companies do not demonstrate that they will protect freedom of expression, particularly for such a high profile event as the Olympics, it will only hasten calls for governments to regulate them and make such protections mandatory for companies because companies would have again demonstrated that they are unwilling or unable to do it themselves.

General Electric may have more invested in the Games than any other company because it owns NBC and because it is a TOP sponsor. It could be a forceful advocate for human rights with the government and could insist that the IOC ensure that the companies involved in constructing Olympics venues and providing the technology and other infrastructure for the Games, also respect the rights of workers and the users of their products and equipment. A starting point would be to publicly and unequivocally state that General Electric, its subcontractors, and suppliers will fully implement its human rights policy in China. It should clearly communicate to the IOC and the Chinese government its expectations that human rights must be respected. It should also advocate for relevant changes in laws or policies to ensure that rights are respected and publicly detail what steps it has taken to ensure compliance with the company's policies and respect for human rights in China.

The Beijing Games are not just China's Olympics, or the IOC's. In very real financial terms, they are the sponsors' and broadcasters' Olympics because they pay for it. Increasingly, anywhere in the world, if corporations ignore human rights or are silent when governments commit abuses, the corporations themselves are complicit. If the veneer of a sporting competition covers a much deeper pattern of abuse and exploitation, it would be hard to call the Games a success for China or for their sponsors and instead would be a source of condemnation for their conduct.

# CHAPTER 15

# China and the Spielberg Effect

BY R. SCOTT GREATHEAD

*In the fields of meteorology and physics, the "butterfly effect" refers to the idea that tiny changes in one part of a system can eventually lead to major unforeseen effects in other far-away parts of the system. Has "Genocide Olympics," an indelible label used in a* Wall Street Journal *op-ed, produced a response that could affect the war-torn region of Darfur and possibly China's approach to foreign policy?* R. SCOTT GREATHEAD *is a lawyer based in New York and chief executive officer of World Monitors Inc., which works with global companies on strategies for responsible business. He is a member of the Board of Directors of Human Rights in China, and Human Rights First (formerly the Lawyers' Committee for Human Rights), which he cofounded in 1978.*

On March 28, 2007, the *Wall Street Journal* published an op-ed titled "The 'Genocide Olympics,'" by actress Mia Farrow and her son, Yale law student Ronan Farrow.[1] The op-ed warned film director Steven Spielberg that he would "go down in history as the Leni Riefenstahl of the Beijing Games" unless he helped push China to change its policy of supporting its client Sudan in resisting a robust UN peacekeeping force for Darfur. Spielberg responded with a letter to Chinese President Hu Jintao urging China to act, and threatened to quit as an artistic advisor to the Olympics if it didn't. In July, China changed its position in the UN

Security Council and supported a resolution to send a peacekeeping force of 26,000 to Sudan with enforcement authority under Chapter Seven of the UN Charter.

The "Genocide Olympics" story illustrates the power of an easily digestible slogan, the growing effectiveness of human rights campaigns, and the role that private actors—committed individuals and corporate players—can play in advancing the human rights reform agenda. The episode also carries an important lesson for global companies doing business in countries like China: what happened to Steven Spielberg can happen to you, and if you value the reputation of your company and its brand, you should be prepared.

## CHINA'S GREAT WALL OF IMPUNITY

The received wisdom has been that China is impervious to "name and shame," the technique employed by human rights and environmental campaign groups to force multinational businesses and governments to change their ways or suffer public condemnation for depredating the environment, grossly violating human rights or other unethical conduct. Oil and mining companies, apparel makers, and Western governments are all reliably nervous about shareholder, consumer, and voter reactions. But China's notoriously opaque government has traditionally been unmoved by exposure and embarrassment of this sort.

According to this thinking, the world's last major Communist regime is here to stay, and can only be successfully prodded to change by subtle engagement. This has led many prominent and usually scrupled Western foundations, educational institutions and nongovernmental organizations to avoid harsh criticism of Chinese government policies and behavior they privately object to, in favor of the ability to maintain programs and offices on the mainland which they hope will lead to the opening of political space for civil society-driven reforms.

Of course, some motives are less philanthropic. Certain corporate titans mesmerized by business opportunities in China have redefined "engagement" to something that looks more like rank appeasement. How else to explain the decision of Time Warner chief executive officer Gerald Levin at *Fortune* magazine's September 1999 blowout for corporate executives in Shanghai to rise to toast his "good friend" Jiang Zemin rather than complain that China's Security Bureau had pulled the latest issue of *Time* magazine off the newsstands in Beijing because it contained essays on human rights by the Dalai Lama and prominent Chinese exiles Wei Jingsheng and Fang Lizhi?[2] Or Rupert Murdoch when he "kicked the BBC World Service Television off his Star TV system in Asia to please the Chinese government and help establish the satellite service there," as reported in 1994 by the *Financial Times?*[3]

Perceptions about China's immunity to outside pressure began to change with the Farrows' March 2007 op-ed in the *Wall Street Journal*. This carefully crafted piece dealt with China, but as leverage focused its sights on film director Steven Spielberg. This strategy set in motion a chain of events that has moved China in its policies toward Sudan and the human tragedy known as Darfur, and along the way may contribute to establishing new standards for global businesses in dealing with Chinese government policies.

With the Darfur crisis unsolved for years, it has attracted legions of dedicated human rights campaigners, among them many celebrities. One is Mia Farrow, who has made six trips to Darfur and its borders with Chad and the Central African Republic, and written extensively about it.[4] Farrow and her son are not the first Darfur campaigners to target China for its support of Sudan,[5] but they were first to draw blood.

## CHINA AND DARFUR

How did the Farrows get from Darfur to China, the 2008 Olympics and Steven Spielberg?

The Darfur conflict has fueled one of the most extensive human rights campaigns ever waged. It centers on the Darfur region of western Sudan, where over the past four years more than 200,000 people have died and 2.5 million have been displaced from their homes, principally as a result of attacks by Arab militias known as Janjaweed, who are armed and supported by Sudan's government in Khartoum.[6] Like many human conflicts, this one involves oil and water—the proceeds of Sudan's rich oil resources and access to scarce water in the Darfur region. The crisis has spread beyond the borders of Sudan, to the Central African Republic and Chad, where as many as 175,000 Chadians have reportedly been displaced by Janjaweed attacks. The conflict in Darfur has been characterized as genocide by the US government, numerous journalists and many (but not all) human rights organizations.[7] Virtually all observers agree that Darfur is one of the world's most serious humanitarian and human rights emergencies.

China is implicated in Darfur because it is Sudan's largest foreign investor and its most important international supporter. According to an April 2007 report by the Sudan Divestment Task Force, despite Sudan's status as a pariah state and the target of international sanctions, China's foreign direct investment in Sudan totals an estimated US $15 billion.[8] Much of this comes through the state-owned China National Petroleum Corporation (CNPC), which has invested at least US $5 billion in Sudan. CNPC owns 40 percent of—and reportedly controls—Sudan's two largest oil consortiums.[9]

Based on China's seemingly unquenchable need for foreign energy resources, China and Sudan have developed a mutually dependant relationship. Oil from Sudan amounts to 52 percent of CNPC's overseas crude reserves and supplies 7 percent of China's oil needs.[10] China in turn has become Sudan's chief supporter in the international arena, where it has opposed the imposition of economic sanctions and an arms embargo. China is also Sudan's largest arms supplier and, according to a UN investigation, the source of most weapons used to attack civilians in Darfur.[11]

Most importantly, China has backed Sudan in blocking efforts in the United Nations to end the Darfur conflict, sanction Sudan and provide meaningful protection to innocent civilians. China has used its UN Security Council veto power to support Sudan in its opposition to sending a robust UN peacekeeping force to protect civilians in Darfur. In 2006, China threatened to veto a Security Council resolution authorizing UN peacekeepers unless language was inserted that effectively required Khartoum's consent for the force to be sent. This condition was inserted into Security Council Resolution 1706, adopted August 31, 2006, with China abstaining, which authorized a deployment of 22,500 police and troops. The force was never sent because Sudan refused its consent.

## THE "GENOCIDE OLYMPICS"

Looking back, it seems inevitable that China's role as Sudan's supporter-in-chief would lead someone to brand the 2008 Beijing Games the "Genocide Olympics." The surprise is that it was not a Darfur campaigner that first came up with it, but the *Washington Post*, in a December 2006 editorial titled "China and Darfur: The Genocide Olympics."[12] The editorial asserted, "Sudan's government feels it can ignore Western revulsion at genocide because it has no need of Western money," citing "sleek new office towers sprouting up" in Khartoum's commercial district, financed by a Chinese–Malaysian–United Arab Emirates oil partnership, along with other Arab and Asian investors. The *Post* called on China to use "its leverage over Sudan" and join Western nations "to broker a cease-fire in Darfur," warning that if it doesn't, human rights campaigners could be taking out newspaper ads calling on the world "to boycott the Genocide Olympics."

The *Washington Post* editorial was read by Smith College Professor Eric Reeves, a relentless and prolific Darfur campaigner. Reeves picked up the "Genocide Olympics" concept in his own op-ed, "Push China, Save Darfur," published three days later in the *Boston Globe*.[13] Noting "China's imperviousness to foreign criticism of its increasingly rapacious behavior abroad," Reeves argued that "Darfur advocacy needs to change this," and that the way to do it is "to link Darfur indissolubly in the world's consciousness with the 2008 Olympic Games in China." According to Reeves, "The Chinese leadership must be forced to make a choice: work now to halt genocide in Darfur, or see the Olympic Games used, at every turn, as a means of highlighting the Chinese role in sustaining the ultimate human crime." Reeves acknowledged that "[t]his sort of advocacy will be difficult." Clearly, the Darfur campaigners needed help getting the "genocide" and Olympics connection noticed in a big way. They got it from show business.

## SPIELBERG AND THE BEIJING GAMES

Three-time Academy Award winner Steven Spielberg became involved in the 2008 Olympics in April 2006, when the Beijing Organizing Committee announced that he would serve as "an artistic consultant" to *House of Flying Daggers* director Zhang Yimou, who had been selected to design the opening and closing ceremonies of the games.[14] In October it was announced that director Ang Lee would join Spielberg as an "arts and culture consultant" for the ceremonies, despite the fact that his Academy Award–winning film, *Brokeback Mountain*, had been banned in China.[15]

At the Beijing news conference marking his selection, Spielberg said the artistic team was "dedicated to making the opening and closing ceremonies the most emotional anyone has ever seen."[16] It was a prescient statement. Emotions started running high with the publication of the Farrows' *Wall Street Journal* op-ed. After pointing out China's support for Sudan and "bankrolling Darfur's genocide," the op-ed asks rhetorically, "Does Mr. Spielberg really want to go down in history as the Leni Riefenstahl of the Beijing Games?"

The reference was, of course, to the infamous director of *Olympia*, the documentary of the 1936 Summer Olympics in Berlin, which, along with the better-known propaganda film, *Triumph of the Will*, glorified Nazi Germany under Hitler. The Farrows called on Spielberg to use his voice to push "the Chinese government to use its leverage over Sudan to protect civilians in Darfur." They made the same demand to corporate sponsors of the Games—specifically Johnson & Johnson, Coca-Cola, General Electric and McDonald's.

As harsh as it may seem, comparing Steven Spielberg to Leni Riefenstahl was an epithet waiting to be thrown. There are dozens of potential disasters stalking the Beijing Games that are guaranteed to provoke someone to play the Leni Riefenstahl card. It is not difficult to imagine a Falun Gong or Darfur or Tibet-inspired demonstration or incident that invites an overreaction by the police or security bureau. The official Xinhua News Agency has quoted Public Security Minister Zhou Yongkang as listing "ethnic splitism [i.e., Tibet], religious extremism, terrorism and Falun Gong" as major threats to the Games, requiring that the police "strictly guard against and strike hard at hostile forces at home and abroad."[17]

And there is always the specter of a public relations fiasco during the opening ceremony of the Games if Olympic athletes from all corners of the world are made to march under the infamous portrait of Mao Zedong that became an icon of totalitarian oppression during the Tiananmen Square demonstration in 1989. (Who wouldn't want to be a fly on the wall in the Politburo debate over whether to insist on this gesture to China's revolutionary past?)

Steven Spielberg may not have fully thought through the range of political and other developments possible around the Beijing Games. Indeed, the members of the International Olympic Committee may not have either. Blame for anything that happens in the course of the Beijing Games because of the nature of the Chinese government will ultimately be shared by everyone who supported the decision.

But accusing Steven Spielberg of being an aider and abettor of genocide is another matter. Spielberg directed the widely revered Holocaust epic *Schindler's List*, and is the founder of the Shoah Foundation Institute at the University of Southern California, which has created a remarkable documentary archive of 52,000 video testimonies of Holocaust survivors from fifty-six countries in thirty-two languages. By his own account, Spielberg regards his work with the Shoah Foundation as his most important professional accomplishment. This work is important, and it has given Steven Spielberg stature in the eyes of the human rights community, and particularly the anti-genocide movement, far exceeding anything attained by the millions of dollars he has also contributed to their cause.

Not surprisingly, the Farrows' op-ed hit its mark, and it hurt.

## SPIELBERG'S LETTER TO PRESIDENT HU JINTAO

Although the "Genocide Olympics" campaign took him by surprise, Steven Spielberg's reaction was swift and direct. Within five days, he had prepared and sent a private letter to China's President, Hu Jintao, calling on China to "change its policy toward Sudan and pressure the Sudanese government to accept the entrance of United Nations peacekeepers to protect the victims of genocide in Darfur."[18] The Spielberg letter did not mention the Farrows' op-ed, but invoked it in saying he had "recently come to understand fully the extent of China's involvement in the region and its strategic and supportive relationship with the Sudanese government." The letter is direct and unequivocal in asserting Spielberg's concerns: "I believe there is no greater crime against humanity than genocide. I feel strongly that every member of the world community has a moral and ethical responsibility to act to prevent such crimes, to eliminate the conditions in which they are bred and to combat them wherever they exist. . . . There is no question in my mind that the government of Sudan is engaged in a policy which is best described as genocide."

The final draft of the letter did not explicitly state what Mr. Spielberg would do if China failed to act, but resigning from his role as an artistic advisor to the Games was certainly the message. This message was explicitly delivered by Spielberg spokesman Andy Spahn in statements to the press in late July, which produced a spate of stories headlined, "Spielberg May Quit Post."[19]

## CHINA RESPONDS

The first sign that Spielberg's letter might be having an effect on China was noted by Helene Cooper in the *New York Times* on April 13, 2007, in a story headlined "Darfur Collides with Olympics, and China Yields." She reported that in the preceding week "[a] senior Chinese official, Zhai Jun, traveled to Sudan to push the Sudanese government to accept a United Nations peace-keeping force."[20] Zhai also visited Darfur to tour three refugee camps, which the *Times* called "a rare event for a high-ranking official from China." According to Cooper, "Credit goes to Hollywood—Mia Farrow and Steven Spielberg, in particular." She cited the "crucial role" played by Farrow's campaign "to label the Games in Beijing the 'Genocide Olympics,'" and her op-ed with its warning to Spielberg, prompting him to write his letter to President Hu.

More evidence that the Farrow op-ed and the Spielberg letter were having an effect came on July 31, with China's vote in the Security Council in favor of sending a UN peacekeeping force to Darfur with 26,000 soldiers and police, making it the world's largest peacekeeping effort. Significantly, the unanimous resolution was passed with enforcement authority under UN Chapter 7, an essential element that allows the force to protect itself and civilians in the violent region of Darfur, and a necessary feature for governments to be willing to contribute military and police personnel to the force.

China's vote represented a reversal of its policy of complete support for Sudan in opposing UN peacekeepers, and the position it took a year earlier when it threatened to veto Security Council Resolution 1706 authorizing such a force unless it was conditioned on requiring Sudan's consent. Darfur campaigners initially praised China's movement and credited it to Spielberg's letter. But hopes that 26,000 peacekeepers would soon be on the ground in Darfur began to fade as months passed with Sudan still stalling on various conditions needed to dispatch the force.

Responding to the growing frustration of the Darfur campaign community, Spielberg sent a second letter to Hu Jintao on November 15, 2007, telling him that "Sudan is continuing to defy the international community, creating obstacles to the deployment of peacekeepers, increasing violent campaigns against Darfuris and expelling humanitarian officials essential to the very survival of millions of desperate citizens." The letter noted that while "China's earlier efforts were encouraging, its silence in the wake of Sudan's recent actions and the resulting chaos on the ground has been disturbing." Spielberg asked President Hu to "urge Sudan to accept - and rapidly facilitate" the UN peacekeeping force.

On February 12, 2008, Steven Spielberg finally announced he was withdrawing from the Olympics. In a statement he noted that "while China's representatives have conveyed to me that they are working to end the terrible tragedy in Darfur, the grim realities of the suffering continue unabated," and said that "my conscience will not allow me to continue with business as usual." Darfur campaigners had expected him to withdraw and had already begun to shift their attention to the major multinational corporations that are sponsoring the Olympics.

## LESSONS FOR GLOBAL BUSINESS

The Genocide Olympics episode marked the beginning of a period that will see many similar initiatives aimed at business, with human rights advocates and campaigners taking advantage of the 2008 Games to push their agendas on both China and corporate social responsibility.

Encouraged by the success of the Genocide Olympics campaign, Darfur campaigners are also turning up the heat on companies sponsoring the 2008 Games. So are campaigners for a seemingly limitless number of other causes: freedom for Tibet; freedom of association for the Falun Gong movement; child labor, mine safety, and the rights of workers to organize; press freedom; treatment for HIV victims and other health issues; the persecution of human rights advocates and legal defenders; air pollution in Beijing and other environmental issues. The list goes on.

This creates a perfect storm for global companies doing business in China, and particularly corporate sponsors of the Olympics: long-standing abuses, resolute campaigners and the global spotlight thrown by the Beijing Games. What is the best approach for these companies, particularly in light of the Genocide Olympics episode? Here are three suggestions.

*First, understand that the ground is shifting, and that global businesses can no longer expect to get away with ignoring the Chinese government's abuses.*

The effect the Spielberg letter had in moving Chinese authorities to shift position on Sudan is compelling evidence that the world's most impregnable power is beginning to care about its international image, and that external pressure can work. Thus expect advocates and campaigners to press even harder on global businesses to speak up. The Farrows' "Genocide Olympics" op-ed did not just exhort Steven Spielberg—it also called on the corporate sponsors of the 2008 Games to raise their voices to push China to act on Darfur. Where do the companies named in the Farrows' op-ed—Johnson & Johnson, Coca-Cola, General Electric and McDonald's—stand on these issues?

Three of these companies are quoted in a June 21 *BusinessWeek* story reporting that "activists upset by Beijing are turning up the heat on sponsors of the 2008 Games."[21] Two of the companies told *BusinessWeek* they had no position on China and Darfur. According to Coca-Cola, the company "does not have a role in the internal policy decisions of sovereign nations such as China and Sudan." McDonald's said that "the Olympics are not the right forum for discussing Darfur." General Electric pointed out that its foundation has given US $2 million to fund humanitarian efforts in Sudan. That seems like a lot of money, but *BusinessWeek* points out that a corporate sponsor can pay "as much as US $80 million for one Winter and one Summer Olympics."

Corporate support for Darfur relief efforts is important, but the "it's none of our business" attitudes are woefully out of date. It is useful to remember the 1994 statement of the Royal Dutch/Shell spokesman when he was asked about the threat of Nigeria's military regime to hang Ken Saro Wiwa and eight other Ogoni tribe members who had campaigned against environmental depredation in tribal lands where Shell was operating. The hanging, he said, was not appropriate "for private companies to comment on." In 1999, after years of consumer and shareholder-driven campaigns against Shell for its indifference to the hangings, a much enlightened Shell Chairman, Mark Moody-Stuart, articulated the modern standard of corporate behavior in the global economy: "The demands of economics, of the environment and of contributing to a just society are all important to a global commercial enterprise to flourish."[22] In short, global business no longer gets a "pass" on these issues—it is no longer acceptable for a Rupert Murdoch or a Gerald Levin to check principles at the Chinese border on the theory that China is immovable and the needs of companies to do business there demand it.

Some prominent companies doing business in China are adopting a principled approach by speaking out on human rights issues that concern their stakeholders. In April 1999, the chief executive officers of three large US-based companies doing business in China—Paul Fireman of Reebok International, Robert Haas of Levi Strauss, and Bruce Klatsky of Phillips Van Heusen—took the bold step of writing a letter to China's President, Jiang Zemin, requesting an opportunity to meet with him to discuss workers' rights. They were concerned about the inability of workers making their products in China to freely exercise their rights to free association, expression and assembly—rights that do not presently exist in China.[23] Citing commitments in their company codes of conduct to respect the rights of these workers "to organize and to bargain collectively," the letter bluntly pointed to reports that the government was preventing workers from exercising these rights, which jeopardized the ability of US companies to continue doing business in China: "These include reports about the arrest and detention of Chinese citizens for attempting peacefully to organize their fellow workers or to engage in non-violent demonstrations concerning the conditions of their employment. These reports have caused a number of our stakeholders to once again question whether it is appropriate to continue to produce products in China."

Sending the letter did not cause the sky to fall on any of the companies, as some insiders (mostly lawyers) predicted it would. No local executives were kicked out of China on trumped-up charges, no orders were mysteriously "lost" or delayed, there were no threatening visits to local offices or factories by the Security Bureau. Although the chief executive officers' letter did not open the door to allow workers to organize independent labor unions in China, it did contribute to a more open discussion of workers rights in China. This opening has in turn led to small but important steps toward reform, such as elections of independent worker committees in some foreign-owned factories. As the CEOs' letter to Jiang Zemin showed, with resolve, global companies can do business in China without having to abandon their principles to do so.

*Second, expect something to happen in China that will put global business on the spot.*

Although many human rights groups openly opposed Beijing's bid to host the 2008 Olympics, they simultaneously had their fingers crossed that China would be selected because of the opportunity to shine a spotlight on one of the world's darkest corners for human rights abuse. Ahead of the Games, advocates and campaigners will be doing everything they can to focus that spotlight squarely on the lack of fundamental rights and freedoms in China.

Advocacy groups have begun issuing reports and press statements to raise the visibility of issues that concern them. The New York and Hong Kong–based Chinese advocacy group Human Rights in China has launched a project called Incorporating Responsibility 2008, which during the run-up to the Olympics is tracking China's progress in respecting freedom of expression and information, civil and political rights and economic, social and cultural rights.

Because of China's public promises that journalists could report freely, one issue already in the forefront is press freedom. In August 2007, two prominent advocacy groups marked the twelve-month period running up to the opening ceremony by issuing well-documented reports charging that China had broken its promises to ease restrictions on journalists. Human Rights Watch released *You Will Be Harassed and Detained*, a report detailing how the Chinese government is violating commitments it made to the IOC on media freedom by continuing to harass, intimidate and detain foreign journalists and their local colleagues. On the same day, the Committee to Protect Journalists issued *Falling Short*, a report urging Beijing to free twenty-nine imprisoned journalists and loosen the restrictions on local reporters. CPJ board chairman Paul Steiger, a *Wall Street Journal* editor-at-large, called on the IOC "to speak out and to encourage the government of China to live up to its commitments."

Some campaign groups will be more provocative in pushing issues. On August 6 in Beijing, French-based Reporters Without Borders unveiled an Olympic banner with the five Olympic rings styled as handcuffs, calling China "the world's biggest prison for journalists and cyber-dissidents." The Associated Press reported that earlier in the week the police detained participants for two hours at the scene of a Reporters Without Borders demonstration on a pedestrian bridge near where the Olympics planning committee was meeting.

Given the nature of the two sides—global campaign groups capable of potentially incendiary tactics and China's authoritarian government—the odds are that some event connected to the Olympics will provoke a repressive response from the government, involving possibly large-scale arrests or detentions, putting Olympic sponsors and other global businesses on the spot. Be prepared for it.

*Third, look for an opportunity to engage with your stakeholder critics.*

Companies with effective social responsibility programs have learned that an essential first step is opening a dialogue with stakeholder critics that are willing to engage with business. Campaign groups fall into two categories: those who rely on bashing business to make a point, and those who seek to engage with companies to address their concerns. A Darfur campaign group looking for opportunities to engage is Dream for Darfur, chaired by Mia Farrow and directed by Jill Savitt, one of the human rights community's leading media professionals.

In July 2007, Dream for Darfur wrote to the twenty-six official Beijing Olympics sponsors to suggest four ways they might help alleviate suffering in Darfur. These included directing private and public appeals to the Chinese government to act on Darfur, with a sample letter to President Hu Jintao; private and public appeals to the International Olympic Committee to engage with the Chinese government on the issue of Darfur; cosigning letters with other corporate sponsors; and signing a Corporate Sponsor Pledge to urge the Chinese government to use its leverage to persuade Khartoum to agree to an "international civilian protection operation for Darfur and a good-faith peace process well before the August 2008 start of the Games." Dream for Darfur also created an Olympic Sponsor Report Card to grade companies on how well they have demonstrated an understanding of the China-Darfur issue, and what they are doing about it. Its first Report card was released on November 26, 2007, and gave Ds and Fs to sixteen out of nineteen top 2008 Olympic sponsors. The highest grade—a C+—went to General Electric, because it contacted the International Olympic Committee about the crisis in Darfur, provided a point person on the issue, and has provided aid to Darfur relief efforts.

Each of the steps Dream for Darfur has suggested is a safe and sensible way for a company to be part of the 2008 Games while reducing the reputational risk that it is ignoring the human suffering in Darfur. Each of these steps would work equally well for companies to communicate other concerns about human rights abuses in China. And for companies uncomfortable acting alone, they should seek out other companies to join in collectively communicating their concerns to the IOC and the Chinese government, as did the three executive officers did who wrote to President Jiang Zemin about labor rights.

A single global company or individual doing business in China may not be able to change Chinese government policy. But expectations of corporate responsibility are changing, and today's stakeholders of global companies do expect them to at least communicate their concerns about government abuses, and where possible to work to end them. Anyone with a reputation worth protecting should heed these new standards and expectations while doing business in China.

# CHAPTER 16

# A Marathon Challenge to Improve China's Image

BY JOHN KAMM

*In November 2003, Zheng Bijian, an advisor to President Hu Jintao, addressed a group of Asian business and government leaders in the city of Hainan in southern China. In his speech, Zheng introduced the term "peaceful rise" ("heping jueqi"), to convey the image of a strong but nonthreatening China. One month later, both Hu Jintao and Premier Wen Jiabao used the term in official speeches. The Chinese leadership sees the Beijing Games as an ideal venue to project the image of a "peaceful rise," but these two words may not suffice to offset the image of another China indelibly represented by the photograph of one man facing a column of tanks in Tiananmen Square.* JOHN KAMM, *former president of the American Chamber of Commerce in Hong Kong, is the chairman of the Dui Hua Foundation, which he established in 1999. The Foundation's work on behalf of Chinese political detainees and human rights reform is based on the concept of dialogue ("dui hua") with the authorities. Kamm was given the Eleanor Roosevelt Award for Human Rights in 2001 and is a recipient of a 2004 MacArthur Genius award.*

In January 2005, the BBC released a 2004 poll of global attitudes toward world powers. Respondents in twenty-two countries around the world were asked whether a country's influence in the world was positive or negative. The poll found that much of the world viewed the United States as having a negative influence due in large part to reports of human rights abuses committed by

American troops in Iraq and Guantánamo. In contrast, China's "positive influence" numbers in a majority of countries polled were good, far better than those of the United States.

The finding attracted big headlines in the world's major newspapers. America's image was so bad that even China's was better. Professor Joseph Nye cited the poll in his pioneering work on China's "soft power"—the influence and attractiveness derived from the country's culture, development models, ideals and foreign policy. The numbers were pointed to as evidence of a successful campaign by China to enhance its standing in the world, at the expense of the United States, by projecting its soft power.

In the middle of 2005, the Chinese government, afraid of what it perceived as a plan on the part of the United States and its allies to foment a "color revolution," began an intensified crackdown on dissent and on the country's restive ethnic populations. Limited political reform stalled as did consideration of important legislative changes to the country's criminal justice system (with the exception of the use of the death penalty.) The Chinese government's most recent crackdown on dissent that began in 2005 dismayed many who had hoped China had turned a political corner.

At the same time that the Chinese government was jailing an increasing number of journalists and dissidents and quelling a rising tide of social protest—sometimes with deadly force—trouble for Beijing was brewing elsewhere in 2005. The *New York Times* columnist Nicholas Kristof—author of the introduction to this volume—and other journalists showed the world what genocide looked like in Darfur, and it wasn't long before the world's spotlight turned to China's involvement with the Sudanese government which was carrying out the genocide. The articles bolstered an international movement for Darfur that has targeted China and has given rise to a slogan hated by China's rulers: "The Genocide Olympics."

## CHINA'S BATTERED IMAGE

Sure enough, when the polls came out in early 2006, China's image had taken a hit. In the words of the BBC: "Views of China have deteriorated sharply over the past year. . . . Among twenty countries polled (in both 2004 and 2005), the number rating China mainly positively dropped from thirteen to eight, while those rating it negatively have risen from three to seven. On average, positive ratings of China have dropped nine points." The one-year drop in the percentage of people who viewed China's influence in the world was especially breathtaking in democracies which respect human rights. In France, China's "positive influence" rating dropped from 49 percent to 31 percent, in Italy it fell 20 points from 42 percent to 22 percent, in Canada, from 49 percent to 36 percent, and in Australia, from 56 percent to 43 percent. In India, those viewing China as having a positive influence in the world fell from 66 percent in 2004 to 44 percent in 2005 and in the Philippines the number was down from 70 percent to 54 percent. In South Korea, those viewing China's influence as negative rose from 47 percent to 58 percent.

In explaining the drop, BBC analyst Steve Kull commented, "Recent stories of a tightening of state controls appear to have hurt China's image in the world." In language that proponents of the "soft power" theory will understand, the world took a good look at China's ideals and much of the world didn't like what it saw.

In 2007 the BBC was able to report a stabilization of China's image, but China's average "positive influence" rating of forty represented a drop from forty-three in 2006 and forty-eight in 2005. In many countries, especially the Olympic powers, a majority of people saw China's influence in the world as negative.

FIGURE 1: IS CHINA'S INFLUENCE IN THE WORLD POSITIVE?

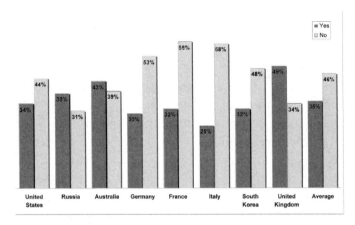

Source: BBC Poll samples of varying size, conducted November 2006 to January 2007

During 2007, a flurry of polls appeared on China's image in the world. (Most have gone unreported by the world's press, and proponents of China's rising "soft power" have chosen to ignore them.) The respected Pew Global Attitude Poll showed that opinions of China in countries as diverse as Lebanon and Spain dropped significantly over two years (2005 to 2007). In only one country—Nigeria—did China register a significant improvement in its favorability rating from 2006 to 2007.

In the Pew Poll, the percentage of Americans with a favorable opinion of China dropped from 52 percent in 2006 to 43 percent in 2007. But it was in the annual Harris Poll released in August 2007 that the damage to China's image in the United States was evident in the starkest terms. Harris reported that the percentage of Americans who considered China a friend or ally stood at thirty, down from forty-six a year before. The percentage of those who saw China as "not friendly" rose from 50 percent to 63 percent. Nearly one in four Americans saw China as an enemy, one of the highest percentages registered by Harris in recent years.

Of special concern to Beijing are the findings of a poll of international opinion towards major countries commissioned by the Chicago Council on Global Affairs. Samples in eighteen countries covering 56 percent of the world's population were asked "Do you trust China to act responsibly in the world?" Fifty-two percent of respondents said no, 38 percent said yes. But if the populations of Olympic powers—defined as the top ten medal winners in 2004 minus China—are considered, it turns out that 58 percent said no, China can't be trusted, and 38 percent disagreed.

FIGURE 2: DO YOU TRUST CHINA TO ACT RESPONSIBLY?

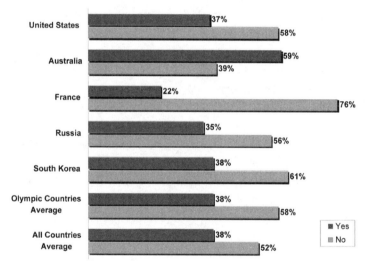

Source: Polling of samples in eighteen countries covering 56 percent of world population. Polls conducted from June 2006 to May 2007 by Chicago Council for Global Affairs.

The question of whether to trust China is a burning one in the United States, and three polls released in mid-2007 contain much bad news for China. According to a UPI/Zogby poll released in May, fewer than 4 percent of Americans believe that human rights reforms introduced prior to the Olympics will be long-lasting. An NBC News/*Wall Street Journal* poll released in July 2007 showed that 65 percent of Americans have little or no confidence that food produced in China is safe to eat. Shortly after that poll was released, a Zogby poll found that 82 percent of Americans are concerned about purchasing goods made in China, and that nearly two-thirds would likely participate in a boycott of Chinese goods until the country implements stricter safety regulations.

Poll numbers attesting to China's sinking popularity are known to be worrying to officials in Beijing charged with making sure the Olympic Games are seen as a great success around the world, the symbol of a peacefully rising China, a benign projector of soft power and a paragon of "harmonious society." The theory is simple. If a country has a poor international image, people, tourists as well as the folks back home, are less likely to be interested in watching a spectacle staged there. Throw in doping scandals, stories of toxic pollution and the probability that one's own athletes won't do well against the Chinese juggernaut, and the global audience at the 2008 Games could well be low, even lower than the audience for the Athens Games in 2004. In fact, the NBC News/*Wall Street Journal* poll published in July 2007 found that two-thirds of Americans had little or no interest in visiting China to see the Olympics. The number is probably much the same in the other Olympic powers.

## AN IMAGE MARRED BY HUMAN RIGHTS ABUSES

The problem of China's bad image revealed by polls of international opinion lies not with the Chinese people but with their government and its policies. When asked by UPI/Zogby in May 2007 if they had a favorable opinion of the Chinese people, 79 percent of Americans said yes. When asked about the Chinese government, an astonishing 87 percent had an unfavorable opinion.

It should also be noted that most of the polls cited above do not take into account the possible impact on China's image of the tainted products row and none of them measure the impact of Beijing's close association with the junta in Myanmar which ruthlessly suppressed monks who marched for freedom in September 2007. Neither of these developments will exert a positive pull on opinion toward China, and the potential for further damage is considerable. Indeed, it is likely that no country with an international image as negative as China's has hosted the Games in the postwar period, with the possible exception of the Soviet Union in 1980.

The experience of China since 2005 is further proof that a country's international image is directly related to how people in foreign countries view the government's policies on human rights—in other words, the country's ideals in practice. China's poor image in South Korea is in no small part the result of its repatriating North Korean refugees to deprivation and death, just as its image in Turkey has doubtless been affected by reports of China's assault on the Uighurs, a Turkic people, in Xinjiang. What Beijing is doing in Tibet, jailing teenagers for writing graffiti calling for independence, demonizing the Dalai Lama and abrogating to itself the power to appoint lamas, has not helped China's image in India, a deeply spiritual country that has traditionally been Tibet's best friend in Asia.

While the drop in China's image can be tied to its human rights policies at home and abroad, it is also the case that unease over China's trade practices and expansive military spending have been contributing factors. According to the May 2007 UPI/Zogby poll, Americans by large majorities blame China for the trade deficit, the loss of jobs in manufacturing, the tightening of energy supplies, and the worsening of global pollution. So troubled are Americans about China that 62 percent favor restrictions on Chinese imports and 67 percent oppose US companies opening more factories in the country. The 2007 Pew Global Attitudes Survey found that majorities in Italy, France, South Korea, the Czech Republic, Germany, Mexico and Morocco view China's economic growth as a bad thing for their country.

As 2007 closed, there were few signs that China's poor reputation would trigger calls for boycotting the Olympic Games. (The UPI/Zogby poll released in May 2007 showed that almost 80 percent of Americans oppose boycotting the Games versus roughly 10 percent who favor a boycott.) Nevertheless, China's links to the Sudanese regime and the Burmese junta have triggered boycott calls from leading politicians in Europe (in the 2007 French presidential election, two of the three leading vote getters voiced support for boycotting the Games over Darfur) and the United States (where presidential candidate Bill Richardson has spoken in favor of a boycott over Darfur and Senator John Kerry has issued a warning over Burma). In the US House of Representatives, members of Congress have introduced resolutions calling for a boycott of the Olympics and parliamentarians in Scandinavia are debating whether or not to send athletes to the Games.

## QUEST FOR A GOOD GLOBAL IMAGE

If China weren't hosting the Olympics in 2008, it could thumb its nose at world opinion, but in a classic case of being careful of what you wish for, China now has little choice but to take steps to help improve its global image. The Communist Party leadership has decided that not only will the Games be a success in terms of the country's medal haul but that the Games will be seen as a success by people around the world. Led by Chairman Hu Jintao, senior leaders at the 17th Party Congress held in October 2007 exhorted the rank and file to "do a good job" on the Olympics, preparations for which will cost China more than US $2 billion. In a tacit acknowledgement that China needs to improve its international image, Hu told a meeting of party propagandists held in Beijing in January 2008 that "We should work hard on overseas propaganda to further display and improve a positive state image."[1]

Since 1990, when China devised a plan for maintaining its trade status in the United States, Beijing has made human rights concessions to achieve foreign policy goals. To maintain "Most Favored Nation," a preferential trade status, gain entry to the World Trade Organization, and deflect criticism of its human rights at the UN, Beijing has released prisoners and provided information on others, agreed to bilateral human rights exchanges and talks with foreign countries on such topics as parole for counterrevolutionaries and jamming of foreign radio broadcasts. The Chinese government has also signed a prison labor memorandum of understanding with the United States and increased access by international observers to the country's prisons and detention centers.

True to form, a number of moves took place to suggest that China's leadership acknowledges the need to improve the country's human rights profile for a successful Olympics. The NBC News/*Wall Street Journal* poll cited above reveals that Americans think that the most important thing China can do in the run-up to the Olympics is to improve its human rights record—well ahead of cleaning up the environment and practicing fair trade. Beijing appointed a special envoy to deal with the Darfur issue, and became the first Permanent Member of the UN Security Council to send military personnel to Sudan to support the joint UN–African Union peacekeeping force. The Darfur special envoy declared that China would halt new investments in Zimbabwe. While opposing strong sanctions, China criticized the crackdown in Burma, called for democracy (!) and successfully pressured the junta into agreeing to receive the UN's envoy on Myanmar (the junta's new name for Burma). It cracked down on manufacturers of shoddy export goods and reached an agreement with the United States on strengthening standards.

On the domestic front, the power to approve executions was returned to the Supreme People's Court in January and reports in the official press by mid-year pointed to a significant drop in the number of executions. The number for the full year is likely to drop by at least 30 percent to a still-horrifying number of 4,000–5,000. The drop was pushed along in September 2007 with the publication of a notice by the Supreme Court ordering that death sentences should be given for only the most serious crimes, and that courts should make more use of a unique feature of the Chinese justice system—death sentence with two-year reprieve. (About 99 percent of people sentenced to death with two-year reprieve have their death sentences commuted to life or a fixed term of imprisonment after the two years are up.) In October 2007, the Chinese government limited the transplant of organs from executed prisoners to family members. If enforced, this new regulation will drive the number of executions down even more. For many years, organs from executed prisoners were used in the great majority of transplants in the country, most for the benefit of foreigners.

In a sign that relations are thawing, Roman Catholic bishops approved by the Vatican have been installed by China's government-controlled Catholic Patriotic Association. Though little progress was achieved, talks between the government and representatives of the Dalai Lama resumed in July 2007 after a hiatus of nearly eighteen months.

## CORRELATION BETWEEN RIGHTS REFORMS AND IMPROVED IMAGE

It remains to be seen if these limited moves will help improve China's image to the point where the success of the 2008

Olympics is ensured. After all, China is still the world's number-one executioner and it remains the chief supporter of reviled regimes in Sudan, Zimbabwe, Burma and North Korea. Hu Jintao, before coming to power, decried the use of prisoner releases to appease foreign governments and public opinion, and since 2005 few political prisoners have benefited from sentence reductions or parole. Yet Chinese diplomats recognize that the large number of well-publicized releases of political prisoners in the three years from early 2002 to early 2005 helped fuel the improvement in China's image that topped out in 2005. If Beijing is to recover at least some of the ground lost since then, it will need to return to the practice of releasing political prisoners before the end of their sentences, preferably in large numbers as the result of amnesties for the remaining counterrevolutionaries and those still in prison for the 1989 political protests in Beijing and hundreds of other cities.

Unfortunately, there has been no let-up in the campaign to suppress dissent and stifle protest. In an especially poignant case, Yang Chunlin, a dissident and community leader in northeast China, was detained in August 2007 for circulating a petition entitled "We want human rights, not the Olympics." Yang's trial on February 19, 2008 lasted less than a day. On March 24, 2008, he was sentenced to five years in prison—the maximum term in these circumstances—for "incitement to subvert state power."

Release of political prisoners should be part of a concerted effort to shift the country's soft power projection away from developing countries in Africa and Latin America (a strategy eerily reminiscent of China's courting of the "Third World" in the 1960s and 1970s) to developed countries with populations that celebrate both sports and respect for human rights. For European audiences, Beijing should release detailed statistics documenting the drop in executions, holding out the promise of even greater drops in the years ahead, with the ultimate aim of abolishing the death penalty. Nothing would help China's image in South Korea more than if Beijing could work out an arrangement whereby North Korean refugees were given shelter and not sent back across the border. Normalizing relations with the Vatican and allowing the Dalai Lama to return for a personal visit to Tibet would be very popular with large audiences in the West and Asia.

To counter the distrust toward China prevalent in many countries around the world, it is vital that Beijing scrupulously honor the promises it made to win the 2008 Olympics. Anyone who wants a visa to watch the Games should be granted one, regardless of whether they're on a blacklist or not. And journalists should be allowed to go wherever they want and write on any subject they choose. If China wants to improve its image, a good place to begin would be to stop beating, harassing and jailing journalists, during the Games and beyond.

# CHAPTER 17

# Clearing the Air

BY CHRISTINE LOH

*China's fast-paced economic growth over the last few decades has been achieved at high cost in terms of environmental damage, including air pollution. Mindful of the potential negative public relations from globally televised images of a smoggy Beijing and gasping athletes, Chinese authorities have belatedly undertaken corrective measures. But only a genuine commitment to the long-term welfare of its own citizens and to enhanced transparency will give the Chinese government a chance of truly "clearing the air."* CHRISTINE LOH *is the founder and chief executive officer of Hong Kong–based public-policy think tank Civic Exchange, a former elected legislator, and cochair of the Board of Human Rights in China. She has worked in many areas, including law, business, politics, media and the nonprofit sector, but is best known as a leading voice in public policy in Hong Kong, particularly in environmental protection.*

"The nation is broken but mountains and rivers are still there." (国 破 山 河 在)
—TANG DYNASTY POET, DU FU (AD 712–770)

"The nation is still there but mountains and rivers are broken." (国 在 山 河 破)
—AN OBSERVATION WHICH COULD BE MADE ABOUT MODERN CHINA (AD 2008)

After decades of downplaying environmental concerns relative to economic development, the Chinese government is at last prioritizing the environment. With the international profile of hosting the Olympics, air pollution has become a signature challenge. Drinking water can be purified and bottled water can be imported. The recent food safety scare can be overcome by better inspection and at a push, food could be imported for the more than 10,000 athletes.[1] The extent of China's own water and soil degradation is serious but for the duration of the Games, can be handled. However, athletes cannot compete carrying oxygen tanks. The Games will be marred if dense smog reduces visibility and television screens around the world show a highly polluted Beijing. Moreover, athletes gasping can only lead to poor performance and fewer records broken.

Beijing has called on Chinese and international air quality scientists to help clean up. The data collection, analysis, modeling and meteorological forecasting being done by experts from a variety of disciplines are helping policy makers to base their strategies on hard evidence. Over the course of the past two years, pollution control measures are also being tested and fine-tuned. The entire experience is the largest collaborative air quality science project ever in China, the results of which will be extremely useful to help clean up air pollution in other parts of the country. It should not be overlooked that the city of Guangzhou in south China, not far from Hong Kong, will host the Asian Games in 2010, and Shanghai will host the World Expo lasting 184 days in the same year. The learning curve from the Beijing Olympics on air-quality management will not be wasted—it could help to improve the health of hundreds of millions of people. It should also help to push the authorities to ensure laws and regulations are not only passed but implemented and rigorously enforced. Environmental improvement will also reduce the Chinese government's contingent liability on public health cost in the longer run.

## BEIJING'S PLEDGES IN BIDDING FOR THE GAMES

In preparing its bid for the Games, Beijing pledged that the city's environmental plans and actions would leave behind "the greatest Olympic Games environmental legacy ever." Moreover, "air quality is expected to be within World Health Organization (WHO) standards at all venues, and in Beijing generally."[2] In April and May 2007, when the Canadian soccer team was playing in Beijing, team members reported breathing problems. The city's air quality was eight times worse than that in downtown Toronto over the same period, according to Canadian Olympic Committee meteorologists, and very much worse than WHO air quality guidelines.[3]

As of August 2007, Beijing's air quality remained far off the mark. With one year to countdown, Jacques Rogge, president of the International Olympic Committee acknowledged that Beijing's air pollution could force the postponement or delay of endurance sports like cycling and the marathon.[4] A page-one article in the *New York Times* on August 26, 2007, was titled "As China Roars, Pollution Reaches Deadly Extremes," and included a map which attributed to Beijing and nine provincial capitals a level of air pollution three times as high as in Los Angeles. However, the 2008 Beijing Olympics Games will have to proceed even if the city's air quality does not improve substantially, as there is no alternative. The pressure to understand the nature and origin of the pollution is going to become a focus of intense national and international interest. Those who are working hard on cleaning up hope Beijing's trials and tribulations will not only produce the necessary short-term results, but also lead to a longer-term improvement of air quality management in China.

Dealing with air pollution was always going to be a hard challenge for Beijing, but China's rapid industrialization and urbanization have exceeded all estimates since 2001, resulting in massive consumption of fossil fuels and vast quantities of polluting emissions. Despite many efforts to clean up Beijing, the problem has been hard to crack. No doubt, the authorities believed they could do it when they prepared their bid for the

Games. Indeed, everyone including nongovernmental organizations wanted Beijing to succeed and leave behind a legacy of a cleaner environment, which would be to the long-term benefit of the Chinese people. By successfully cleaning up, Beijing would also set a positive example for other cities across China to protect the environment and improve public health. However, air pollution remains very bad today and renewed efforts are necessary in a final push over the remaining months.

## BEIJING'S CHALLENGING ECOLOGICAL CONDITIONS

The municipality of Beijing has a total area of 16,800 square kilometers of which 1,040 square kilometers fall within the urban planning area, which has 7 million residents (50 percent of the population), 80 percent of its buildings, and consumes about 60 percent of the city's energy usage. In other words, within a relative small area, there are high levels of emission-generating activities. August in Beijing can be extremely hot, with daytime temperatures in the upper nineties Fahrenheit, or more. The city's annual average precipitation is less than twenty inches with about 75 percent falling between June and August. The summer months can be uncomfortably humid. Moreover, Beijing is surrounded by mountains in the west, north and northwest. Summer winds from southerly directions carrying pollution from far away can get trapped by the surrounding mountains.

The mix of heat, humidity, pollution and windless conditions can create a thick smog soup. The massive four-day vehicle limitation test in August 2007, when more than a million vehicles were taken off the road, only managed to cut vehicle emissions and improve air quality slightly but it represented an important learning exercise for Beijing. Government officials said, "If we had not had the traffic controls we could not have maintained this level because the temperature and humidity were very high. So we see the restrictions worked."[5] These undesirable conditions have been described by physiologists as "borderline hazardous" for endurance sports. There is an immediate impact on an athlete's performance. For example, nitrogen dioxide, sulfur dioxide, and particulate matter cause exercise-induced asthma and "airway hyper-responsiveness," either of which can suddenly strike athletes with no history of susceptibility. Ozone has similar effects and is tricky to predict because its formation depends on sunlight and heat. Sulfur dioxide burns the eyes, with implications for sports like shooting and archery. All these effects are aggravated by high respiration rates.[6]

With the IOC chasing Beijing Olympics officials for contingency plans, a new package of measures was announced in August 2007. The latest plan divides the pre-Games preparation process into three stages—pre-February 2008, February to May 2008, and June to August 2008—with different tasks assigned to each period. The plan includes specific measures to improve air quality during August 2008, such as reducing the number of vehicles on the road during the Games, eliminating dust from construction sites and cutting industrial emissions. Beijing's neighboring cities and provinces, particularly Tianjin, Shandong, Hebei, Shanxi and Inner Mongolia must join in the efforts. For instance, construction sites that might spread dust should be closed down at the end of 2007 and not be reopened until after the Games have finished. Petrol stations that would not have installed vaporization equipment by June 2008 will be shut down. Factories will be asked to either stop production or reduce output. There is also an emergency plan if pollution is high during the Games. That plan includes an even wider ban on vehicles, giving people extra holidays so they do not need to travel to work, shutting down even more factories, as well as shooting chemicals into the air to seed rain so as to damp down pollution and hopefully clear the skies.[7]

From China's first unsuccessful Olympic bid in 1993, through its success in 2001, convincing the IOC that Beijing could clean up its environment was critical to winning the prize to host the Olympics. In 1993, Beijing lost to Sydney, with an important aspect of Sydney's bid highlighting an environmentally friendly experience. In 2001, Beijing finally beat Paris and Toronto to play host in 2008, promising a "Green Olympics" which would promote sustainable development. The city's "green" bid was jointly endorsed by the Beijing 2008 Olympic Games Bid Committee, the Beijing Municipal Environmental Protection Bureau and more than twenty nongovernmental environmental organizations.[8]

The Beijing Sustainable Development Plan committed the city to spend US $12.2 billion on many projects, including twenty key projects and various anti-pollution measures, such as preventing coal burning pollution by retrofitting power plants with scrubbers.[9] Natural gas pipelines and storage tanks would be constructed for natural gas usage, electricity distribution would be improved, the city's power supply structure would be upgraded, vehicular emission standards would be tightened, and thousands of taxis and buses would be powered by natural gas. Beijing would speed up the development of facilities for treatment and dumping of domestic waste, and improve sewage systems and urban waterways. There would also be energy efficient street lighting. In the area of ecological protection, major forestation projects would be undertaken in the mountain and plains areas surrounding the city, as well as in the "three rivers and two sandbanks" (namely the Yongding River, the Chaobai River, the Dasha River, Kangzhuang in Yanqing County, and Nankou in Changping) in order to reduce the effects of sand storms in Beijing. According to the plan, massive greenbelt of trees surrounding the entire metropolitan area would be developed. Urban forestation and beautification projects would be implemented throughout the city with the goal of 45 percent greens coverage in Beijing proper.

Also, there would be a push to move hundreds of factories and plants operating within the city center to surrounding areas, the most famous being Shougang, the city's famous steel mill.

## AN AMBITIOUS OLYMPIC ACTION PLAN

After winning the right to host the Games, Beijing worked on specific plans to fulfill its pledges. In 2002, it released the Olympic Action Plan, which foresaw that Beijing would become an "ecological city" and referred to improvements over the next five years that would lead to "pollution-free burning, geothermal-operated pumps, solar energy power generating, solar energy heating, fuel cells, and nanometer materials."[10] Indeed, many of the pledges have been carried out or are being put in place.

Even before 2001, Beijing had recognized the need to improve environmental conditions. From February 1998, Beijing published weekly Air Pollution Index (API) figures, and daily API figures became available the following year. China took note of a 1998 WHO study of 272 cities around the world that reported that seven out of the ten most severely polluted cities were in China. The nation's own evaluation showed two-thirds of the 338 Chinese cities for which air quality data were available were polluted, and two-thirds of those were moderately to heavily polluted.[11] Moreover, bad sand storms resulting from deforestation caught the attention of top Chinese leaders.

In 2000, the Standing Committee of the National People's Congress (NPC) approved sweeping amendments to the nation's Air Pollution Control law with the intent to improve enforcement, address critical air-quality problems in key urban areas and make broader use of market-based methods for cutting emissions. Penalties are stiffer, coverage is broader and lines of authority are clearer than before. The amendments reflect a shift in strategy from controlling the concentration of pollutants from particular sources to controlling the total volume of pollutants entering an airshed.[12] This revision in the law provided a new vision of the future direction of Chinese pollution control approach, even though the legislation left much to be dealt with by administrative regulations.

Ultimately the success or failure of new plans, laws and regulations depends on how effectively they are implemented and enforced, especially at the local level. Municipal environmental protection authorities, who bear the lion's share of enforcement responsibility in China, are more beholden to local governments than to the national State Environmental Protection Agency (SEPA), China's top regulatory body. Those local governments are often major shareholders of polluting enterprises, creating an inherent conflict of interest. Many local governments are also concerned about unemployment if they closed down polluting industries. China's enduring systemic problem is how to deal with local officials who ignore the law. The fact that even in Beijing and in its neighboring provinces, the government has not managed to clean up satisfactorily says a lot about how difficult the clean-up challenge has been.

By 2005, it had already become clear to Beijing that despite all its efforts more had to be done to clean up. Beijing called upon the help of the nation's top air quality experts to use science to better inform processes of air quality control and to identify how pollution generated from afar affects Beijing. Under the coordination of the Beijing Environmental Protection Bureau and Peking University, experts from Hong Kong, Taiwan, Japan, South Korea and Germany were also invited to help, dividing themselves into several teams using a variety of methods to collect data and analyze it, as well as to carry out modeling, and simulation exercises to understand how pollution can disperse or be transported a long distance, in order to gain in-depth understanding and insight. Meteorological analysis, data interpretation and weather forecasting were also done alongside tests on emissions. While emissions from power plants, chemical factories and steel plants in neighboring provinces remain problems affecting Beijing, evidence also showed that vehicular emissions in Beijing itself had become a major contributor to the city's air quality.

In 2006, a complementary project named CAREBEIJING coordinated testing among more than one hundred scientists, engineers and students from some twenty universities and institutes.[13] It was the largest ever atmospheric chemistry testing exercise done in China. The information collected provided a new foundation of understanding of the air quality problems affecting Beijing. It will be critical for Beijing to work closely with its neighboring provinces to limit emissions arising from their industrial activities if the nation's capital is to have a chance to enjoy better air-quality during the Games in 2008.

Armed with the knowledge that the city's own vehicular emissions must be controlled, it was clear that policy makers needed to know more about how tough they need to be to deal with the problem. Thus, in 2007, the science teams collected and analyzed data from the four-day vehicle limitation trial so that policy makers would have solid data to consider control strategies going forward in working out the new three-stage pre-Games preparation process. No doubt Beijing will need to roll out even tougher plans. As this book goes to print, scientists and policy makers in China are continuing to scrutinize new data to assist in the clean-up fight.

In many ways, the quality of Beijing's air has become the signature challenge for China's battle to improve the nation's environmental conditions. What is heartening is that policy makers have become directly engaged in trying to understand the science of air quality.

Working on evidence-based solutions is a step in the right direction. China's policy makers now understand just how complex the environment is. Those who are involved in the science are hopeful that these policy makers will want to continue the practice of evidence-based approaches. The insights gained from three years of intense testing, analyzing, verifying and modeling may well take China's understanding of atmospheric science a notch or two up. It is hoped that the data and information gained from the exercises will be shared after the Games are over so that a long-term plan can be devised to clean up pollution nationwide.

## WORRIED MARATHONERS, CYCLISTS AND TRIATHLETES

Meanwhile, athletes from around the world must prepare for poor air quality and take steps to minimize air pollution risks to their performance. Sports coaches are recommending unusual and even unprecedented measures, including the wearing of activated-charcoal face masks. Other tips include using over-the-counter ibuprofen or indomethacin to partially block pollution's lung-searing effects.[14] Athletes may also want to get exemptions from the IOC to use these drugs and other inhalers to stay clear of anti-doping rules. Coaches may well find living sites elsewhere in the region—Japan or South Korea, for example—and to wait until the last moment before flying the athletes into Beijing to compete. Several weeks in Japan or South Korea in the summer will help athletes to acclimatize to the heat and humidity. According to experts, American swimmers and track-and-field athletes set up bases in Majorca and Crete before the 2004 Athens Games in order to stay away from dirty urban air, and felt that the strategy helped them to win more medals than other US teams that did not do the same.[15]

There is much skepticism as to whether Beijing can substantially clean up the air before the Games, even with a Herculean effort. For example, Beijing must find a way to deal with old diesel trucks that are highly polluting. Armed with solid data, sports events can be more appropriately timed. For example, some events may be scheduled in the evening to avoid high ozone levels. In a visit to Beijing in August 2007, the president of the International Olympic Committee, Jacques Rogge, even indicated that some endurance events like the marathon might have to be postponed if the air pollution level was not brought down further by the time of the Games. Indeed, news stories are noting that the Beijing air poses a triple threat to marathoners, cyclists and triathletes: there are particulates like carbon monoxide and sulfur dioxide, pollutants to which some athletes might be allergic, and excessively high levels of heat and humidity.[16]

Most importantly, and with a long-term view beyond the Olympics, the Chinese authorities need to take a hard look at the environmental costs of meeting Premier Wen Jiabao's target of quadrupling the Chinese gross domestic product by 2020. Sixteen of the world's twenty most polluted cities are Chinese. One quarter of China's territory—including vast expanses of agricultural land—is exposed to the acid rain caused by sulfur dioxide emissions.[17] The time for action is now.

Some Chinese officials have spoken up: Pan Yue, a vice minister of China's State Environmental Protection Administration said in 2005, "The [economic] miracle will end soon because the environment can no longer keep pace." China can clean up but genuine and sustainable environmental progress will require the type of long-term strategy, central coordination, and determination the Chinese government brought to another massive effort: winning the right to host the Olympic Games.

PART IV

# THE POLITICAL BACKDROP
# OF THE BEIJING GAMES

# CHAPTER 18

# Modern Games, Old Chinese Communist Party

## BY BAO TONG

*The Beijing Games will be held in thirty-seven venues across China. The cost of just six of these venues—among them the National Stadium (or "Bird's Nest") and the National Aquatics Center (or "Water Cube")—is expected to total some US $2.5 billion. The venues will dazzle with state-of-the-art technology such as computational fluid dynamics simulations designed to calculate temperature and airflow speeds. But this modern image the China government seeks so hard to project is just one side of the coin. The other side is the authoritarian political culture inherited from the founding days of the Chinese Communist Party. BAO TONG is a former Director of the Office of Political Reform of the Chinese Communist Party Central Committee and Political Secretary to Premier Zhao Ziyang, the highest-ranking official to offer support for the Tiananmen Square democracy movement in 1989. Bao Tong was arrested for his support of the Tiananmen Square demonstrators. Officially charged with "revealing state secrets and counter-revolutionary propagandizing," he was sentenced to seven years in prison plus deprivation of his political rights for two years. He has been under virtual house arrest since his release in 1996, but continues to address the need for reform from his home in Beijing.*

What makes the Beijing 2008 Summer Olympics different from previous Olympic Games held in other countries? The answer is that no other government has been quite as eager to use the Games as a ploy to enhance its international prestige. The

Chinese government fervently hopes thereby to boost its domestic support and to regain people's trust.

The implied but highly effective message of a successful hosting of the Olympics would be that the anticipated rise in national prestige will be a result of the preservation of the Communist Party's authoritarian rule. It is this disproportionate internal political significance that creates an irony for the Beijing Olympics: it marries an event symbolizing international peace and cooperation with rising nationalism.

The current regime was founded in the pursuit of Communism, now a bankrupt ideology. Today the Chinese government continues to demand sacrifices from the majority of the people, but no longer in exchange for a future Communist society. Instead, the new purported goal is a stronger nation, one to be reckoned with on the international stage.

## A PYRAMID OF SACRIFICES

Yet the Chinese government's desire for improved international standing is, at present, essentially an aspiration of the elites. In contrast, the majority of the people, particularly in rural areas, are still overwhelmed by poverty, disease and economic insecurity. The glory of a nation will be beamed down via television to the rural millions who have sacrificed their well-being to pay for a half century of industrialization while seeing in their own futures little improvement from their ancestors. I hope the world will remember them and be reminded of their share in the pride. Yet, that hope is dim.

So far, what we have witnessed are the low wages paid to migrant construction laborers who work on the infrastructure projects that will serve the Olympics and the continued acquisition of land for new construction projects through administrative means without consultation or adequate compensation to the displaced. Unfortunately, these are not the first examples of government demands on the disadvantaged to pay for China's international image, nor will they be the last.

There is no doubt in my mind that any good fortune brought by the forthcoming international sporting gala has fallen only into the hands of China's ever-richer urban elites. The economic stimulant that has resulted in unconstrained government spending, huge infrastructure projects and the influx of foreign investment produces a few very rich people. In theory the "trickle down" effect should spread these benefits throughout the economy. But the growing income disparity in China suggests a systematic inequality fostered by a government whose motto could be "for the elites, by the elites and of the elites." The Olympic Games are the ultimate example of the kind of policies that end up serving only a small group of the population. When the shiny new buildings and temporarily clear skies of Beijing are displayed to the world at the 2008 Summer Olympics, let us not forget that they were built on a pyramid of sacrifices, made by people who are most likely to be carefully shuffled out of view for the event.

There is sadly little hope that the Beijing Games will push China any closer to an open society, though temporary permission has been given to foreign journalists to interview Chinese citizens without official sanction as of January 1, 2007, permission set to expire or be reevaluated upon the end of the Games. Since then, while rules have indeed been relaxed for foreign journalists, the crackdown on Chinese journalists and lawyers has continued unabated.

## HOPING FOR COLLECTIVE AMNESIA

The modernity of China that will be showcased during the hosting of the Olympics stands in stark contrast with the Chinese Communist Party's antiquated way of ruling. Too much of the government's legitimacy is based on misconceptions and historical untruths. To keep up its increasingly twisted and complicated version of truth, censorship and the systematic induction of mass memory loss has been necessary.

Will the enthusiasm of millions of Chinese television viewers captivated by the Games erase the dark memory of the government's crackdown on protestors in Tiananmen Square? No one knows for sure, but the Chinese government apparently thinks it can achieve this goal of collective amnesia. This explains why the government is so fixated on the hosting of the 2008 Games and also the reason for the international focus on what China's future role on the world stage will be beyond 2008. Using the Games as an instrument of propaganda can only serve the government to improve its image cosmetically in the short term, but it will help very little to resolve China's real problems in the long run.

China's true problems lie beyond the 2008 Olympics or any other showcase of success. After 50 years of major policy U-turns, the Chinese Communist Party has not delivered any kind of equality or basic universal social programs for education, medical care and economic security, though it did nationalize all lands and huge sectors of the economy during Mao's reign. Endless promises to the rural poor have been made and forgotten, while in fact their hard work ended up being siphoned off to build industries and modern cities. Government funds have built state-of-the-art sports complexes, opera houses and Internet firewalls, but have failed to build roads in the nation's poorest villages or keep the nation's social-security system from bankruptcy. On top of all that, there has been no progression of civil liberties, which is the only way adequately to address issues of injustice in an open and equitable way.

Deng Xiaoping has been credited for undoing Mao's policies, but he was also the one to come up with the inherently unjust idea of allowing elites to prosper through economic expansion. So far, no Chinese politicians have been able to systemically resolve or even reduce China's social injustice, despite lip service to the disenfranchised. The result is that the Chinese government is growing increasingly reliant on coercive powers to keep down the disgruntled while at the same time growing addicted to tactical cosmetic patches, such as hosting the Olympics.

# CHAPTER 19

# Democracy with Chinese Characteristics

BY MARTIN LEE

*A consistent theme in President Hu Jintao's speeches is the concept of "harmonious society" (和谐社会, or "hexie shehui"). Officially introduced during the 2005 National People's Congress, this slogan is designed to blend concepts of economic growth and social welfare. In February 2005, President Hu listed the virtues of a "harmonious society": democracy, the rule of law, equity, justice, sincerity, amity and vitality. Hong Kong was handed over from Britain to China in 1997, yet has long enjoyed the rule of law and basic freedoms. Today its citizens are fighting a vital battle for democracy in order to preserve these rights under Chinese rule.* MARTIN LEE CHU-MING *is an elected legislator and the founding chairman of the Democratic Party of Hong Kong. A barrister, Lee was appointed Queen's Counsel in 1979 and was chairman of the Hong Kong Bar Association. He was first elected to the Legislative Council in 1985 and has been overwhelmingly reelected in every election since. From 1985 to 1989, he served as a member of the Beijing-appointed Basic Law Drafting Committee to draw up Hong Kong's post-1997 constitution, until his expulsion from the body following the 1989 Tiananmen crackdown.*

In his speech to the 17ᵗʰ National Congress of the Chinese Communist Party, President Hu Jintao made a point of talking about "democracy." Party Congresses occur only once every five years, and in China's nondemocratic system, they are the way new leaders, cadres and directions for the party and the country are selected. So for those looking for clues to the future of China, the tea leaves of President Hu's speech were studied very closely. The word "democracy" was mentioned in President Hu's keynote speech no fewer than sixty-one times, leading to optimistic speculation that perhaps the tide of democracy might at last be seeping into the world's most populous country and largest remaining Communist state.

But what exactly do China's leaders mean when they say "democracy"? They mean democracy . . . "with Chinese characteristics." In short, elections Beijing can control. Of course, China has had little experience with genuine democracy, so to understand democracy with Chinese characteristics, it is useful to look at Hong Kong, our small but vibrant society that was transferred from colonial Britain to China on July 1, 1997.

On December 19, 1984, the Sino-British Joint Declaration was signed, setting out the terms of the resumption of sovereignty of Hong Kong to China. In this important treaty, the Chinese government pledged to the international communities and to Hong Kong people that our freedoms, "autonomy," and way of life would continue unchanged for fifty years.

## TRANSFERING SOVEREIGNTY . . . AND PEOPLE

Indeed, to reassure Hong Kong's jittery people, Deng Xiaoping famously promised us that under his "one country, two systems" policy, the "horse-racing and dancing" would continue without Communist interference. At the time, I thought his statement was insulting—as if these were the only freedoms Hong Kong citizens cared about. But of course Deng proved to be correct, and even prophetic, at least about the horse-racing: Hong Kong will host all equestrian events for China's Olympic Games.

Hong Kong's 7 million people were also promised "a legislature constituted by elections" and that all of our rights and freedoms would continue. These solemn guarantees were used to seek the support of the international and Hong Kong communities. Hong Kong people have had democratic elections for some seats in the Legislative Council since 1991, and we have a free press, an independent judiciary and a lively civil society.

China wanted to win the support of the international community for the handover of Hong Kong, so both the Joint Declaration and the Basic Law, Hong Kong's mini-constitution, envision a gradual process of democratization, with full democracy as the stated ultimate goal. Indeed, the Basic Law would have allowed the election of our chief executive in 2007 and of the entire Legislative Council in 2008 by universal suffrage. For more than a decade, public opinion surveys uniformly have shown that Hong Kong people want to participate directly in selecting their own leaders for both the legislative and executive branches. And that they believe democracy is necessary to protect basic freedoms.

But we did not have the hoped for elections in 2007, as Beijing overruled the wishes of the Hong Kong people, and used powers of "interpretation" to block that opportunity for democratic advancement. On December 30, 2007, the Chinese government through the Standing Committee of the National People's Congress blocked any democratic progress for at least another decade. In doing so, Beijing rejected poll after poll confirming the majority of Hong Kong people wanted full democracy by 2012. Now the earliest we will be able to choose our chief executive by popular vote is 2017, and we must wait until 2020 or later until there is any hope of a fully democratic legislature.

## WHY DOES DEMOCRACY MATTER TO HONG KONG PEOPLE?

Freedom and the rule of law are not just abstract theories to those of us who live in Hong Kong. Most Hong Kong families are only one or two generations away from escaping brutality and political upheaval in Communist China. Thus we understand that a free society protected by the rule of law will enable us to plan and lead our own way of life without arbitrary interference from the government, to become prosperous by our own hard work and to provide good opportunities for future generations. This is what enabled Hong Kong to become the eighth largest trading center in the world.

So when the Beijing-selected Hong Kong chief executive and Beijing put forward a bill that would roll back basic rights, including press freedom, religious freedom and freedom of association, the Hong Kong people demonstrated—literally—how much they value their freedoms, and their peaceful aspirations for democracy. On July 1, 2003, three-quarters of a million Hong Kong people took to the streets to protest against proposed national-security legislation, known as Article 23, and to demonstrate in favor of democratic elections. The number of people protesting—men, women and children—was one tenth of the entire population of Hong Kong. The chief executive, C. H. Tung, was forced to amend, then withdraw the bill. He was soon after forced by Beijing to resign due to "health problems," which is another way of saying that from Beijing's point of view, Mr. Tung totally mismanaged controlling Hong Kong by fanning the flames of people's democratic aspirations rather than pouring water on them.

For ordinary citizens in Hong Kong, this near-passage of a pernicious bill was a catalyst for recognizing that the freedoms we have long taken for granted could not be protected over the long term without democracy. For the Chinese leaders in Beijing, it was also a catalyst, and led to a change in policy where control of Hong Kong—and especially of our political system—became paramount. China took control of our political development through an "interpretation" of our constitution in 2004, and it appears that Chinese officials will try to keep control until they are sure that the pro-Beijing parties will win.

When they first arrived on the political scene, leaders President Hu Jintao and Premier Wen Jiabao won the admiration of many people in Hong Kong. They dealt with the SARS crisis (after being forced to admit to an earlier official cover-up which worsened the outbreak's spread) and in a speech to the Australian Parliament, President Hu asserted that the government was increasingly involving the Chinese people in decision-making and would take concrete steps to safeguard the legitimate rights of the people. President Hu said, "Democracy is the common pursuit of mankind, and all countries must earnestly protect the democratic rights of their people."

I couldn't agree more. After a decade of stability since China's resumption of sovereignty of Hong Kong and despite the latest setbacks for democracy, we still hope to embark on a path of mutual trust and cooperation with the Chinese leaders.

## A "SPECIAL POLITICAL ZONE"

In the early 1980s, when Deng Xiaoping wanted to roll back Communism and allow market forces to help the Chinese people rebuild their lives after the upheaval of the Cultural Revolution, the government created a revolutionary "Special Economic Zone" in Shenzhen, in southern China near Hong Kong. In a short two decades, by copying many of Hong Kong's free-market practices, this small village became a booming manufacturing metropolis, and by example led the way to other prosperous economic zones in China and practices in the country as a whole.

Deng called his reversal of Mao's deadly economic policies "socialism with Chinese characteristics." Deng's economic loosening in effect got rid of Communism in China by bringing in a market economy that has lifted millions out of poverty. But Deng wanted the fruits of democracy without the tree, and he left in place the Communist political controls that even he and his family had previously been victimized by.[1]

What China urgently needs now is a good example to follow of an open political system, with reforms to the rule of law and other key areas to sustain the market opening. For the time being, Chinese leaders obviously fear such a system. But I would encourage them to take a page out of Deng's visionary playbook and to make Hong Kong a "Special Political Zone," where we would be allowed the full democracy long promised to Hong Kong people—a test tube of sorts for expanding political reforms on the mainland.

For Hong Kong people, the crucial question is what kind of democracy will we have? Beijing's proxies in Hong Kong have suggested that an election where Beijing picks two candidates and then Hong Kong voters can choose between them would be acceptable. Certainly such an election would qualify as "democracy with Chinese characteristics" but it would not meet international standards, and would be an insult to Hong Kong's highly educated and sophisticated population, which is ready to select and elect their own leaders as China has promised since 1984.

## HONG KONG AND THE OLYMPIC GAMES

This should be possible, since Chinese rulers have promised to make these improvements anyway. In their pledges to the International Olympic Committee while bidding for the Games and since, China's leaders at all levels repeatedly assured the world that they would use the Games to go beyond improving the country's physical infrastructure.

"'By applying for the Olympics, we want to promote not just the city's development, but the development of society, including democracy and human rights,' Deputy Mayor Liu Jingmin, a key Olympic official, told the *Washington Post* in 2001. 'In the past few years, we've improved a lot. . . . There are fewer poor people, grass-roots democracy is developing bit by bit, and the media have more freedom and criticize the government regularly.' Then, Liu held out a tantalizing promise of what might happen if China gets the Olympics: 'Eight years is a long time. . . . If people have a target like the Olympics to strive for, it will help us establish a more just and harmonious society, a more democratic society, and help integrate China into the world.'"[2]

The Chinese government wants the world to see an open and tolerant China, and thus an opening should exist to encourage Beijing not to backslide on its promises, including those to Hong Kong.

One reason for optimism about the possibilities for progress in China is recent Olympic history. When South Korea bid for the 1988 Games, the country was a military dictatorship. Due in good part to the prospects for embarrassment and international engagement, the Olympics helped kick off an overdue peaceful political transformation in South Korea just six months before the launch of the Seoul Games. Since then, South Korea has endured as one of Asia's most stable and vital democracies. The parallels between South Korea and China are not exact, but the lesson is that the Olympics certainly present an opening to raise these issues in the context of the Chinese government's own promises.

In the United States and elsewhere, there are campaigns to boycott the Beijing Games over the Chinese government's trade with and support for regimes in Sudan and Burma. As a Chinese person, I would encourage backers of these efforts to consider the positive effects Olympic exposure could still have in China, including scrutiny by the world's journalists. This is certainly the time for Chinese leaders to step up and constructively use their clout in Asia and Africa. In so doing, Beijing should open a new chapter of responsible foreign policy and convince the world it is not oblivious to these issues.

Chinese people in Hong Kong and around the world are proud that China will host the Games. China has the world's fastest growing economy, and may indeed put on history's most impressive Olympic Games. But how does it profit our nation if it wins gold medals but suffers from the continued absence of democracy, human rights and the rule of law?

It is my hope that the Games will have a catalytic effect on the domestic and foreign policies of the Chinese government, and that the Chinese people will remember the Games long after they are held—not merely for medals won, but also because they were a turning point for human rights and the rule of law in China, and democracy in Hong Kong. That would be something worth cheering.

# CHAPTER 20

# Authoritarianism in the Light of the Olympic Flame

BY LIU XIAOBO

translated from Chinese by Tong Yi

*China has launched an unprecedented effort to make the Beijing Games the most successful in Olympic history. But a closer look at the country's history since 1949 reveals that each Communist leader has sought to skillfully exploit nationalist fervor, particularly through the staging of successful sports events, to enhance the regime's popularity and distract from its authoritarianism and lack of true legitimacy. LIU XIAOBO is a Chinese writer born in Changchun in 1955. Formerly a teacher at Beijing Normal University, Liu lives in Beijing, is the director of the Independent Chinese PEN Center, and has been honored by Reporters Without Borders as a "defender of press freedom."*

In April 2007, Beijing announced its grand plan for the Olympic Torch Relay. The official theme, "Harmonious Journey," was clearly meant as an indirect reference to the "harmonious society" advocated by President Hu Jintao soon after he assumed office in 2003. The planned relay will break many Olympic torch records, as the torch will cover the longest route and the broadest territory, reach the highest altitude (through the Tibetan Himalayas), and engage the largest number of participants. The torch will pass through twenty-two cities on five continents, as well as 113 domestic cities and regions throughout China. The route's inclusion of

Hong Kong, Taipei, and Macao is intended to symbolize the great "unity" of the Chinese ethnicity.

Words such as "the first," "the best," "the pride of Chinese around the world," "harmony," and "dream" frequently appeared in media reports and comments in mainland China regarding the torch relay. The official Beijing Olympic website states: "From March to August 2008, the world will focus on this route—the glorious Olympic torch will carry the spirit of the Olympics and the dream of the people around the globe, lightening the voyage of ancient civilizations and evolving into the brand new 'harmonious journey.'"

Yet these inspirational words mask a harsher reality—the authoritarian nature of the Beijing political regime. For the Chinese government, the Olympic Games are less about "harmony" than about promotional opportunities and huge financial gain. The slogan is "One World One Dream"—but the "dream" is that China will be recognized and accepted as a world player, with the world's attention focused on spectacular sports events rather than the continuing human rights abuses which every day cause suffering to thousands of ordinary Chinese citizens.

The 1936 Berlin Games—the first to stage a torch relay—illustrate the need for vigilance when a regime uses the Olympics for propaganda purposes. Adolf Hitler skillfully exploited the Games in a dual fashion: on the one hand, he sought to cover up his military buildup and intentions by presenting to the world the image of a peaceful, sports-loving nation; on the other hand, he used the Olympic stage to showcase Nazi theories of Aryan superiority. Hitler's gamble paid off like so many of the risks he took in his first years of power: an international boycott was averted, and Germany won the most medals in the Berlin Olympics—eighty-nine, far more than the fifty-six won by the second-ranked United States. The Berlin Games were the first Olympics where television was used, and were further glorified by Leni Riefenstahl's film *Olympia*.

Yet only three short years after the Berlin Olympics, Nazi Germany invaded Poland, thereby igniting the Second World War and the Holocaust. A few months before the 1980 Moscow Olympics, the Soviet Union invaded Afghanistan. This time, because the invasion flagrantly violated the Olympic spirit and the Berlin precedent was not forgotten, many countries boycotted the Moscow Olympics. Even China, which had just been readmitted as a participating nation, followed the lead of the United States and chose not to attend the Moscow Games. At that time, 147 countries were Olympic members; only eighty participated in the Moscow Games, nearly two-fifths of the member countries having decided to join the boycott.

In the early years of the twenty-first century, the most powerful authoritarian country in the world has won its bid to host the Olympics. No other city in Olympic history has matched Beijing's efforts in terms of propaganda, mass mobilization, investment and efforts to arouse nationalist fervor.

## A "HOT WOK" OF NATIONALISM

On July 13, 2001, Beijing's surprise victory over Toronto, Paris, Istanbul and Osaka was announced at a meeting of the International Olympic Committee in Moscow. In Beijing the news sparked massive rejoicing. That same evening, more than a million Beijingers poured into the streets to celebrate. Millions of people in other Chinese cities also stayed up all night to celebrate. With crowded streets, brandished flags, joyful tears, hoarse voices due to constant shouting, China instantly became a hot wok of boiling nationalism.

The top Communist leaders headed by Jiang Zemin made their way to Tiananmen Square to celebrate with the exhilarated masses. Slogans such as "realizing the dream of a hundred years," "the grand revitalization of Chinese," "the bankruptcy of

Western anti-China forces" were chanted throughout the night. This was sweet revenge after "the shame endured for more than a century" and "the sick man of Asia" derogatory label which instilled in many Chinese a sense of insecurity, coupled with the ambition to rise again.

The official Beijing launch ceremony for the one-year Olympic countdown on August 8, 2007, undoubtedly broke Olympic records in terms of investment, scale, and mass participation. On that morning, more than 1 million residents participated in the great morning exercise simultaneously taking place in ten parks, including Chinese Century Park and Yuyuan Park, as well as twenty other sites in Beijing.

From 7 p.m. to 9 p.m that evening, the Beijing Olympic Committee hosted a mass countdown celebration at Tiananmen Square. The top leaders in the Central Government and Beijing Municipal Government, the president of the International Olympic Committee, Olympic representatives from 205 countries, diplomatic luminaries, and main corporate sponsors for the 2008 Olympics all showed up for the event. Performances by domestic and international artists were telecast to China and the rest of the world.

A Beijing Olympic Committee spokesman explained the mass rejoicing by stating that the purpose of the Beijing Games was quite simply to allow modern China, inheritor of the wealth of the ancient Chinese civilization, to bring happiness to the world. The theme song "We Are Ready," performed by one hundred Chinese singers, expressed confidence in a successful Olympics.

Ever since the East clashed with the West in the 1840s, the empire that once considered itself the center of the world—the Chinese word for China is "Zhong Guo," or "Empire of the Middle"—was first defeated by the West, and then was conquered by Japan. The shameful "sick man of Asia" became a Chinese taboo. After the Communist Party took power, it used every social resource, including an appeal to nationalist sentiments extending to sports events, to buttress its dictatorship. By encouraging strong performances in sports, the regime sought to create the image of a "strong man of Asia" which would supersede the cliché of the "sick man of Asia," and thereby enhance its own popularity and legitimacy.

## NATIONALISM AS A TOOL FOR THE PARTY

In the Mao era, nationalism was distilled in a slogan, "From now on, the Chinese people stand up." This resurgence was manifested not only in the quest to become a nuclear power, but also in the realm of sports, in particular table tennis. When the Chinese table tennis team defeated the Japanese team in the 1960s, the victory left my generation with an indelible memory. The so-called "Ping-Pong diplomacy" would also play a famous role in paving the way for Nixon's historic visit to China in 1972.

In the Deng era, nationalism was embodied in the slogan, "Strengthening China." The formidable rise of the Chinese Women's Volleyball Team (CWVT), winner of the gold medal at the 1984 Los Angeles Olympics, was saluted by the Central Party Committee and by Chinese citizens from all walks of life. Even in academic centers such as Beijing University, students amended Deng's slogan to: "Strengthening China by learning from CWVT."

Following the Tiananmen massacre of June 4, 1989, the Chinese government faced mounting domestic and international pressure. Once again, the government turned to sports to whip up nationalist fervor and enhance its own popularity, while distracting from its lack of true legitimacy. The hosting of the 11th Asian Games, or Asiad, in 1990, was a successful step in this direction: China won a total of 341 medals, far ahead of South Korea and Japan which each garnered fewer than 200 medals.

Encouraged by this success, China engaged in an all-out effort in 1991–93 in bidding for the right to host the 2000 Olympics. However, the 1989 Tiananmen massacre was still fresh in the memories of most observers, and Beijing's bid was strongly opposed by the United States and several other countries.

In September 1993, Beijing lost out to Sydney in one of the closest votes in Olympic history. This was perceived by many Chinese as a stinging humiliation, and spurred a nationalist backlash which was perhaps best expressed in the 1996 bestseller *The China That Can Say No*. This book—a collection of essays by various authors—urged an uncompromising rejection of American values such as individualism, and excoriated the "pro-Western" stance of certain intellectuals such as the astrophysicist Fang Lizhi and journalist Liu Binyan. The book also renewed calls for war reparations from Japan, as a belated compensation for this country's actions in the Second Sino-Japanese War of 1937–45.

The party state's reliance on nationalism during the Jiang Zemin era from 1989 to 2002 was expressed by the slogans "Diplomacy of a Great Nation" and "the Grand Renaissance of Chinese Ethnicity," instead of Deng's "Strengthening China by Avoiding to Being Top Guns." The Jiang regime never passed up a chance to promote nationalism, which became more and more fervent. In 2001, the bid for the 2008 Olympics once again became a paramount goal for the government. The regime needed the bid to promote its own legitimacy, while the mass population wanted this chance to average the 1993 shameful failure. By mobilizing all resources, the Communist Party not only played its usually effective trade card when facing political pressure, but mobilized even more resources than for the earlier bid, hiring top international public relations companies to polish its image. This was a crucial factor, in light of China's dismal record in human rights, including freedom of speech. Behind such devotion to winning the bid was the fear of losing again.

The 2008 Olympics will be the most important event staged by the Chinese Communist Party since Hu Jintao's accession to power in November 2002. For Hu, the opportunity to host the Olympics is even more important than the 17th Congress of the Central Party Committee which took place in October 2007. No matter how fierce a fight to get into the top leadership, the party conference will not affect Hu's leadership. However, hosting a successful or unsuccessful Beijing Olympic Games will affect the political image of the current leadership—and even affect Hu's legacy in history. No doubt, to host an Olympic Games of unprecedented success is the prime political priority for the current regime, which mobilized all resources to seek the Games.

## PROPAGANDA MACHINE ON OVERDRIVE

Mindful of this scrutiny, the Chinese government has adopted a four-pronged approach to make the Beijing Games a dazzling success. First, the propaganda machine for the Olympic Games has been in full swing to drum up internal support. Since 2001 when Beijing won the bid, the mainland media have been encouraged to stir up nationalist fervor, for example through a multitude of Olympics-related special programs on government controlled television stations. Non-stop sports competitions and art performances have had Olympics related themes, while advertisements and billboards related to the Games are plastered in large and small cities throughout the country. Chinese athletes participating in international sports competitions need to talk about the Olympics if they wish to be perceived by the authorities as "politically correct."

Moreover, the government has mobilized its public relations machine to create a benign image. In November 2006, an unprecedented government-sponsored exhibition on human rights was held in the Beijing Cultural Palace for Nationalities. The exhibition was clearly geared to an internal audience, chronicling "human rights developments" in China since 1949, such as medical care programs in impoverished rural areas.

To burnish its image abroad, the government loosened the restrictions affecting foreign media for the first time, and the Committee to Protect Journalists—an American nonprofit organization which had opposed Beijing's bid—came to visit China.

At the opening ceremony of the International Sports Conference in Beijing in April 2007, Premier Wen Jiabao spoke of the Beijing Olympics as a means to present a democratic, open, civilized, friendly and harmonious China to the world.

China has invested unprecedented sums in preparing the Olympics. In August 2007, with one year to go before the opening ceremony, the total investment for the Beijing Games already reached US $40 billion. Major financial outlays are required for the implementation of the Chinese Sports Committee's "Olympic Honor" plan, which concerns an estimated 17,000 athletes, officials and coaches. The Committee's "119 blueprint" spells out China's objective of becoming the country with the most medals in 2008 by vastly exceeding the sixty-three medals won at the 2004 Athens Olympics, where China ranked second behind the United States which had garnered 103 medals.

Finally, to ensure social stability during the Olympics, the government is nipping any emerging sign of dissent in the bud. Law enforcement organs continue to abuse their power by tightly controlling the media—particularly domestic outlets—and Internet, constraining nongovernmental organizations as well as individual petitioners, and imprisoning people for merely exercising their inherent right to free speech. This of course is in complete contradiction with the second point mentioned above, whereby the authorities are seeking to create the image of a government genuinely concerned with human rights. In fact, the main international human rights organizations released reports as the one-year countdown to the Olympics began, alerting the world that the Chinese government had not honored its pledge to improve its human rights record.

## THE TRUE MEANING OF "ONE WORLD, ONE DREAM"

As the one-year countdown started, some voices of dissent were also heard within China. On August 8, 2007, forty-two Chinese liberal writers, scholars and rights defenders published an open letter addressed to President Hu Jintao and entitled "One World, One Dream, Equal Human Rights—Our Call for the 2008 Beijing Olympics." I signed this letter, along with the leader of "Tiananmen Mothers," Ding Zilin, journalists Dai Qing and Gao Yu, and the former top Communist Party official Bao Tong (who has also contributed a chapter to this book).

The open letter stated that "when the world focuses on China, the Chinese Government should realize its solemn promise to improve human rights." The reasoning was simple: "Without the protection of the human rights of all Chinese citizens equally— i.e., without abolition of the rural-urban residential control system, without an end to discrimination against women and sexual, ethnic, and faith minorities, and without ending the suppression of political dissent—it is senseless to talk about 'One Dream' for all of China." The letter called for basic rights reforms including amnesty for all prisoners of conscience and an end to the forced evictions and land appropriations undertaken to construct Olympic facilities.

The Beijing Olympics will probably benefit both the government, which will see its prestige enhanced if it delivers a spectacular and successful show, and the elite class which will be enriched by both the Olympic effect and the underlying corruption. Nationalist pride may swell in the short term, but the long-term interests of the Chinese and even the cause of peace will not be served. Unless the Chinese government can be per-

suaded to undertake meaningful human rights reforms, the flick-
ering hope for a truly better China could vanish once the flame of
the Olympic Torch has been extinguished.

# CHAPTER 21

# Dragons Win: The Beijing Games and Chinese Nationalism

BY EMILY PARKER

*Beijing literally means "northern capital," consisting of the Chinese characters 北 (bei, meaning northern) and 京 (jing, meaning capital). The red and white emblem of the Beijing Olympics, shaped liked a traditional Chinese seal, depicts a dancing figure cleverly based on the second character (jing). According to the official website of the Beijing Games, this logo is designed to "portray the feelings of friendly and hospitable Chinese people and expresses the sincerity of the city." This spirit of openness has not always been on display during previous sporting events, which instead often provided an outlet for Chinese nationalist fervor. Once released, patriotism turns out to be a difficult genie to stuff back in the bottle.* EMILY PARKER, *an assistant editorial features editor at the* Wall Street Journal, *previously worked for the* Asian Wall Street Journal *in Hong Kong. She holds a master's degree in East Asian Studies from Harvard University, and wrote her thesis on how Chinese nationalism affects Japanese companies in China. She has spent almost six years living in both China and Japan, and speaks Mandarin Chinese and Japanese.*

If you are looking for a picture of the real situation on the ground in China, the 2008 Beijing Olympics might be the worst place to start. Beijing has had years to devote to its acrobatic efforts to ensure that in August 2008, visitors will descend upon an unpolluted, dissident-free city with a remarkably polite, English-speaking population. What the Olympics will provide is a window into China's self-image and global ambitions.

China's long awaited "coming out party" will present the world with a relatively clear picture of how Beijing *wants* to be seen. When the world arrives on its doorstep for the "One World, One Dream" Olympic Games, Beijing will play the part of a gracious host. This will likely entail keeping the Games free of the ugly displays of Chinese nationalism that have marred sporting events in the past.

The Chinese, after all, have not always been so hospitable toward foreign athletes. When China hosted the final round of the 2004 Asian Cup in Beijing versus Japan, Chinese fans rioted, shouted out anti-Japanese slogans, booed the Japanese national anthem and burned Japanese flags. It's true that soccer fans are notoriously rowdy, and it certainly didn't help when China lost to Japan. But the fans' rage underscored a much deeper problem. The Chinese reaction wasn't so much about soccer as it was about history—and national pride. The jeering was just another way of venting a long-held grievance that Japan has yet to take responsibility for its World War II–era brutality toward China.

After spending so much time primping and preening for the Games, it's no surprise that Beijing wouldn't want the ugly side of Chinese nationalism to show up and crash its party. Besides being a major embarrassment, it would also make it a lot harder for the Communist Party to convince the world of China's "peaceful rise." Incidents like the unseemly Asian Cup, not to mention the virulent anti-American and anti-Japanese protests that have erupted in China over the past decade, have already raised eyebrows abroad.

If the 2008 Games are indeed free of such antics, it may be in part because many ordinary Chinese don't want to show the world a face that is contorted with anger. But even if China's citizens are inclined to replay the Asian Cup debacle, they probably wouldn't get very far. "The Chinese government will take every measure to prevent this kind of thing from happening," Shi Yinhong, professor of international relations at the People's University in Beijing, told me on the phone. Japan's *Asahi* newspaper took this even further in March 2007, reporting that "Huajiadi Elementary School in northeast Beijing has been chosen by the Chinese authorities to cheer and support athletes from Japan."[1] China's attempts to adopt an appropriate level of nationalistic sentiment at the Games are not simply a public relations campaign. The Olympics are landing in Beijing at a time when China is struggling to define its own patriotism. What does it mean to love China, and how is that sentiment expressed? And who decides the answers to these questions, the Communist Party or the Chinese people themselves?

The fact that there are no easy answers to these questions says a great deal about China today. Perhaps at some point in the past, *aiguozhuyi* (patriotism, or love of country) did translate roughly into love of party. But that's not necessarily the case now. It hasn't been hard to find Chinese people who love their motherland but disagree with the people in charge. More important, it is not clear who is driving China's nationalist agenda. Questions remain over just how big a role the government played in China's anti-American protests following the 1999 NATO bombing of the Chinese Embassy in Belgrade, or during the anti-Japanese protests of 2005. Even if the government did initially encourage these demonstrations, Beijing may have been caught off guard by their intensity.

Beijing may now be ruing the effects of years of strident rhetoric decrying the evils of Japan, which brutalized China before the people were "liberated" by the Communist Party. This narrative has been a cornerstone of Chinese nationalism: loving China meant hating Japan. This means that when Beijing's more pragmatic leaders want to pursue a friendlier, more constructive foreign policy toward Japan, the government has to worry about being accused by the Chinese people of being too "soft" on its rival. The idea that the Chinese public is simply swayed by Beijing's nationalistic whims is not entirely accurate. On the contrary, public Internet petitions may have the ability to push the government's hand. This is why Beijing wants to take back the reins over a nationalistic fervor that has, at several points over the past decades, threatened to veer out of its control. And thanks to the Internet, the people have a powerful new capacity to gather online and make their voices heard.

## *AIGUOZHUYI*: LOVE OF COUNTRY

While the Chinese people struggle to define what it means to love their country, those outside of China are asking their own questions. Perhaps what they want to know most is this: will China's "love of country" somehow amount to hostility toward us? There have been several moments over the past decade when the answer to this question, at least as far as Americans and Japanese were concerned, appeared to be yes.

Over the past decade, there have been too many eruptions of Chinese nationalist outrage to name them all here, but several stand out for their intensity. One of the most frightening outbursts took place in 1999, when NATO bombed the Chinese Embassy in Belgrade, killing three Chinese people. Many Chinese refused to believe fervent United States pleas that the bombing was a tragic accident, and tens of thousands took to the streets, shouting and throwing bricks and Molotov cocktails, even burning the consul general's residence in Chengdu. US Ambassador Jim Sasser was trapped in the American embassy for four days as demonstrators pelted the building with stones. The Chinese media chimed in to vilify the United States.

Then in 2005, thousands of Chinese people took to the streets again, this time in reaction to Japan's bid for a permanent seat on the UN Security Council. The emotional, occasionally violent demonstrations were also protests against what many Chinese felt was Japan's failure to address the past, including textbooks that whitewashed Japan's historical atrocities and then Prime Minister Junichiro Koizumi's repeated visits to Yasukuni Shrine, where war criminals are enshrined. The message of the demonstrations was clear: "We can't let Japan get away with this!"

In the eyes of many Chinese, these expressions of outrage may have had one similar cause: China was victimized by the acts of a foreign country. It wouldn't have been the first time. This idea of a wounded, defeated nation has deep roots in official education and propaganda over the past century. In his book, *China's New Nationalism,* Peter Gries discusses how the narrative of China's "Century of humiliation" has framed its interactions with the West. This period starts, he says, with China's defeat in the First Opium War and the British acquisition of Hong Kong in 1842, and covers unequal treaties signed with the British and the Japanese in the nineteenth century, the Sino-Japanese War of 1894–1895, and the "War of Resistance" against Japan in the 1930s and 1940s.

While the state has sponsored various alternative, "heroic" narratives over the past century, Gries argues that during the 1990s the official Maoist "victor narrative" was superseded by a "victimization narrative" that blamed the West and Japan for China's suffering. Running through this victimization narrative is a potent streak of pride and indignation, a sense that such treatment is an insult to China's national dignity.

The combination of pride and victimization makes for a potent blend, and has shaped attitudes toward both the United States and Japan. While Chinese attitudes toward the United States seem to be reactions to certain events that are seen as acts of aggression against China, such as the Belgrade bombing, anger at Japan runs deeper. China's widespread anti-Japanese sentiment is fueled by a deep feeling of being historically wronged, because Japan has yet to seriously repent for the abuses that it committed in China during wartime, in particular the brutal "Rape of Nanking" of the late thirties.

After conducting substantial research on Chinese opinion, Harvard University Professor Alastair Iain Johnston and Daniela Stockmann, an assistant professor at Leiden University, found a difference in the nature of sentiment toward the United States and Japan. When it came to attitudes toward the United States, "there is a substantial amount of distrust, even anger (an issue of what people do), but those attitudes are still quite different from the level of hatred and bias (an issue of who people are) that is directed at Japan and the Japanese." They proceeded to argue that the "century of humiliation" historical memory plays a key role in some Chinese attitudes toward the United States: "The anger manifests itself in perceptions that the United States is bullying China, is trying to keep China weak, and employs double standards in its policies toward China."[2]

One way for either the United States or Japan to anger Chinese nationalists is to threaten to interfere with the status quo of Taiwan. For many Chinese, an independent Taiwan symbolizes the dissolution of the Chinese nation, and otherwise cool-headed Chinese might flatly state that an attempt at Taiwanese independence would be a justification for war.

## LEBRON JAMES VS. THE DRAGONS

In China, you don't need a political incident to strike a nationalist chord, and the same feelings of pride and victimization bleed into the business sphere as well. Some American and Japanese companies have learned the hard way the perils of appearing to treat China as an "inferior" nation. In 2004, Nike made the mistake of running an ad on the mainland that featured American basketball star LeBron James battling, and defeating, Chinese symbols such as dragons and a kung-fu master. Memo to Nike: if you want to run this kind of an ad in China, the dragons better win. A brouhaha erupted, Chinese "national dignity" was wounded, and the Nike ad was promptly banned. In 2005, a McDonald's television ad that showed a Chinese man begging for a discount was taken off the air as the act was considered to be humiliating.

In the consumer field, Japanese companies have had their share of trouble in the Chinese market. A year before the Nike incident, Toyota had a similar misstep. The Japanese company ended up pulling—and formally apologizing for—advertisements featuring stone lions bowing to a Prado SUV. This time the issue was that lions, ancient symbols of Chinese power exemplified by the carved lions guarding Tiananmen Gate in front of the Forbidden City, were bowing to a Japanese product. Several years before that, some Chinese accused Toshiba of treating them as inferior, because following accusations of a laptop defect the company compensated US consumers, but not their Chinese counterparts. Chinese consumers cried foul, outrage erupted on the Internet, and Toshiba sales saw a steep drop in the Chinese marketplace.

Japanese companies have been particularly vulnerable in China, not least because Chinese nationalists are so quick to view product defects against a much larger historical backdrop of Japan's historical misdeeds. When I interviewed a Toshiba manager in 2002 about the laptop incident, he told me: "As for Sino-Japanese relations, the war issue is always present. This is the context in which we are conducting business activities with China . . . Before that incident, we had never had a single quality problem in China. Not one. In spite of that, this trouble occurred and brought up these issues of Chinese pride."

## THE BATTLE FOR THE SOUL OF CHINESE PATRIOTISM

*"The title 'patriot' should be reserved for people who love the party.*
*It is an inaccurate description of me, a perpetual misfit in China."*
—KANG ZHENGGUO, THE AUTHOR OF CONFESSIONS, WHO IN
1968 WAS SENTENCED TO THREE YEARS IN LABOR CAMPS FOR
THE "CRIME" OF REQUESTING A COPY OF DR. ZHIVAGO FROM
MOSCOW UNIVERSITY LIBRARY

Once upon a time, in theory at least, the paradigm was simple: the Communist Party decided what it meant to love China. It then determined how that sentiment should be expressed. State media reflected these views, and the public took their cues from there. The reality is much more complex. In fact, the widespread popularity of the Internet may be allowing the people to influence the state media. A conversation I recently had with a Chinese journalist who worked for a major state-media outlet provides evidence that this is happening. The journalist, who requested that he not be named, described his own experience covering Japan's bid for a permanent seat on the Security Council, which played a key role in sparking the anti-Japanese protests of 2005.

"At the very beginning, the Chinese delegation in the UN was not so strong in their opposition to Japanese efforts," the journalist told me. "Later on they changed their mood, because the reaction on the Internet was so strong." An Internet petition opposing the bid reportedly obtained over 40 million signatures.

Apparently, the Chinese government did not want to appear as being too soft on the Japanese. "They asked us to be more strong," he said of the authorities. "To make people feel we are very strong in fighting against these efforts. So we changed our tune." Public opinion may have played a decisive role in determining the state media reporting, not the other way around. "After the reactions on the Internet, the government changed, so we had to change. We had to report every day on how these efforts [to gain a seat on the Security Council] were going. Before this era, government could act unilaterally. Now, when something happens on the Internet, the government has to change policy."

For Beijing, the public leading the nationalist agenda is not the biggest problem. A much greater threat is the fact that there have been moments when the people's patriotic agenda seemed to be out of sync with Beijing's goals. Ironically, expressions of ostensibly sought after "national unity" with Hong Kong and Taiwan has not always served Beijing's interests. In September of 1996, Hong Kong activists and more than 10,000 Taiwanese citizens staged an enormous rally against Japan's occupation of the Diaoyu islands. "We believe that finding a solution to the Diaoyu Islands problem will bring all Chinese people together," wrote Hong Kong legislator Albert Ho in the *Asian Wall Street Journal*. But rather than celebrating this national unity, Beijing showed signs of uneasiness, and authorities reportedly took steps to cool down public anti-Japanese sentiment.

As Beijing has tried to forge friendlier, more pragmatic relations with Japan, a major trade partner, public patriotism has more than once threatened to get in the way. Some would argue that China's anti-Japanese sentiment is nothing more than a tool of the Communist Party to shore up its own legitimacy, and maybe this was once the case. But there have been several incidents over the past decade or so that have given reason to believe that Beijing wished it could shove that genie right back into the bottle. In an attempt to strike a more conciliatory tone after the anti-Japanese protests of 2005, the state media notably softened its rhetoric toward Japan. This wasn't the first sign that Beijing was worried about anti-Japanese sentiment spinning out of control.

In 2004, the Chinese authorities shut down the Patriots' Alliance Web site, a popular, nationalist site founded two years earlier. The site had criticized Japan, the United States and occasionally the Chinese government for being too weak. The site apparently crossed the line after it launched an online petition protesting the Railways Ministry's decision to award contracts to Japanese companies. The petition obtained over 67,000 online signatures in under twenty-four hours.

Some Chinese might tell you that one particularly proud moment in recent history was in August of 1984, a mere six years after Deng Xiaoping opened China's doors to the world. The moment was the Los Angeles Olympic Games, where China took home fifteen gold medals. For a country that had once been called "the sick man of Asia," this was a truly historic moment, and even those who suffered dearly during Mao's Cultural Revolution that ended in 1976 may have felt pangs of national pride. It goes without saying that China has come a long way since then. Over the past decade its impressive economic growth has caused rivals like Japan to consider it a threat, and then later an enormous opportunity.

If love of party doesn't entirely define love of country, and China can no longer realistically play the "humiliation" card, then what does it mean to love China today? The Beijing Olympics, a time for the host country to both celebrate itself and show its best face to the world, is a prime opportunity for the Chinese people to examine their own "love of country." Hopefully, this examination will pave the way for a new *aiguozhuyi* that reflects a more confident nation whose patriotism in no longer dictated from the top down. Let the Games begin.

# CHAPTER 22

# Challenges for a "Responsible Power"

### BY SOPHIE RICHARDSON

*In October 2002, the* Straits Times *published an article entitled "A More Self-Confident China Will Be a Responsible Power." Coauthored by Zhang Yunling of the Chinese Academy of Social Sciences, the article painted a reassuring picture of Chinese foreign policy: "While the world will see a more self-confident China, it will not see an aggressive China. Instead, the country is more likely to behave like a 'responsible power' with its growing strength." As Beijing prepares to host the 2008 Summer Olympics, the world is certainly seeing a "more self-confident China." The degree to which it is also a "responsible power" is a vital open question.* SOPHIE RICHARDSON *is the Asia Advocacy director for Human Rights Watch, where she oversees the research on a number of Asian countries and advocacy in and on the region. Her book on Chinese foreign policy is forthcoming from Columbia University Press.*

In recent years, China's harsher critics across the world have pointed with alarm to its growing international presence, highlighting what they describe as its preference for doing business with abusive and autocratic governments like itself, its export of hazardous toys and tainted medicines, and its rapacious quest for energy resources across the defenseless developing world. Chinese officials paint a very different picture, describing their foreign policy as a "process of forging [China's] destiny with the international community in a closer and more genuine way," insisting it is a "responsible power," and suggesting that such relentless criticism violates the rights of China's 1.3 billion citizens.

One thing is certain: as China becomes ever more enmeshed in the international system, its foreign policy is changing in small ways and is under more scrutiny than ever. As the 2008 Beijing Olympic Games approach, which Chinese officials consider a unique opportunity to show off a modern China to the world, the leadership may be more willing to factor human rights considerations into their decisions. Successfully encouraging them to be more open to human rights promotion, however, will require understanding several key dimensions of Chinese foreign policy and what they mean for human rights globally.

Human rights activists expect all governments to uphold internationally recognized human rights obligations, regardless of borders. But China's approach is one of noninterference, respect for sovereignty, unconditional development aid, refusal to base international relations on regime type or commitments to reform, and resistance to international scrutiny of domestic affairs. This leads to some key questions: How does the Chinese government's approach harm international human rights promotion? In particular, will China's policies of noninterference and unconditional aid obstruct crucial traditional human rights instruments and institutions, such as UN Security Council–imposed pressure and sanctions? Is there a particular logic to Chinese foreign policy? Has recent international pressure prompted the Chinese government to respond more constructively in the face of human rights crises, such as in Darfur and Burma? And, ultimately, can a government that assiduously represses rights at home be expected to work for their defense elsewhere?

# HOW CHINESE FOREIGN POLICY UNDERMINES INTERNATIONAL HUMAN RIGHTS PROTECTION

Few bother to note that it is a tenet of Chinese foreign policy to have relations with, and provide aid (a considerable amount of it for a developing country) to, rights-respecting governments on the same basis as it provides aid to abusive ones. This is a reflection of China's core policy of "noninterference" in the internal affairs of other states. As a growing power, China's close relations with abusive governments come in for great criticism, as they should, but there is little evidence in recent years that the Chinese government actively encourages human rights abuse by others. China's willingness to provide aid and political support regardless of a recipient's human rights record may, depending on the situation, deserve criticism, but no more so than other countries that do the same thing.

Yet there are many ways in which the model and practice of Chinese foreign policy crucially undermines international efforts to defend human rights. First, the Chinese Communist Party model of development—rapid economic growth without a commensurate increase in civil or political rights, alongside general resistance to international pressure—is hardly a positive example. Economic development in China has brought a greater degree of social freedoms, and of course reduced the number of people in poverty, but the fact remains that it is a government highly repressive of its critics, often on the grounds that their criticism jeopardizes state stability and growth. In addition, that rapid growth has been enabled by gross violations of labor rights, rampant expropriation by officials of land and other public resources, environmental devastation, and suppression of public discontent about these developments. In this sense, the Chinese model is, needless to say, not one rights activists wish to see replicated.

Second, after regaining UN membership in 1971 and spending about twenty years reinvigorating its international diplomacy, Chinese diplomats have become more adept at undermining or obstructing the work of international institutions important to the promotion of human rights. For example, Chinese officials consistently block UN Security Council resolutions that entail sanctions, such as, along with other countries, a proposed resolution in January 2007 on Burma and a later resolution condemning the Burmese junta's September 2007 assault on thousands of peaceful demonstrators. By obstructing a means of swiftly disciplining an abusive government or impeding investigations into the nature and scope of human rights abuses, such actions directly contribute to the misery of those who are already suffering.

China's actions at the UN Human Rights Council also demonstrate a concerted effort to roll back structures and procedures for protecting rights. China was one of several countries to propose that country mandates and "special procedures" be abandoned or restricted. It suggested that only governments should be able to submit statements in the universal periodic review process. Chinese diplomats have complained that nongovernmental organizations' involvement in the Human Rights Council should be "controlled." In 2006, China objected to the Human Rights Council accepting a report on human rights conditions in Darfur on the grounds that the authors had not actually been inside the country and therefore its report could not be accurate. That entry into the country had been denied by precisely the people thought to be responsible for human rights abuses (and precisely in order to evade scrutiny) seemed immaterial to China.

Third, while Beijing may have deep philosophical differences with the rest of the international community on the efficacy of conditioning aid, it has indisputably provided a crucial financial lifeline to countries with poor human rights records. This has often undermined efforts made by other international actors to use financial pressure to improve rights. Without steady flows of Chinese aid, investment, weapons, and political support, it is possible that the governments of Burma's General Than Shwe, Sudan's President Omar Bashir, and Zimbabwe's President Robert Mugabe, among others, would either already have been consigned to history or would have had their ability to abuse their citizens dramatically limited by a lack of resources.

It is these kinds of actions that earn the Chinese government its reputation as the patron of abusive regimes. Beijing defends its decisions to maintain these relationships with three arguments: first, that to alter them would be to discriminate on the basis of "internal affairs," which it insists it will not do; second, that withdrawing such support would only worsen at least the economic situation of the countries in question, particularly for ordinary people; third, that developed countries at various points continue to support equally abusive governments when it suits them, and thus China's approach cannot be criticized. That these arguments find sympathy in some quarters around the world does nothing to relieve China of complicity in the human suffering that results from its relations with abusive governments.

## THE LOGIC BEHIND CHINESE FOREIGN POLICY

Many assume that Chinese diplomats simply do not care about the human rights of other people. After all, they argue, the Chinese government does not care about the rights of its own citizens. Its leaden rhetoric about international human rights and noninterference often sounds callous and seems to eschew any sympathy or responsibility for victims. But those who make assumptions about China's global agenda—that it only supports dictatorships or Communists, that its aid brings no benefits to ordinary people, that it seeks to dominate its region—do so at their own peril, as they ignore much evidence to the contrary. More important, these arguments fail to apprehend the internal logic and thinking of Chinese leaders about their international role and aspirations.

China's leaders often point to their efforts to lift hundreds of millions of Chinese out of poverty as evidence of their commitment to human rights domestically. Rather than seeing all rights as equally important, the CCP continues to argue that economic and social rights, which it often equates with economic development, take precedence over civil and political rights. Poverty, they argue, causes serious instability and makes it impossible for any rights to be secured. Even assuming that poverty reduction is their overarching priority, the logic of Chinese officials is flawed. Respect for civil and political rights can also assist poverty reduction efforts, but one does not hear Chinese officials arguing that China must immediately remove barriers to free expression and the free flow of information so as to free up space for more robust public criticism of bad governance and policy failures. This failure to acknowledge the importance of such civil and political rights, it is worth noting, has created a domestic threat to the CCP more serious than it has grappled with in decades, as unprecedented numbers of Chinese protestors and petitioners spill into China's streets to make their complaints known.

China's foreign policy employs a similar logic—that economic development is key to real independence and therefore securing individual countries' "rights" in the international community. This thinking is augmented by several other closely held beliefs, including a half-century of hostility towards the principles and practices of American foreign policy, which China continues to see as profoundly imperialistic, hypocritical, and, directly or indirectly, the cause of conflict. Beijing also remains skeptical about the merits of international institutions and norms, many of which were developed in the two decades during which China was frozen out of the international system, and which the CCP believes were created in part to criticize, take advantage of, and marginalize developing countries. As long as the United States remains committed to defending Taiwan, the CCP also believes it remains vulnerable to actual threats to its territorial security. Finally, by forgoing its claim to examine other countries' human rights conditions, it is much easier for Beijing to reject scrutiny of its own.

These convictions and rhetoric often sound—and are—obstructionist, particularly when deployed in the face of gross human rights abuses. Yet they remain popular in many parts of the developing world, where China is now seen as almost as desirable a partner as the United States, the European Union, and international financial institutions.

The term "noninterference" seems to contradict other Chinese foreign policy rhetoric, which regularly states the importance of China's membership in the international community. But many Chinese officials genuinely do not believe that pressing countries to adopt rights-respecting political or economic systems, or selecting aid recipients based on their human rights records, let alone deposing a particular political leader, achieves progress. To many Chinese leaders, noninterference does not mean uninvolved or uninterested, but rather conducting international relations in a highly circumscribed way so as not to alter the domestic balance of power or induce significant change other than that which local authorities want—it also means reducing the role of international organizations to talk shops for deferential governments, not activist bodies.

Whether local leaders are human rights heroes or war criminals, and regardless of how they came to power or what sort of system they run, China believes it is best to leave crucial decisions about human rights policies to domestic politics. This is the opposite of the approach the United States, European Union, UN, and others often adopt (though with glaring exceptions and highly inconsistent emphases). Many Chinese foreign policy officials, however, view any intervention as distorting domestic politics and relieving domestic actors of responsibility for their actions, ultimately making those countries less independent and stable.

China's insistence on sovereignty also seems in tension with its own rapidly growing interconnections with the rest of the world. But one has to bear in mind Chinese leaders' obsession with maintaining control of Tibet and Hong Kong, and gaining control of Taiwan. These goals are inextricably linked to the CCP's lore about its own legitimacy: that it came to power and has stayed in power because it has popular support, and no foreigners have the right or even the information needed to make good decisions about what happens inside China. Similarly, in the international arena, Chinese leaders view conditioned aid and pressure for major economic or political change as undermining sovereignty by leaving too many important decisions to foreigners. Those leaders also believe that international interventions are likely to fail because the people pushing for intervention often lack an adequate understanding of ground reality or a sufficient commitment to remain involved long enough, or are actually using human rights as a Trojan horse for hidden political agendas.

## ARE THINGS CHANGING?

As it has increasingly come under the international spotlight for its foreign policy positions, China has recently made modest policy adjustments that appear to promote human rights. It is too soon to tell whether they constitute a shift away from the traditional policy of noninterference, or whether they are idiosyncratic changes made in response to intense international pressure.

One sign of change is that, in response to considerable international pressure, China has taken some steps to respond to the human rights crisis in Sudan. China has been harshly criticized for not making better use of its leverage as the primary purchaser of Sudanese oil to discipline a government that is almost certainly guilty of—at a minimum—crimes against humanity. From 2004 to 2006, China helped shield Sudan from the threat of individual and other types of sanctions at the Security Council. It provided diplomatic support to Sudan's refusal of a UN deployment in Darfur, for instance, by abstaining on resolution 1706 in August 2006, which authorized such a force.

Yet just months later, in November 2006, Chinese diplomats apparently took a more assertive position at a key meeting to discuss Darfur deployment in Addis Ababa. In March 2007 China removed Sudan from a list of countries in which Chinese investors were encouraged to do business. In May, Beijing took the highly unusual step of appointing a special envoy for Africa with a focus on Darfur, tapping veteran diplomat Liu Guijin. In August, China supported resolution 1769 at the Security Council, which authorized the deployment of a hybrid UN–African Union peacekeeping force. In October, it sent 300 engineers to join the peacekeeping operation.

What changed? China says that it was quietly pushing Sudan all along to resolve the Darfur crisis. But the Chinese government clearly was deeply dismayed over the international focus on its role—which was concentrated, in the words of one Chinese diplomat, "in a way we have never before experienced"—and efforts to link the abuses in Sudan to the 2008 Beijing Olympics. As a result, it decided to more actively intervene with Khartoum, and to be more visible in doing so. The Chinese government made more public statements explaining how it was trying to convince the Sudanese government to accept international demands. The tone and timing of Chinese statements and actions also suggest growing concern in Beijing that ongoing instability in southern Sudan would jeopardize China's plans for oil development across the country. There is, of course, a great deal more China should push Khartoum to do: rapidly deploy the hybrid force, ensuring that it is fully equipped with a robust protective mandate; surrender the International Criminal Court indictees; end rape and ethnic cleansing; and create conditions for voluntary safe return of the displaced. These actions will have far more of an impact than a special ambassador ever will.

News also began to trickle out in June 2007 of an "unprecedented" effort by Chinese diplomats to bring together leaders of Burma's exile government with members of the ruling State Peace and Development Council. Since the Burmese military government solidified its grip on power after annulling elections in 1990, it has been increasingly isolated by Western sanctions. Yet China has provided a crucial financial and diplomatic lifeline even in the face of attacks on peaceful democratic opponents, continued brutal assaults on ethnic minorities, the systematic use of rape as a weapon of war, and ongoing recruitment of child soldiers. After the government used force to break up street protests led by monks in September 2007, China publicly called for restraint and dialogue on all sides and agreed to a Security Council statement critical of the government. It gained credit for quietly pressuring the Burmese government to allow a special UN envoy access to opposition leader Aung San Suu Kyi and supporting the "good offices" of the UN secretary-general. However, China failed to halt arms transfers or publicly challenge the Burmese rulers over the killing and arrest of protestors.

This relative assertiveness is far more likely a function of China's desire not to have a large border state deteriorate into chaos than a shift in loyalties—although China has long had a relationship with Burma's military leaders, it had no trouble congratulating the pro-democracy forces for their electoral victory in 1990. If Burma implodes, not only would China's considerable investments there be compromised, but so would its ability to manage a border area already rife with drug trafficking and serious public health crises. Of course, should China want to work for a truly stable Burma, it should recognize that the source of instability in Burma is a deeply unpopular, repressive and rapacious military government that has done almost nothing to address the economic needs of its own people. So long as it stays in power, the country is likely to remain unstable.

Another interesting development came in late August 2007, when a senior British diplomat suggested that China was taking a harder line against Zimbabwean President Robert Mugabe through a highly unusual reduction in aid. After a flurry of articles in the international press, China vehemently denied that the total amount of its aid would be reduced. It later emerged that the amount going to economic programs that China had deemed unsuccessful was being cut, while commensurate increases were being made in humanitarian aid. It is unclear why the change was made—whether it was a political message or a more technical decision relating to the efficacy of the use of development aid by Mugabe's government—and therefore whether it signaled a new willingness to use aid to press a recipient government to change its policies. But it is a noteworthy episode that should be further explored.

In international fora, China has been a marginally more cooperative player recently. It is increasingly inclined to abstain on, rather than veto, some international initiatives with which it is uncomfortable, such as the Security Council's referral of Darfur to the International Criminal Court or the Asia-Europe Meeting's communiqué harshly criticizing the Burmese junta. China is contributing larger numbers of troops to international peacekeeping efforts, including 1,000 to efforts in Lebanon, which shows a growing level of comfort with such initiatives.

## WHAT CHINA CAN DO DIFFERENTLY

Senior Chinese foreign policy makers' core beliefs remain largely unchanged, and it will be at least another decade until younger, more progressive diplomats come to the fore. Consequently, it is unlikely that China will significantly change its approach in the near future and embrace some of the practices most relied upon by other influential governments—international scrutiny, political pressure on abusive governments, sanctions, conditioned aid.

Yet there are some steps China can take that are consistent with its current worldview which will help victims of human rights abuses. At a minimum, Beijing should reconsider its aid strategies. It is highly unlikely that China will begin "attaching strings," but it can at least suspend gratuitously inappropriate projects, such as the new presidential palace for Sudanese president Omar Bashir, and reallocate those funds to other projects that would help those most in need. In the direst circumstances, such as the crackdown in Burma in September 2007, it should suspend some aid to send a political signal. Should it fail to do so, the Chinese government must recognize that its actions will give others legitimate grounds to criticize its agenda and question its motives. Simply being more transparent about aid, particularly in countries with serious human rights issues, would also be a significant improvement.

China could also articulate the conditions under which it will set aside its insistence on sovereignty and noninterference, particularly with respect to human rights crises. Some argue persuasively that by ratifying legally binding international human rights treaties, China's obligations are clear.[1] When in 2005 it signed up to the "responsibility to protect" at the UN, China agreed that member states are obliged to intervene when a government fails to protect its own population against serious human rights abuses. It is not yet clear under what circumstances China will endorse the doctrine's use—if it is serious, the discussion in China (and elsewhere) should move on from *whether* to treat state sovereignty as an impregnable boundary to *how* it will join with other countries to intervene in the most egregious humanitarian crises when circumstances require. In order for the responsibility to protect to be implemented, the capacity to prevent and respond to mass atrocities must be created, both within countries and at the international level. For example, the UN secretary-general should have the ability to deploy human rights monitors if alerted to a developing situation which implicates the doctrine, and the UN should have a standby force ready to deploy immediately when mass atrocities loom. Chinese support for such measures would indicate true international responsibility.

Finally, China should be truer to its own rhetoric that it is a devoted friend of the developing world. It should see its foreign policy as not just about relations with other governments, but about helping improve the well-being of the people of those states. This would earn China the gratitude of people around the globe. But it will require a policy that accepts that human beings need civil and political rights as well as economic development. If it wants to be seen as a responsible power, China should be willing to act decisively when people suffer at the hands of their own governments. Putting human dignity at the core of Chinese foreign policy would indeed constitute revolutionary change for China and the rest of the world.

# CHAPTER 23

# A Dual Approach to Rights Reform

BY KENNETH ROTH

*In August 2007, the historian Xu Guoqi explained that for the Chinese government, the Beijing Games represent "weiji"—a word translated as "crisis" in English but which is more nuanced in Chinese. The Chinese word consists of two characters: 危 (wei, meaning danger) and 机 (ji, meaning opportunity). The character "wei" could refer to the risk of unrest and violence that has marred past Olympic Games in Mexico City, Munich, and other host cities. On the other hand, the character "ji" symbolizes the historic opportunity that the Games present to both the Chinese government, which yearns for greater prestige on the world stage, and to human-rights advocates, who seek durable rights reforms in China.* KENNETH ROTH *is the executive director of Human Rights Watch, a post he has held since 1993. Roth has conducted human-rights investigations around the globe, devoting special attention to justice and accountability for gross abuses of human rights. A former federal prosecutor with a degree from Yale Law School, he is the coeditor of* Torture, *an anthology of essays published in 2005.*

Is there anything that outsiders can possibly do to help the people of China change their country? That is not a question that human-rights activists usually ask about a country. They assume that, with sufficient pressure, any government can be convinced to change. But if any government challenges that assumption, it is China's. With more than a billion people—one-fifth of humanity—China has historically been difficult to influence. The prospect of external impact has only dimmed as China's economy has expanded and the nation has emerged as a superpower in its own right.

Yet, difficulty does not warrant despair. Outside actors may never be able to change China overnight, but with the proper approach, they can make their influence felt and in the process help the Chinese people improve China's respect for the rights of its own people and those of its governmental partners in countries such as Sudan and Burma.

In making this point, I do not subscribe to the facile platitudes of constructive engagement. Rubbing shoulders with political and business leaders, many of whom believe in human rights at some level but rarely allow their supposed convictions to interfere with their profitable relations, will not convince anyone to pursue a more rights-respecting path. If anything, these business leaders provide a lesson in hypocrisy—in not practicing what one preaches whenever there is a cost—that Chinese leaders seem all too eager to embrace.

Nor is there evidence to support the only slightly more sophisticated view that trading with China will help build a middle class that will soon insist on democracy and human rights. China has been growing now for quite some time—its middle class is formidable—but Beijing has successfully fended off whatever pressure it may feel to improve its human-rights practices. It has long learned how to permit economic freedom and even a significant degree of personal freedom without allowing political freedom.

That said, I would hardly advocate cutting off China, either economically or politically. Rather, the question is how best, while engaging with China, to promote human rights in a way that might help to influence the leadership in Beijing.

The Chinese government is no more altruistic than others. It will enhance its respect for human rights when it finds doing so to be in its self-interest. But such reasons exist, and in my view, an effective human-rights policy toward China would seize any possible occasion to point them out. A two-pronged strategy based on an analysis of both domestic and foreign policy factors could prove especially productive.

## RAISING THE COST OF DOMESTIC REPRESSION

Take domestic policy. Beijing's overwhelming preoccupation is to avoid large-scale popular unrest—especially the kind of massive uprising that it saw during the Tiananmen Square democracy movement of 1989. Yet, today, according to China's own security services, there are already tens of thousands of small-scale incidents of public unrest throughout the country each year. Most are triggered by corrupt or abusive local officials who seize land, pollute the environment, or extort funds at will. Beijing must know that these protests are so numerous and widespread that it is only a matter of time before they begin feeding off each other and sparking a larger uprising.

So far, China's leaders have tried to control abusive local officials through their usual system of command and control. But the incentives for corruption and abuse exist at all levels of government, and the farther one is from the Beijing leadership, the weaker is the central government's influence. It is extraordinarily difficult for a small group of officials in the capital to control a bureaucracy as vast and far-flung as China's.

Here, external voices might productively suggest an alternative route. The best way to rein in local officials is to empower those with the greatest incentive to do so—the very people these officials are victimizing. But that requires giving them the tools they need to fight back—namely, the freedom to speak out, to publish in the press, to meet and discuss their common persecutor, to protest, and to enlist the courts. In short, it requires loosening the constraints on civil society, allowing journalists and lawyers to do their jobs, and permitting, at least at the local level, the emergence of the rule of law.

That is no small task. Chinese leaders are obviously wary that if such political and legal activity were permitted, it might move beyond an initial focus on the local target and aim for the higher-ups in Beijing. Indeed, precisely that fear seems to have led to the backsliding in rights protection that has characterized the government of President Hu Jintao. Persuading Chinese leaders otherwise requires convincing them that the risk of doing nothing, with the chance that it will gradually fuel a violent explosion of discontent, is greater than the prospect that a modest easing of liberties at the local level will come back to seriously haunt central leaders in Beijing. Chinese leaders may be reluctant to permit even a modest shifting of power to independent institutions such as the judiciary, but if they can be convinced that the alternative may be a large-scale uprising and a dramatic power shift, they might be persuaded to take their rhetorical endorsement of the rule of law seriously.

One important way to do that is through the message accompanying human-rights advocacy. Human-rights activists should move beyond simply protesting the suppression of demonstrations or the arrest of lawyers. We should always note that Beijing, by tolerating such repression, is tacitly endorsing the abusive activity that is the subject of protest. Stop farmers demonstrating against the corrupt seizure of their land? That means that Beijing in effect supports the seizure. Arrest lawyers challenging environmental degradation? That means that Beijing effectively sides with the polluter. By connecting rights violations against protesters to the abuses being challenged, human-rights activists can refocus popular discontent toward the top, and raise the cost of repression. As independent protesters around the country start connecting the dots between local abuses and the central leadership, the balance of considerations in Beijing might tip toward a loosening of restraints on civil society.

## CHALLENGING BEIJING'S TIES WITH ROGUE REGIMES

A different kind of persuasion might play out with respect to China's foreign policy. China traditionally has equated the promotion of human rights with interference in a country's internal affairs. Having suffered interference, including military intervention and colonialism, China has not been eager to endorse interventionist international policies. Even as China emerged from its shell and began trading with partners around the world, it embraced what President Hu calls a policy of dealing with governments with "no strings attached."

But the consequences of this rather callous approach have often been calamitous. While China purchased two-thirds of Sudan's oil, Khartoum used the enormous revenue generated to fund the Janjaweed militia that was killing, raping, and displacing the people of Darfur. A similar logic found China supporting governments from Zimbabwe to Burma that were wreaking havoc with the lives of their people. It turns out that when dealing with highly abusive governments, there is no such thing as neutrality: to trade with government-dominated businesses or to provide those governments with significant aid is to become complicit in their atrocities.

That raises a critical question for Beijing as it aspires to greater leadership in international affairs. Will it act like a responsible global partner, or does it want to be seen as the supporter of thugs and murderers around the world? Human Rights Watch has raised that question on every occasion—in part because we think it will appeal to the elements of the Chinese government that do aspire for a more constructive global role, and in part because it raises the reputational cost of the status quo. The prospect that China's tacit endorsement of unsavory regimes will come back to tarnish its prized Beijing Olympics has only heightened the stakes.

That is not to say that China might suddenly become a global champion of democracy. It can hardly promote a free civil society or the rule of law when it denies these basic rights to its own people. But at least since 1989, China has not engaged in mass murder. It thus can, without hypocrisy, stand up to other governments that commit mass atrocities against their own people, particularly the killers in Khartoum and the butchers in Burma. At the very least, it can make sure not to provide them support.

It bears pointing out that China can afford to be less concerned about interference in its internal affairs because that fear is an attribute of the weak, and China today is hardly weak. It is an emerging superpower. No one is about to invade. The colonial intrusions of the past are an increasingly distant memory. There is no real reason why China should fear that challenging the most serious human-rights abuses abroad will give rise to pressure for it to change internally.

And there are signs that China is beginning to rethink its attitude toward its most abusive allies. Since December 2006, China has helped to persuade the Sudanese government to permit the deployment of a large peacekeeping force to protect the people of Darfur. In October 2007, Beijing even allowed the UN Security Council to "strongly deplore" the Burmese military crackdown on monks and other protesters demonstrating against military misrule, although as of this writing China has not permitted Security Council-imposed sanctions. The action on Burma was particularly important in light of Beijing's fear of similar protests in China.

No one believes that it will be easy to transform China in human-rights terms. But today's circumstances suggest that the task is not impossible. China's interests, chief among them the desire to successfully host the 2008 Olympics, do not align neatly with the adoption or endorsement of repression. It is conceivable that strategies geared to those new interests might work to nudge Beijing in a more rights-respecting direction.

# Notes

## CHAPTER 1 Overview: China's Race for Reform

1. Li Datong, "Beijing's Olympics, China's Politics," OpenDemocracy.net, August 22, 2007. Li is a Chinese columnist and a former editor of *Bingdian* (*Freezing Point*), a weekly supplement of the *China Youth Daily* newspaper. http://www.opendemocracy.net/democracy_power/china_inside/beijing_oly mpics_china_politics.

2. From the final—successful—candidacy presentation speech in Moscow in July 2001 by Beijing Mayor and the Beijing 2008 Olympic Games Bidding Committee president Liu Qi. When the International Olympic Committee votes were tallied, Beijing defeated the other candidate cities of Paris, Toronto, Osaka, and Istanbul. http://en.beijing2008.cn/spirit/beijing2008/ candidacy/presentation/n214051410.shtml.

3. Nien Cheng, *Life and Death in Shanghai* (Penguin, 1986), for example, is a harrowing account of Cheng's 1966 detention by Red Guards who murdered her daughter.

4. Jung Chang and Jon Halliday, *Mao, The Unknown Story* (Random House, 2005), p. 609.

5. Nick Mulvenney, "Olympics: Beijing Has Some Success with Rain Prevention: Official," Reuters, January 30, 2008. The Beijing Meteorological Bureau has been tasked with preventing wet weather for the opening ceremony of the Games. Zhang Qian, head of weather manipulation at the bureau, told a news conference, "For clouds above zero degrees we use the seeding agent silver iodide to accelerate the droplets' collision and coalescence, producing a downdraft which suppresses the formation of clouds."

6. Perry Link, "China: The Anaconda in the Chandelier," *New York Review of Books*, Vol. 49, Number 6, April 11, 2002. The Anaconda is also a useful metaphor for how the International Olympic Committee and many governments are cowed into adjusting their own positions in the face of Beijing's intransigence and failure to honor its pledges on human rights.

7. Teng Biao was detained by the Chinese police on March 6, 2008, only to be released two days later as human rights advocates began to mobilize on his behalf. As noted in a Reuters article on March 8, 2008 ("Chinese Police Release Rights Lawyer Teng Biao"), Teng's detention was "threatening to take

off as another focus for human rights campaigners as Beijing readies for its Olympic Games starting on August 8. Local supporters were already collecting signatures for a petition demanding his release."

8. Peter Simpson, "BOCOG Has Promised the World's Media Freedom to Roam At Will . . . ," *South China Morning Post*, October 1, 2006.

## CHAPTER 2 From Mao to Now: Three Tumultuous Decades

1. Associated Press, "Reports: Top Salt Lake Olympics Officials to Step Aside," January 8, 1999. The Salt Lake City bribery scandal ultimately caused ten members of the International Olympic Committee to resign or be expelled in 1999.

2. Christopher Clarey, "Olympics; I.O.C. Officials to Scrutinize Sydney Bid," *New York Times*, January 26, 1999.

## CHAPTER 3 The Promise of a "People's Olympics"

1. The author thanks Victoria Kwan and Charlie McAteer for service beyond the call of duty in providing invaluable research assistance and support.

2. Salt Lake Olympic Committee, Board of Ethics, "Board of Ethics Report to the SLOC Board of Trustees," February 1999.

3. International Olympic Committee, "Candidature Acceptance Procedure for the Games of the XXIX Olympiad in 2008," March 13, 2002, http://multimedia.olympic.org/pdf/en_report_295.pdf.

4. International Olympic Committee (IOC) Candidature Acceptance Working Group, "Report by the IOC Candidature Acceptance Working Group to the Executive Board of the International Olympic Committee," August 18, 2000. http://multimedia.olympic.org/pdf/en_report_287.pdf

5. International Olympic Committee (IOC) Evaluation Commission for the Games of the XXIX Olympiad in 2008, "Report of the IOC Evaluation Commission for the Games of the XXIX Olympiad in 2008," April 3, 2001, http://multimedia.olympic.org/pdf/en_report_287.pdf.

6. Tibet Brief, *Law Firm Chooses Beijing Olympic Contract Over Tibetans*, Winter 2003, available at http://www.tibetjustice.org/reports/tibetbrief/winter_2003.pdf.

7. See Scott Greathead's chapter in this volume for a description of the concerted pressure on Spielberg which followed his appointment as artistic adviser of the Beijing Games, particularly by activists concerned with China's role in the Darfur crisis. Spielberg ultimately resigned from this position in February 2007, stating that "my conscience will not allow me to continue with business as usual."

8. "One World, One Dream," *Washington Post*, August 10, 2007, http://www.washingtonpost.com/wp-dyn/content/article/2007/08/09/AR2007080902009.html.

9. Human Rights in China; see http://hrichina.org/public/PDFs/CRF.3.2007/CRF-2007-3_Rogge.pdf.

10. "Beijing Games Should Make Profit: Consultant," *ABC News* (Reuters), September 26, 2007, http://abcnews.go.com/Sports/wireStory?id=3651500.

11. He Qinglian, "Human Rights: the True Gold Standard," in *China Rights Forum*, No. 3 (2007) citing an article, "Aoyun jinpaide xianjing," posted on a number of Internet bulletin boards since 2004, including http://bbs.lasg.ac.cn/cgi-bin/forum/view.cgi?forum=10&topic=438.

12. "Beijing Offers Free Vaccinations to Migrant Workers," *China Daily*, April 6, 2007, http://www.chinadaily.com.cn/2008/2007-04/06/content_844951.htm.

13. "Fair Play for Housing Rights: Mega-Events, Olympic Games and Housing Rights," Center for Housing Rights and Evictions (COHRE), June 5, 2007, http://www.cohre.org/store/attachments/Fact percent20Sheet%20-%20Beijing.doc.

14. "Nearly One Hundred Relocated Households in Qingdao Protest Land Seizure for Olympics," *Huaxia Dianzibao*, July 26, 2007, No. 202.

15. Audra Ang, "China Land Activist Tortured in Prison," Associated Press, October 8, 2007, http://news.yahoo.com/s/ap/20071008/ap_on_re_as/china_activist_arrested.

16. Howard French, "China: Advocate Said to Be Tortured," *New York Times*, October 9, 2007, http://select.nytimes.com/mem/tnt.html?emc=tnt&tnt-get=2007/10/09/world/asia/09briefs-china.html&tntemail1=y.

17. "China: One Olympics, One Voice?" *Global Voices*, August 9, 2007, http://www.globalvoicesonline.org/2007/08/09/china-one-olympics-one-voice/.

18. "China: Blogs Deleted, Barred and Officially Backed," *Global Voices*, August 18, 2007, http://www.globalvoicesonline.org/2007/08/18/china-blogs-deleted-barred-and-officially-backed.

19. Jonathan Watts, "Olympic Artist Attacks China's Pomp and Propaganda," *The Guardian*, August 9, 2007, http://arts.guardian.co.uk/art/news/story/0,,2144692,00.html.

CHAPTER 4 The Ghosts of Olympics Past

1. Shirley Povich, "The Echo of Shots That Rang Through the Dawn," *Washington Post*, July 9, 1992, http://www.washingtonpost.com/wp-srv/sports/longterm/general/povich/launch/munich.htm.

2. Andrew Jennings, *The New Lords of the Ring: Olympic Corruption and How to Buy Gold Medals* (Pocket Books, 1992), chapter 3.

3. Kate Doyle, "Tlatelolco Massacre: Declassified US Documents on Mexico and the Events of 1968," http://www.gwu.edu/~nsarchiv/NSAEBB/NSAEBB10/intro.htm.

CHAPTER 7 Physical Strength, Moral Poverty

1. Congressional-Executive Commission on China (CECC), Political Prisoner Database, *2006 Annual Report*. This database is supplied by the Dui Hua Foundation and the Tibet Information Network. See http://www.cecc.gov/

pages/annualRpt/annualRpto6/PoliticalPrisonerDatabase.php?PHPSESSID
=73ed5341d09e93dc4943a2a71f0c2867.

2. Committee to Protect Journalists, *Falling Short: As the 2008 Olympics Approach, China Falters on Press Freedoms* (2007), p. 9.

3. World Bank statistic cited in *Financial Times*, "750,000 A Year Killed by Chinese Pollution," July 2, 2007, http://www.ft.com/cms/s/0/8f40e248-28c7-11dc-af78-000b5df10621.html.

4. Joseph Kahn, "Rioting in China over Labels on College Diplomas," *New York Times*, June 22, 2006. This article described a protest described a protest by students in Xinzheng and noted: "China has been engulfed in other types of unrest, including nearly 80,000 mass protests recorded in 2005 alone. Most such events involve peasants, migrant workers or workers laid off from state enterprises."

5. Minxin Pei, "The Dark Side of China's Rise," *Foreign Policy*, March–April 2006, http://www.carnegieendowment.org/publications/index.cfm?fa=view&id=18110.

CHAPTER 8 A Gold Medal in Media Censorship

1. Congressional-Executive Commission on China (CECC), Political Prisoner Database, *2006 Annual Report*. This database is supplied by the Dui Hua Foundation and the Tibet Information Network. See http://www.cecc.gov/pages/annualRpt/annualRpto6/PoliticalPrisonerDatabase.php?PHPSESSID =73ed5341d09e93dc4943a2a71f0c2867.

2. Committee to Protect Journalists, *Falling Short: As the 2008 Olympics Approach, China Falters on Press Freedoms* (2007), p. 9.

3. World Bank statistic cited in *Financial Times*, "750,000 A Year Killed by Chinese Pollution," July 2, 2007, http://www.ft.com/cms/s/0/8f40e248-28c7-11dc-af78-000b5df10621.html.

4. Joseph Kahn, "Rioting in China over Labels on College Diplomas," *New York Times*, June 22, 2006. This article described a protest described a protest by students in Xinzheng and noted: "China has been engulfed in other types of unrest, including nearly 80,000 mass protests recorded in 2005 alone. Most such events involve peasants, migrant workers or workers laid off from state enterprises."

5. Minxin Pei, "The Dark Side of China's Rise," *Foreign Policy*, March–April 2006, http://www.carnegieendowment.org/publications/index.cfm?fa=view&id=18110

6. Committee to Protect Journalists, *Falling Short: As the 2008 Olympics Approach, China Falters on Press Freedom*, August 2007, http://www.cpj.org/Briefings/2007/Falling_Short/China/china.pdf; Human Rights Watch, *"You Will Be Harassed and Detained": China Media Freedoms Under Assault Ahead of the Beijing Olympic Games*, vol. 19, no. 12 (C), August 2007, http://china.hrw.org/issues/media_freedom.

CHAPTER 9 High Hurdles to Health in China

1. World health leaders and human rights advocates have explicitly examined how to balance the protection of human rights with the restrictive measures sometimes necessary for infectious disease control. The Siracusa Principles, conceptualized at a meeting in the Italian city of Syracuse in 1984, are widely recognized as a legal standard for measuring valid limitations on human rights, including the response to disease threats. The principles do not prohibit the restriction of human rights, but seek to ensure that such restrictions are in accordance with the law, based on a legitimate objective of general interest, strictly necessary, the least restrictive and intrusive means available, and are not arbitrary, unreasonable or discriminatory.

2. Thankfully, Chinese physicians who conducted the exams frequently recommended universal precautions, so quarantine was rare.

3. The 2003 Human Rights Watch report *Locked Doors: The Human Rights of People Living with HIV/AIDS in China* provides a detailed examination of the Henan blood scandal and the spread of HIV through unsafe, state-run blood-collection centers in the 1990s. The report also documents restrictions on freedom of expression, assembly, association and the right to information of those living with HIV/AIDS and persons seeking to help them; arbitrary detention of injection drug users; discrimination based on HIV status by government hospitals, clinics and government employees; and lack of access to AIDS treatment in China's health care system. The report is available at http://www.hrw.org/reports/2003/china0803.

4. The Chinese government has continued to insufficiently address the safety of the blood supply or compensation for those infected by unsafe transfusions and donation. In 2007, Asia Catalyst, a US-based NGO, published a report examining China's blood-safety practices and the lessons learned from other countries. The report, entitled "AIDS Blood Scandals: What China Can Learn From the World's Mistakes" is available at: http://www.asiacatalyst .org/AIDS_blood_scandals_rpt_0907.pdf.

5. On February 21, sixty-four-year-old Dr. Liu Jianlun, a professor and physician from Guangzhou, Guangdong Province, who had been treating patients with "atypical pneumonia" arrived in Hong Kong to attend a wedding. Although he felt feverish, Dr. Liu went sightseeing with his brother-in-law and then retired to his room on the ninth floor of the Metropole Hotel. That night Dr. Liu felt worse and called ahead to the hospital to warn them that he had a communicable disease, and upon arriving was placed in a pressurized room. However, in the short time that he had been at the hotel Dr. Liu infected sixteen people, including a resident of Hong Kong, an American national with business interests in Vietnam, Singaporean nationals, and two Canadian nationals. Dr. Liu died March 4 and his brother-in-law died shortly thereafter.

6. In June 2003, BOCOG Vice President Wang Wei was quoted as saying: "SARS or not, Chinese athletes have always made every effort to achieve good results in their competitions, for honor and for sportsmanship." In August the Chinese government was able to finally hold a public ceremony

to unveil the 2008 Olympic Games emblem. The release had been delayed for months because of the SARS epidemic.

7. *Restrictions on AIDS Activists in China*, a 2005 Human Rights Watch report, documents the detention and harassment by local authorities in Henan province of AIDS activists, the harassment of activists working with persons at high risk of HIV transmission, such as injection drug users and sex workers, and censorship of websites that provide AIDS information to men who have sex with men. The report is available at http://hrw.org/reports/2005/china0605.

8. Counterfeit drugs are a global crisis. It is estimated that up to 15 percent of all drugs are fake, and in parts of Africa and Asia this figure exceeds 50 percent. In 2001, 192,000 people are reported to have died in China from counterfeit drugs. The World Health Organization estimated that there were 500 illegal medicine manufacturers in China. A good overview of counterfeiting is a 2005 article entitled: "The Global Threat of Counterfeit Drugs: Why Industry and Governments Must Communicate the Dangers" by Robert Cockburn et al., *PLoS Medicine* 2, no. 4, doi:10.1371/journal.pmed.0020100.

9. Chinese doctors have also performed partial lobotomies on patients in order to address drug addiction. The operation, which has been performed on more than 500 patients in China, involves inserting a heated needle into a half-inch diameter hole in the patient's head. After seven days with a surgical clamp holding it in place, the needle is removed from the patient's head and the area of the brain responsible for addictions and craving is said to be destroyed. In 2003, Chinese doctors published a paper ("Clinical Study for Alleviating Opiate Drug Psychological Dependence by a Method of Ablating the Nucleus accumbens with Stereotactic Surgery," by Guodong Gao, et al., *Stereotactic and Functional Neurosurgery*; 81(2003), 96–104) which described the procedure and reported 39 percent relapse by six months. The study was widely criticized in the international media and by Western addiction experts; see Wayne Hall in *Addiction* 101, no. 1–3 (2006), p. 1–2.

10. A meeting of experts in economics, epidemiology, ethics, human rights, public policy, and public and animal health met in Bellagio, Italy, in July 2006, to discuss human rights and social-justice concerns surrounding an influenza pandemic and response. The "statement of principles" resulting from the meeting emphasized access to information, the participation of marginalized groups, and public involvement in surveillance and reporting activities (without fear of discrimination or uncompensated loss of livelihood), and can be found at http://www.hopkinsmedicine.org/bioethics/bellagio/Bellagio_Statement.pdf.

## CHAPTER 10 Worship Beyond the Gods of Victory

1. Constitution of the People's Republic of China, article 36.
2. "Religion mentioned in CPC Constitution," Xinhua, in *China Daily*, October 22, 2007, http://www.chinadaily.com.cn/china/2007-10/22/content_6194537.htm.

3. "The Basic Viewpoint and Policy on the Religious Question During Our Country's Socialist Period," Central Committee of the Chinese Communist Party, Asia Division of Human Rights Watch, *Freedom of Religion in China* (January 1992), p. 33–45; original from Donald E. MacInnis, *Religion in China Today: Policy and Practice* (Maryknoll, NY: Orbis, 1989).

4. The Chinese government has stated that family and friends may meet in a private home for prayer and Bible study without having to register. The scope of the exception is unclear; practice varies by locale. US Department of State, International Religious Freedom Report 2007, released by the Bureau of Democracy, Human Rights, and Labor, http://www.state.gov/g/drl/rls/irf/2007/90133.htm.

5. Beijing 2008, The Official Website of the Beijing 2008 Olympic Games, http://en.beijing2008.cn/spectators/beijing/religion.

6. Wu Jiao, "Church to be built in Olympic village," *China Daily*, p. 1, September 4, 2007.

7. Gareth Powell, "Church for the Olympic Village," *China Economic Review*, September 11, 2007, http://www.chinaeconomicreview.com/olympics/2007/09/11/church-for-the-olympic-village.

8. "Religion mentioned in CPC Constitution," Xinhua, in *China Daily*, October 22, 2007, http://www.chinadaily.com.cn/china/2007-10/22/content_6194537.htm.

9. Ibid.

10. "Trials of a Tibetan Monk: The Case of Tenzin Delek," Human Rights Watch, February 2004, http://hrw.org/reports/2004/china0204/.

11. US Department of State, International Religious Freedom Report 2007, released by the Bureau of Democracy, Human Rights, and Labor, http://www.state.gov/g/drl/rls/irf/2007/90133.htm.

12. During the early morning of April 25, 1999, more than 10,000 well-disciplined Falun Gong practitioners peacefully surrounded Zhongnanhai, the compound where China's leaders live and work, to protest against attacks on the organization's integrity.

13. See *Dangerous Meditation: China's Campaign Against Falungong*, Human Rights Watch, January 2002, http://hrw.org/reports/2002/china/.

14. International Covenant on Civil and Political Rights, article 18. China signed the covenant in 1998 but has yet to ratify it.

## CHAPTER 14 The Race for Profits

1. From 1993 to 1996, ticket sales to the Olympics totaled about US $451 million, or 17 percent of overall revenue. But from 2001 to 2004, ticket sales fell sharply to US $411 million, representing only 9.8 percent of total revenue.

2. Geoffrey Fowler, "Olympians Turn Up Heat Over Darfur," *Wall Street Journal*, February 4, 2008.

3. Rebecca Blumenstein, "Venture to Focus on Managing Crises in China," *Wall Street Journal*, September 25, 2007.

## CHAPTER 15 China and the Spielberg Effect

1. Mia Farrow and Ronan Farrow, "The 'Genocide Olympics,'" *Wall Street Journal*, March 28, 2007.

2. Seth Faison, "China Fetes Capitalists, But the Air is Tense," *New York Times*, September 29, 1999.

3. Raymond Snoddy, "Murdoch Cut BBC to Please China," *Financial Times*, June 14, 1994.

4. Mia Farrow, "No Hopes for Us," *Wall Street Journal*, July 27, 2007.

5. The first appears to have been Roberta Cohen, a Senior Fellow at the Brookings Institute, who in an August 5, 2004, letter to the *Washington Post* called on China to "use even a small part of its leverage to call Sudan to account" on Darfur, citing its position as "Sudan's largest trading partner and the main foreign investor in Sudan's oil industry."

6. "A First Step to Save Darfur, editorial, *New York Times*, August 3, 2007. The toll of 200,000 dead is a conservative estimate, with many human rights campaigners asserting that the true figure is as high as 400,000.

7. US Department of State, "Darfur: A 'Plan B' to Stop Genocide?," April 11, 2007; "A First Step to Save Darfur," editorial, *New York Times*, August 3, 2007.

8. Sudan Divestment Task Force, "PetroChina, CNPC, and Sudan: Perpetrating Genocide," April 15, 2007, 4. The Sudan Divestment Task Force included researchers from the University of California at San Diego and the Monterey Institute of International Studies. Copies of the report are available at www.sudandivestment.org.

9. Ibid., p. 4–5.

10. Ibid.

11. Ibid.

12. "China and Darfur: The Genocide Olympics," *Washington Post*, December 14, 2006, p. A30.

13. Eric Reeves, "Push China, Save Darfur," *Boston Globe*, December 17, 2006.

14. Clifford Coonan, "Olympics Rings in Helmers," *Variety*, April 16, 2006. "Helmer" is *Variety*-speak for "director."

15. Clifford Coonan, "Lee Gets Games Gig," *Variety*, October 17, 2006.

16. Clifford Coonan, *Variety*, April 16, 2006.

17. Quoted in "China Braces For Olympics Demonstrations," Associated Press, August 3, 2007.

18. Spielberg's letter was dated April 2, 2007, but it was not made public until late July. See, "Darfur Activists Push Spielberg to Pressure China," *All Things Considered*, National Public Radio, July 24, 2007, www.npr.org.

19. "Spielberg May Quit Post," *New York Times*, July 28, 2007, citing reports by ABC News and Reuters.

20. Helene Cooper, "Darfur Collides with Olympics, and China Yields." *New York Times*, April 13, 2007.

21. Burt Helm, "An Olympic PR Challenge," *BusinessWeek*, June 21, 2007.

22. Quoted in "A Green Oil Baron?," *Wall Street Journal*, October 19, 1999, p. B1.

23. Tony Emerson, "A Letter to Jiang Zemin," *Newsweek International,* May 29, 2000.

CHAPTER 16 A Marathon Challenge to Improve China's Image

1. Emma Graham-Harrison, "China's Hu Wants Propaganda Surge at Home and Abroad," Reuters, January 22, 2008.

CHAPTER 17 Clearing the Air

1. Beijing will establish a monitoring system to track all the food for the athletes during the Games. See Shi Jiangtao, "Games Hurdles Still Loom Large, Organizers Say," *South China Morning Post,* August 7, 2007.

2. Report of the IOC Evaluation Commission for the Games of the XXIX Olympiad in 2008, International Olympic Committee, Lausanne, Switzerland, April 3, 2001, p. 62.

3. Matthew Chung, "Breathing an Olympian Effort for our Athletes in Beijing," *Toronto Star,* August 4, 2007.

4. "IOC President: Beijing Air Pollution Could Cause Events to be Delayed During 2008 Olympics," Associated Press, August 7, 2007.

5. Jonathan Watts, "China Prays for Olympic Wind as Car Bans Fail to Shift Beijing Smog," *The Guardian,* August 21, 2007. During the four-day trial, cars with odd and even numbered plates were supposed to stay off the roads on alternate days and violators were liable to a fine of RMB 100.

6. Assessment by Randy Wilbur, sports physiologist, see Spencer Reiss, "Smog and Mirrors: China's Plan for a Green Olympics," *Wired Magazine,* 15, no. 8 (August 2007), http://www.wired.com/science/planetearth/magazine/15-08/ff_pollution?currentPage=1.

7. "3-Stage Plan to Ensure Clear Skies," *China Daily,* http://english.sepa.gov.cn/zwxx/hjyw/200708/t2007824_108421.htm, accessed August 26, 2007.

8. Olympic Bid Drives Environmental Improvements in Beijing," *People's Daily,* December 11, 2000.

9. Report of the IOC Evaluation Commission for the Games of the XXIX Olympiad in 2008, International Olympic Committee, Lausanne, Switzerland, April 3, 2001, p. 62.

10. Spencer Reiss, "Smog and Mirrors."

11. Statements from Qu Geping, chairman of the NPC's Environment and Resources Committee, *China Environment News* (Zhongguo Huanjing Bao), May 2, 2000.

12. The revised legislation aimed to cut the total volume of pollution back to 1995 levels by 2010 and deal with air pollution more comprehensively than before. It included measures to reduce $SO_2$ levels and create acid-rain control zones; improve air quality in various designated cities; and reduce construction dust. The total cost was estimated to possibly top 1.5 percent of gross domestic product.

13. CAREBEIJING stands for Campaign for Air Quality Research in Beijing and Surrounding Region.
14. Suggestions from Randy Wilbur, sports physiologist. See Spencer Reiss, "Smog and Mirrors."
15. Ibid.
16. "Endurance Athletes Worry about Pollution in Beijing," *International Herald Tribune*, August 26, 2007.
17. Elizabeth Economy, "China's Great Leap Backwards," *Foreign Affairs*, September/October 2007.

## CHAPTER 19 Democracy with Chinese Characteristics

1. During the Cultural Revolution, Deng Xiaoping's son, Deng Pufang, was tortured by Red Guards and fell or was thrown out of a window, becoming a paraplegic. Deng Pufang now chairs the China Disabled Persons' Federation, which he helped found in 1988.
2. Philip P. Pan, "China Using Rights Issue To Promote Olympic Bid; Potential Gains Cited As Inspectors Arrive," *Washington Post*, February 21, 2001.

## CHAPTER 21 Dragons Win: The Beijing Games and Chinese Nationalism

1. "International Exchange Programs at the Olympic Games in Nagano, Sydney, Salt Lake City and Turin Proved to Be a Great Success," *Asahi Shimbun*, March 28, 2007.
2. Quoted from their chapter in Peter J. Katzenstein and Robert O. Keohane, eds., *Anti-Americanisms in World Politics* (Cornell University Press, 2007), p. 193.

## CHAPTER 22 Challenges for a "Responsible Power"

1. As a member of the United Nations, China is expected to uphold the Universal Declaration of Human Rights (UDHR), but it is also a party to the Convention Against Torture (CAT), the Convention to Eliminate All Forms of Discrimination (CEDAW), the Convention on the Rights of the Child (CRC), and the International Covenant on Economic, Social, and Cultural (ICESCR) Rights. It has signed but not ratified the International Covenant on Civil and Political Rights (ICCPR).

# Suggestions for Further Reading

## BOOKS ON CHINA

### ON THE CHINESE PEOPLE AND RECENT CHINESE HISTORY

Jasper Becker, *The Chinese* (Free Press, 2001).

Ian Buruma, *Bad Elements: Among the Rebels, Dissidents, and Democrats of Greater China* (Random House, 2001).

Sharon Hom and Stacy Mosher, *Challenging China: Struggle and Hope in an Era of Change* (New Press, 2007).

Nicholas Kristof and Sheryl WuDunn, *China Wakes: The Struggle for the Soul of a Rising Power* (Vintage, 1995).

James McGregor, *One Billion Customers: Lessons From the Front Lines of Doing Business in China* (Free Press, 2005).

Orville Schell and David Shambaugh, editors, *The China Reader: The Reform Years* (Vintage, 1999).

Jonathan Spence, *The Search for Modern China* (W.W. Norton and Co., 1990).

### ON CHINA'S POLITICAL AND ECONOMIC SYSTEM

George Black and Robin Munro, *Black Hands of Beijing: Lives of Defiance in China's Democracy Movement* (John Wiley & Sons, 1993).

Gordon Chang, *The Coming Collapse of China* (Random House, 2001).

Ted Fishman, *China Inc.* (Scribner, 2006).

Ian Johnson, *Wild Grass: Three Portraits of Change in Modern China* (Pantheon Books, 2004).

Joshua Kurlantzick, *Charm Offensive: How China's Soft Power Is Transforming the World* (New Republic Books, 2007).

James Mann, *The China Fantasy: How our Leaders Explain Away Chinese Repression* (Viking, 2007).

Robin Munro, *China's Psychiatric Inquisition: Dissent, Psychiatry and the Law in Post-1949 China* (Wildy, Simmonds and Hill, 2006).

Andrew Nathan and Perry Link, editors, *The Tiananmen Papers* (Public Affairs, 2002).

Orville Schell, *Discos and Democracy: China in the Throes of Reform* (Pantheon Books, 1988).

## ON MAO AND OTHER CHINESE POLITICAL LEADERS

Jasper Becker, *Hungry Ghosts: Mao's Secret Famine* (Owl Books, 1998).

Jung Chang and Jon Halliday, *Mao: The Unknown Story* (Random House, 2005, and Knopf, 2005).

Andrew Nathan and Bruce Gilley, *China's New Rulers: The Secret Files* (Granta Books, 2003).

## ON MEDIA CENSORSHIP IN CHINA

Committee to Protect Journalists, *Falling Short: As the 2008 Olympics Approach, China Falters on Press Freedom* (CPJ, August 2007).

Human Rights Watch, *"You Will Be Harassed and Detained": China Media Freedoms Under Assault Ahead of the Beijing Olympic Games*, vol. 19, no. 12 (C), August 2007.

Human Rights Watch, *Race to the Bottom: Corporate Complicity in Chinese Internet Censorship*, vol. 18, no. 8 (C), August 2006.

## ON THE RULE OF LAW IN CHINA

Human Rights in China, *State Secrets: China's Legal Labyrinth*, June 2007.

Human Rights Watch, *"A Great Danger for Lawyers": New Regulatory Curbs on Lawyers Representing Protesters*, vol. 18, no. 15 (C), December 2006.

Human Rights Watch, *"We Could Disappear At Any Time": Retaliation and Abuses Against Chinese Petitioners*, vol. 17, no. 11 (C), December 2005.

ON THE ENVIRONMENT AND HEALTH IN CHINA

Elizabeth Economy,\* *The River Runs Black: The Environmental Challenges to China's Future* (Cornell University Press, 2004).

Human Rights Watch, *Restrictions on AIDS Activists in China*, vol. 17, no. 5 (C), June 2005.

ON HONG KONG

Jonathan Dimbleby, *The Last Governor: Chris Patten and the Handover of Hong Kong* (Little Brown, 1997).

Christopher Patten, *East and West: China, Power and the Future of Asia* (Times Books, 1998).

Mark Roberti, *The Fall of Hong Kong: China's Triumph and Britain's Betrayal* (John Wiley & Sons, 1994).

Frank Welsh, *A History of Hong Kong* (Harper Collins, 1997).

ON TIBET

Robert Barnett, *Lhasa: Streets with Memories* (Columbia University Press, 2006).

Melvyn Goldstein, *A History of Modern Tibet, 1913-1951: The Demise of the Lamaist State* (University of California Press, 1991).

Human Rights Watch, *"No One Has the Liberty to Refuse": Tibetan Herders Forcibly Relocated in Gansu, Qinghai, Sichuan, and the Tibet Autonomous Region*, vol. 19, no. 8 (C), June 2007.

---

\*Also the author of the article "The Great Leap Backwards?", *Foreign Affairs*, September–October 2007.

Human Rights Watch, *Trials of a Tibetan Monk: The Case of Tenzin Delek*, vol. 16, no. 1 (C), February 2004.

Steven Marshall, Orville Schell et al., *Tibet Since 1950: Silence, Prison, or Exile* (Aperture / Human Rights Watch, 2000).

Tsering Shakya, *The Dragon in the Land of Snows: The History of Modern Tibet since 1947* (Pimlico, 1999).

Elliot Sperling, *The Tibet-China Conflict: History and Polemics* (East-West Center, 2004).

## ON XINJIANG AND OTHER CHINESE REGIONS

Sara Davis, *Song and Silence: Ethnic Revival on China's Southwest Borders* (Columbia University Press, 2005).

Human Rights Watch, *Devastating Blows: Religious Repression of Uighurs in Xinjiang*, vol. 17, no. 2 (C), April 2005.

James Millward, *Eurasian Crossroads: A History of Xinjiang* (Columbia University Press, 2006).

S. Frederick Starr, *Xinjiang: China's Muslim Borderland* (M.E. Sharpe, 2004).

## MEMOIRS:

Nien Cheng, *Life and Death in Shanghai* (Penguin, 1986).

Frank Ching, *Ancestors: 900 Years in the Life of a Chinese Family* (William Morrow and Co., 1988).

Tim Clissold, *Mr. China: A Memoir* (Collins, 2005).

Peter Hessler, *Oracle Bones: A Journey Through Time in China* (Harper Perennial, 2006).

Peter Hessler, *River Town: Two Years on the Yangtze* (Harper Perennial, 2001).

Perry Link, *Evening Chats in Beijing: Probing China's Predicament* (W.W. Norton & Co., 1992).

Liu Binyan, *A Higher Kind of Loyalty* (Pantheon, 1990).

Anchee Min, *Red Azalea* (Anchor Books, 1994).

John Pomfret, *Chinese Lessons: Five Classmates and the Story of the New China* (Henry Holt and Co., 2006).

Harry Wu (with Carolyn Wakeman), *Bitter Winds: A Memoir of My Years in China's Gulag* (Wiley, 1993).

FICTION

Gao Xingjian,* *Soul Mountain* (Harper Perennial, 2001).

Ha Jin, *Waiting: A Novel*** (Vintage, 1999).

Ha Jin, *A Free Life* (Pantheon, 2007).

## BOOKS ON THE OLYMPICS

Allen Guttmann, *The Olympics: A History of the Modern Games* (University of Illinois Press, 2002).

David Clay Large, *Nazi Games: The Olympics of 1936* (W.W. Norton, 2007).

Richard Pound, *Five Rings Over Korea: The Secret Negotiations Behind the 1988 Olympic Games in Seoul* (Little, Brown and Company Wiley, 1994).

Richard Pound, *Inside the Olympics: A Behind-the-Scenes Look at the Politics, the Scandals, and the Glory of the Games* (Wiley, 2004).

Alfred Senn, *Power, Politics and the Olympic Games* (Human Kinetics, 1999).

## ON HUMAN RIGHTS IN GENERAL

Human Rights Watch, *Human Rights Watch World Report 2008* (Seven Stories Press, 2008).

Kenneth Roth and Minky Worden, editors, *Torture: Does It Make Us Safer? Is It Ever OK? A Human Rights Perspective* (New Press, 2005).

* Nobel Prize in Literature, 2000.
** National Book Award, 1999.

# Acknowledgments

Producing an anthology is like planning a dinner party—you imagine the people you'd most like to have around a dinner table, and how their expertise and life experiences will combine to make the most interesting and engaging discussion possible. Then you cajole, barter, and shamelessly hassle these one-time friends and colleagues to help you get the book to publication.

Thus my first thanks must go to the contributors from China, the United States, Canada and the Netherlands whose voices, analysis and diverse backgrounds make this book such a engaging portrait of China today. Several contributors wrote and edited chapters from inside China, proof that at least in some respects, the country is more free than it once was.

Close readers of this book may tire of sports puns. But it is no exaggeration to say that it was truly a team effort, and an Olympian one at that. One friend and colleague, however, gets the gold medal for helping carry *China's Great Leap* across the finish line: Peter Huvos. Unfailingly cheerful, resourceful and hard-working, Peter was also a relentless taskmaster as my research assistant, project manager and right-hand editor from the book's genesis to publication.

Human Rights Watch provided time for me to conceive this book, and infinite staff patience in the process. The Human Rights Watch Asia and China teams bear much credit for the book's content, and no responsibility for any errors. In particular Sophie Richardson and Dinah PoKempner, who edited Human Rights Watch contributor chapters, were essential reviewers. Phelim Kine, Nicholas Bequelin, Mickey Spiegel, and Brad Adams all gave timely brainstorming, editing, and vetting assistance.

The Human Rights Watch communications team, especially Emma Daly, Stacy Sullivan, Carroll Bogert, Lance Lattig, Brian Griffey and Conor Fortune pitched in moral support and editing advice. Other colleagues, including Kay Seok, Joe Saunders, Peggy Hicks, Steve Crawshaw, Lawrence Moss, Laura Boardman, Jean-Marie Fardeau, Marianne Heuwagen, Miriam Mahlow, Tara Golden, Michele Alexander, Glen Galaich, Liba Beyer, Susan Fulwiler, Emma Cherniavsky, Tiffany Siart, Libby Marsh, Jasmine Herlt, Jim Murphy, Amha Mogus and Enrique Piraces were great support.

My creative team gets kudos for design advice and brilliant ideas that improved the project at all stages; thanks to Veronica Matushaj, Claudine Boeglin, Sam Ottenhoff, Anna Lopriore, Ella Moran, Yael Gottlieb, and Fitzroy Hepkins. Cover and web graphic designers Wai Hung Young and Martin Bell of Fruitmachine Design have extraordinary creativity—and patience. John Emerson of Apperceptive LLC designed the map of China which graces the opening pages of this book. Special thanks to Kadir van Lohuizen for his iconic photographs of China in transition, and to Ian Teh of Panos Pictures for the cover photograph.

At Seven Stories Press, publisher Dan Simon, Theresa Noll, Ruth Weiner, Anna Lui, Veronica Liu and Jon Gilbert gambled that I could finish the book in time. Their enthusiasm and faith in our project gave me motivation to complete the project practically by the deadline.

Special thanks go to Ken Sheffer, for the South Korea Olympics tales that sparked the idea for this book, to Meg Davis for the Olympic mascots, to writer Peter Hessler for his portraits of China today, to Perry Link and Tong Yi for her translation of Liu Xiaobo's chapter, to Elaine Wang and Dugar Hotala for translation assistance, to Jill Savitt for solidarity and to Josh Prager for the perfect chapter title. Jim Ottaway provided essential support at a key moment. Robert, Helen, Peter and Amy Bernstein are invaluable advisers on this and so many other projects.

My family—my late mother, my father and brothers David and John—has always been the greatest anchor in my life. Final thanks to my husband Gordon Crovitz, who knew I felt compelled to do this book, and to my two sons, Jack and James, who love *cha siu bau*, with the hope they will grow up speaking Cantonese and Mandarin and feeling as I do that China is a second home.

# Index

## ABOUT THE EDITOR

As Media Director of Human Rights Watch, MINKY WORDEN monitors crises, wars, human rights abuses and political developments in more than seventy countries worldwide. From 1992–1998, Ms. Worden lived and worked in Hong Kong as an adviser to Democratic Party chairman Martin Lee. Ms. Worden is a member of the Council on Foreign Relations, speaks Cantonese and German, and is an elected member of the Overseas Press Club's Board of Governors. She is the coeditor of *Torture*, published in 2005 by the New Press.